ON FREUD'S
"BEYOND THE PLEASURE PRINCIPLE"

CONTEMPORARY FREUD
Turning Points and Critical Issues

Series Editor: Leticia Glocer Fiorini

On Freud's "Analysis Terminable and Interminable"
    edited by Joseph Sandler

Freud's "On Narcissism: An Introduction"
    edited by Joseph Sandler, Ethel Spector Person, Peter Fonagy

On Freud's "Observations on Transference-Love"
    edited by Ethel Spector Person, Aiban Hagelin, Peter Fonagy

On Freud's "Creative Writers and Day-Dreaming"
    edited by Ethel Spector Person, Peter Fonagy, Sérvulo Augusto Figueira

On Freud's "A Child Is Being Beaten"
    edited by Ethel Spector Person

On Freud's "Group Psychology and the Analysis of the Ego"
    edited by Ethel Spector Person

On Freud's "Mourning and Melancholia"
    edited by Leticia Glocer Fiorini, Thierry Bokanowski, Sergio Lewkowicz

On Freud's "The Future of an Illusion"
    edited by Mary Kay O'Neil & Salman Akhtar

On Freud's "Splitting of the Ego in the Process of Defence"
    edited by Thierry Bokanowski & Sergio Lewkowicz

On Freud's "Femininity"
    edited by Leticia Glocer Fiorini & Graciela Abelin-Sas Rose

On Freud's "Constructions in Analysis"
    edited by Sergio Lewkowicz & Thierry Bokanowski, with Georges Pragier

ON FREUD'S
"BEYOND
THE PLEASURE PRINCIPLE"

Edited by

Salman Akhtar and Mary Kay O'Neil

CONTEMPORARY FREUD
Turning Points and Critical Issues

LONDON AND NEW YORK

Chapter 2, R. Caropreso & T. Simanke, "Life and Death in Freudian Metapsychology: A Reappraisal of the Second Instinctual Dualism", *International Journal of Psychoanalysis, 89*: 977–992. Copyright © 2008. Reprinted by permission of the publisher, John Wiley & Sons Ltd.

Chapter 6, O. Kernberg, "The Concept of the Death Drive: A Clinical Perspective", *International Journal of Psychoanalysis, 90*: 1009–1023. Copyright © 2009. Reprinted by permission of the publisher, John Wiley & Sons Ltd.

Chapter 7, B. Joseph, "Addiction to Near-Death", *International Journal of Psychoanalysis, 63*: 449–456. Copyright © 1982. Reprinted by permission of the publisher, John Wiley & Sons Ltd.

First published 2011 by Karnac Books Ltd.

Published 2018 by Routledge
2 Park Square, Milton Park, Abingdon, Oxon OX14 4RN
711 Third Avenue, New York, NY 10017, USA

Routledge is an imprint of the Taylor & Francis Group, an informa business

British Library Cataloguing in Publication Data

A C.I.P. for this book is available from the British Library

ISBN: 9781855757851 (pbk)

Edited, designed, and produced by Communication Crafts

CONTENTS

CONTEMPORARY FREUD

IPA Publications Committee

This significant series was founded by Robert Wallerstein and first edited by Joseph Sandler, Ethel Spector Person, and Peter Fonagy, and its important contributions have greatly interested psychoanalysts of different latitudes.

The objective of this series is to approach Freud's work from a present and contemporary point of view. On the one hand, this means highlighting the fundamental contributions of his work that constitute the axes of psychoanalytic theory and practice. On the other, it implies the possibility of getting to know and spreading the ideas of present psychoanalysts about Freud's *oeuvre*, both where they coincide and where they differ.

This series considers at least two lines of development: a contemporary reading of Freud that reclaims his contributions and a clarification of the logical and epistemic perspectives from which he is read today.

Freud's theory has branched out, and this has led to a theoretical, technical, and clinical pluralism that has to be worked through. It has therefore become necessary to avoid a snug and uncritical coexistence of concepts in order to consider systems of increasing complexities that take into account both the convergences and the divergences of the categories at play.

Consequently, this project has involved an additional task—that is, gathering psychoanalysts from different geographical regions representing, in addition, different theoretical stances, in order to be able to show their polyphony. This also means an extra effort for the reader that has to do with distinguishing and discriminating, establishing relations or contradictions that each reader will have to eventually work through.

Being able to listen to other theoretical viewpoints is also a way of exercising our listening capacities in the clinical field. This means that the listening should support a space of freedom that would allow us to hear what is new and original.

In this spirit we have brought together authors deeply rooted in the Freudian tradition and others who have developed theories that had not been explicitly taken into account in Freud's work.

In *Beyond the Pleasure Principle* Freud puts forward a new dualism and introduces the dichotomy between the life and death drives. He emphasizes that the death drive reveals the repetitive character of the drives. Masochism, melancholia, negative therapeutic reaction, and sense of guilt are explained by Freud in a new way. The concept of the death drive has been discussed among post-Freudian analysts from different viewpoints, and there is no an agreement about its significance, with some emphasizing its speculative character, others pointing out its clinical importance.

The editors, Salman Akhtar and Mary Kay O'Neil, together with the contributors to this volume, accepted the challenge to consider Freudian ideas and update this debate.

Special thanks are due to Charles Hanly, the President of the IPA, for his support, and to the editors and contributors to this volume, which enriches the Contemporary Freud's series.

Leticia Glocer Fiorini
Series Editor
Chair of the Publications Committee of
the International Psychoanalytical Association

ACKNOWLEDGEMENTS

First and foremost, we wish to thank the distinguished colleagues who contributed to this volume. We deeply appreciate their efforts, their sacrifice of time, and, above all, their patience with our requirements, reminders, and requests for revisions. With sincerity and affection, we acknowledge the guidance of the members of the current IPA Publications Committee, especially its Chair, Leticia Glocer Fiorini. We are also thankful to Rhoda Bawdekar for keeping track of all sorts of matters during the book's actual production.

Salman Akhtar & Mary Kay O'Neil

EDITORS AND CONTRIBUTORS

Salman Akhtar is Professor of Psychiatry at Jefferson Medical College and a training and supervising analyst at the Psychoanalytic Center of Philadelphia. His more than 300 publications include 11 books—*Broken Structures* (1992), *Quest for Answers* (1995), *Inner Torment* (1999), *Immigration and Identity* (1999), *New Clinical Realms* (2003), *Objects of our Desire* (2005), *Regarding Others* (2007), *Turning Points in Dynamic Psychotherapy* (2009), *Comprehensive Dictionary of Psychoanalysis* (2009), *Immigration and Acculturation* (2011), and *Matters of Life and Death* (2011)—well as 30 edited or co-edited volumes in psychiatry and psychoanalysis, and 7 collections of poetry. He is also a Scholar-in-Residence at the Inter-Act Theatre Company in Philadelphia.

Ira Brenner is Clinical Professor of Psychiatry at Jefferson Medical College, and a training and supervising analyst at the Psychoanalytic Center of Philadelphia. He is also the Director of the Adult Psychotherapy Training Program at the Center, where he teaches courses on trauma to students in both the psychoanalytic and psychotherapy curricula. He has lectured nationally and internationally and has written extensively on the topic of psychological trauma, dissociation, and the devastating long-term impact of the Holocaust upon its survivors and their subsequent generations. His published works include four books, *The Last Witness: The Child Survivor of the Holocaust* (1996) co-authored with Judith Kestenberg, *Dissociation of Trauma: Theory, Phenomenology, and Technique* (2001), *Psychic Trauma: Dynamics, Symptoms, and Treatment* (2004), and the Gradiva Award-winning *Injured Men: Trauma, Healing, and the Masculine Self* (2009). He was awarded the Pierre Janet Writing Prize by the International Society for the Study of Dissociation for his 2001 book, and the Gradiva Award Honorable Mention for his 2004 book. He maintains a private practice in suburban Philadelphia.

Fátima Caropreso is Professor of History and Philosophy of Psychology at the Federal University of Juiz de Fora (Brazil). She is also a professor and MA supervisor in the Programme of Graduate Studies in Psychology at the same university. Her main publications include the books *O nascimento da metapsicologia: Representação e consciência na obra inicial de Freud* [The birth of metapsychology: Representation and consciousness in Freud's early works] (2008); *Freud e a natureza do psíquico* [Freud and the Nature of the psychical] (2010); *Entre o corpo e a consciência: Ensaios de interpretação da metapsicologia freudiana* [Between body and consciousness: Essays on Freud's metapsychology] (2011—co-authored by Richard Theisen Simanke]; as well as many articles and essays in the epistemology of psychoanalysis.

Michael Feldman is a Training and Supervising Analyst of the British Psycho-Analytical Society. In addition to his clinical work, private practice, and teaching in London, he regularly works with analysts in several European countries and in the United States. His papers explore theoretical and technical issues in the interplay of transference and countertransference, the patient's use of projective mechanisms, and the pressures on both patient and analyst towards defensive action rather than thought. He has published a number of papers and has co-edited, with Elizabeth Spillius, *Psychic Equilibrium and Psychic Change: Selected Papers of Betty Joseph*. A selection of his own papers, edited by Betty Joseph and with a preface by Roy Schafer, was published in 2009 under the title, *Doubt, Conviction and the Analytic Process*.

Betty Joseph is a distinguished psychoanalytic clinician in London who has worked with children and adults in full-time analytic practice since the 1950s. Miss Joseph's seminal papers were published under the title *Psychic Change and Psychic Equilibrium* (1989). Her main interest throughout a long and distinguished analytic career has been in the clinical and technical areas of psychoanalysis. Working within the Kleinian tradition, she has developed a distinctive approach to technique that has been widely influential. With her sensitive focus upon the precise details of the clinical situation, Ms Joseph has demonstrated and drawn out the technical implications of Kleinian concepts, particularly those of projective and introjective identification. She is interested in the way the patient's need to maintain psychic equilibrium may permeate the analytic situation and in how psychic change may occur in the face of this. Her most notable papers include "The patient who is difficult to reach" (1975), "Addiction to near death" (1982), "On understanding and not understanding" (1983), "Transference: The total situation" (1985), "Projective identification: Some clinical aspects" (1987), and "Psychic change and the psycho-analytic process" (1989). She has served as a member of the British Psychoanalytical Society and a Training Analyst at the British Psychoanalytic Institute. She has lectured throughout Europe, North and South America, Australia, and India.

Otto Kernberg is Director of the Personality Disorders Institute at the New York Presbyterian Hospital, Westchester Division, and Professor of Psychiatry at the Weill Medical College of Cornell University. He is also a training and supervising analyst at the Columbia University Center for Psychoanalytic Training and Research. He was Director of the General Clinical Service of the New York State Psychiatric Institute and Professor of Clinical Psychiatry at the College of Physicians and Surgeons of Columbia University. He has also held the position of Associate Chairman and Medical Director of the New York Hospital–Cornell Medical Center, Westchester Division. A past President of the IPA (1997–2001), he is a prolific contributor to psychoanalytic literature and is the author of *Borderline Conditions and Pathological Narcissism* (1975), *Object Relations Theory and Clinical Psychoanalysis* (1976), *Internal World and External Reality* (1980), *Severe Personality Disorders* (1984), *Aggression in Personality Disorders and Perversions* (1992), *Love Relations* (1995), *Ideology, Conflict, and Leadership in Groups and Organizations* (1998), *Aggressivity, Narcissism, and Self-Destructiveness in the Psychotherapeutic Relationship* (2004), and *Contemporary Controversies in Psychoanalytic Theory, Technique, and Their Applications* (2004), as well as a number of co-authored and edited volumes.

Joshua Levy, is a Training and Supervisory Analyst, Canadian Institute of Psychoanalysis and is on the faculty of the Toronto Institute of Contemporary Psychoanalysis. His publications focus on the understanding and interpretation of dreams within the various phases of analytic treatment and on analytic supervision. He is much sought after as a supervisor and teaches on dream theory, among other topics.

Ashok Nagpal is Professor of Psychology at the University of Delhi and also holds the office of the Dean of the School of Human Studies at Ambedkar University in New Delhi. He is the founder of the Centre for Psychoanalytic Studies at the University of Delhi and has served as its first Director. His academic interests involve the development and application of psychoanalytic ideas to the Indian cultural context. He has devoted much effort to ensure an interdisciplinary orientation in humanities, especially relying upon the works of Freud, Winnicott, and Erikson. He has published on social change in India, aspects of the nation's popular culture, and the contribution of transitional phenomena in the texture of India's cultural psychology.

Mary Kay O'Neil, a supervising and training analyst of the Canadian Institute of Psychoanalysis is in private practice in Montreal, Quebec. She completed her PhD at the University of Toronto. Currently, she is Director of the Canadian Institute of Psychoanalysis (Quebec English) and secretary—treasurer of the Canadian Institute of Psychoanalysis. She is author of *The Unsung Psychoanalysis: The Quiet Influence of Ruth Easser,* and co-editor of *Confidentiality: Ethical Perspectives and Clinical Dilemmas* and of *On Freud's "The Future of an Illusion".* Her research and publications include areas such as depression and young adult development, emotional needs of sole-support mothers, post-analytic contact, and psychoanalytic ethics. She has served on a number of IPA committees as well as ethics committees at the local, national, and international levels and is currently on the Editorial Board of the International Journal of Psychoanalysis.

Henri Parens is Professor of Psychiatry, Thomas Jefferson University, and a Training and Supervising Analyst at the Psychoanalytic Center of Philadelphia. He is the author of over 200 scientific and lay publications and multi-media programs, including 18 books, 9 of which he authored—*Dependence in Man* (1971), *The Development of*

Aggression in Early Childhood (1979 [2008]); *Aggression in Our Children* (1987; German edition, 1994; Russian edition, 1997); a four-volume set of *Parenting for Emotional Growth* (1995–1997); *Renewal of Life? Healing from the Holocaust* (2004; German edition, 2007; French edition, 2010); and *Handling Children's Aggression Constructively: Toward Taming Human Destructiveness* (2010). His nine co-edited books include *Prevention in Mental Health* (1993; with S. Kramer); *The Future of Prejudice: Psychoanalysis and the Prevention of Prejudice* (2007; with A. Mahfouz, S. W. Twemlow, & D. Scharff); and *The Unbroken Soul: Tragedy, Trauma, and Human Resilience* (2008; with H. Blum & S. Akhtar). He has also made five scientific films, one documentary entitled *The Urgent Need for Parenting Education* and one television series for CBS: 39 programmes entitled, *Parenting: Love and Much More*. He is the recipient of many honours and awards, including Miriam Brown World of the Child Award (1993), Lifetime Achievement Award, Philadelphia Psychiatric Association (1999); Pennsylvania Psychiatric Society's Presidential Award (2004); Dean's Citation for Significant Contributions to the Advancement of Education at Jefferson Medical College (2004); Lifetime Achievement Award, Regional Council of Child and Adolescent Psychiatry (2005); and The Arnold Lucius Gesell Preis (Munich, 2008). His principal research efforts include the prevention of the development of aggression in early childhood, of violence and malignant prejudice, and of experience-derived emotional disorders as well as methods of education for parenting. Dr Parens is a Holocaust survivor.

Richard Theisen Simanke is Associate Professor at the Federal University of São Carlos, Brazil. He has been professor and supervisor (M.A. and Ph.D.) in the Program of Graduate Studies in Philosophy since 1997 and in the Program of Graduate Studies in Psychology since 2009, both at Federal University of São Carlos. His main publications include the books *A formação da teoria freudiana das psicoses* [The development of Freud's theory of psychoses] (1994; second ed. 2009), *Metapsicologia lacaniana: Os anos de formação* [Lacanian metapsychology: The early years] (2002), *Mente, cérebro e consciência nos primórdios da metapsicologia freudiana* [Mind, brain, and consciousness in the beginnings of Freud's metapsychology] (2007), *Entre o corpo e a consciência: Ensaios de interpretação da metapsicologia freudiana* [Between body and consciousness: Essays on Freud's metapsychology] (2011; with Fátima Caropreso), and *Ciência, teoria e metáfora: Estudos em* *filosofia da psicanálise* [Science, theory and metaphor: Studies in the philosophy of psychoanalysis] (forthcoming), as well as many other articles and essays published in Brazil and abroad. He also co-edited *Freud na filosofia brasileira* [Freud in Brazilian philosophy] (2005), *Perspectivas em Psicanálise* [Perspectives in psychoanalysis] (2009), and *Filosofia da psicanálise: Autores, diálogos, problemas* [Philosophy of psychoanalysis: Authors, dialogues, problems] (2010).

W. Craig Tomlinson is an Assistant Clinical Professor of Psychiatry and is on the faculty of the Center for Psychoanalytic Training and Research at Columbia University. He has written on the history of psychoanalysis in America in the twentieth century and on the development of psychology in eighteenth-century Germany, and has also translated works from the German on psychoanalysis, art, and music.

Elisabeth Young-Bruehl practiced psychoanalysis in Philadelphia and New York, and now lives in Toronto, where she is a member of the Toronto Psychoanalytic Society. She has written many books, including biographies of Hannah Arendt and Anna Freud, *Creative Characters* (1991), *The Anatomy of Prejudices* (1996), *Subject to Biography* (1999), *Cherishment* (2000), as well as essays collected into three volumes. *Childism* is forthcoming in 2011.

ON FREUD'S
"BEYOND THE PLEASURE PRINCIPLE"

Introduction

Salman Akhtar

Like the Masud Khan saga, the emergence of the "death-instinct" concept is a turn in the history of psychoanalysis that remains somewhat unfathomable. Both events trouble us. Both stir up wishes to deny and repudiate. We want to say that "this did not happen", "let us forget about it", "it is not really that important", or "it does not matter in the long run". However, the very fact that we are traumatized by them makes us revisit them. We bring renewed epistemic vigour to them. We want to understand what happened. Why? How? And, with what great or small consequences? We are also pulled to re-examine these two narratives by the mysterious and ever so slightly eroticized allure all psychic wounds possess. The tale of Masud Khan and the notion of "death instinct" have indeed cut through the skin of psychoanalysis.

The former is not our concern here, though. The latter is. That this should be so is hardly surprising, since our book is built around *Beyond the Pleasure Principle*, the essay in which Freud (1920g) introduced the concept of the "death instinct". Before delving into the controversy surrounding this heuristic leap, however, let us take a step back and put matters into their context. The reason that text is a crucial turning point in the evolution of

1

psychoanalytic thought is that it radically altered Freud's theory of human motivation. His original view (Freud, 1905d, 1915c) was that there were two fundamental motivating forces: "sexual instinct" and "self-preservatory instinct". The former sought erotic pleasure through discharge and served the goal of species propagation; the latter sought safety and growth and served the goal of self-preservation. With Freud's change of heart in 1920, this perspective came to be retrospectively known as his "first dual-instinct theory". His "second dual instinct theory", enunciated in *Beyond the Pleasure Principle*, classified instincts into "life instinct" and "death instinct". The former subsumed the prior categories of "sexual" and "self preservatory" instincts. The latter was a new concept: it referred to a "daemonic force" (p. 35), which searched for psychosomatic quiescence and, at its deepest core, sought to reduce the animate to its original inanimate status.

The shift from the first to the second dual instinct theory sent a seismic shock wave through the foundations of psychoanalytic theory. Many concepts now warranted reconsideration. The original formulation that sadism was primary and masochism was its inverted form was reversed, with the concept of death instinct placing masochism to be the primary phenomenon and sadism to be its externalized consequence. The operative supremacy of "pleasure principle" (Freud, 1911, 1916–1917) in mental life was also brought into question. Indeed, the definition of "pleasure" itself became muddled. If the aim of the death instinct was to make the subject inanimate, then how and by whom could the discharge of this instinct be felt as pleasurable? Yet another conundrum was in the realm of repetition, which in 1920 received an explanation that was entirely different from the one given to it in the 1914 paper, "Remembering, Repeating and Working-Through" (1914g). And then there were traumatic dreams that defied the erstwhile solid wish-fulfilment hypothesis and needed to be reconsidered. The list goes on.

Three major consequences of the changed instinct theory

Three other consequences of the revised instinct theory had an even greater impact upon the subsequent evolution of psychoanalytic thought and praxis. These include (a) the elevation of aggression to an independent instinctual drive, (b) the unintended marginalization of self-preservatory instincts, and (c) the pronouncement that death—with or without an accompanying "instinct", so to speak—was a life-long existential concern. Now let us take a careful look at these three issues.

The elevated status of aggression

It was in *Three Essays on the Theory of Sexuality* that Freud (1905d) began to develop his instinct theory, though it was a few years later that he first explicitly referred to the "instincts of self-preservation and of sex" (1909b, p. 140). In the 1905 trilogy, Freud focused attention on sadism and masochism. He regarded sadism as a component of sexual instinct and masochism as sadism turned around upon the subject's own self. Freud correlated sadism with the instinct of mastery as well and spoke of masochism as a passive "instinct of cruelty" (1905d, p. 193). However, only four years later he declared that he could not bring himself "to assume the existence of a special aggressive instinct alongside the familiar instinct of self-preservation and sex, and an equal footing with them" (1909b, p. 140).

In later works, especially *Instincts and Their Vicissitudes*, Freud (1915c) held on to the dichotomy between sexual and self-preservatory instincts, again assigning sadism to the sexual instinct. However, as Parens (1979) has cogently argued, a tension similar to that in the *Three Essays* between viewing aggression as a component of sexual instinct and viewing it as a component of self-preservatory instinct exists here as well. This dilemma was automatically laid to rest with Freud's postulation of his "second dual instinct theory". He now relegated both sexual and self-preservatory instincts to the "life instinct" and elevated aggression to an independent instinctual drive. In a "startling" (Jones, 1957, p. 266) theoretical move, he declared this aggressive drive to be the derivative of the death instinct, which, together with the life instinct, formed the two main forces in the struggle of life. Over the subsequent years, Freud became increasingly committed to this view. In *The Ego and the Id* (1923b), he repeated this theory. In *Civilization and Its Discontents*, he emphasized that "aggression is an original, self-subsisting disposition in the man" (1930a, p. 122). In polar opposition to his 1905 view that destructive aggression was not an independent instinct but a reaction to thwarted self-preservatory instinct, Freud now suggested that "the instinct of destruction, moderated and tamed, and, as it were, inhibited in its aim, must, when it is directed towards objects, provide the ego with the satisfaction of its vital needs and with control over nature" (1930a, p. 121).

This exalted status of aggression led subsequent psychoanalysts to pay great attention to it; prominent theoreticians (e.g. C. Brenner, 1971; A. Freud, 1972; Hartmann, 1939; Hartmann, Kris, & Loewenstein, 1949), who did not concur with Freud's proposal of death instinct, found the "aggressive instinct" to be a face-saving compromise that allowed them at least partial loyalty to the master. The securely established central place of aggression also provided an anchor to the view that man was inherently destructive—an idea upon which Freud elaborated further a decade later, in *Civilization and Its Discontents* (1930a). Freud's grim take on the nature of man, in turn, discouraged generations of psychoanalysts from studying the positive and "good" aspects of human beings (Akhtar, 2009a). All in all, the elevated status of aggression had major consequences for the subsequent development of psychoanalytic thought.

The unintended marginalization of self-preservatory instincts

An unintended consequence of the dramatic juxtaposition of life and death instincts in *Beyond the Pleasure Principle* was that their more noisy constituents—that is, sex and aggression—grabbed all the investigative attention, and the "quieter" (Modell, 1975) instincts of self-preservation came to be ignored. The latter were the forces aimed at self-protection and self-seeking. They operated under the reality principle and carried an energy of their own that was not libido but "interest" (Freud, 1905d, 1915c). Freud's elevation of aggression in the hierarchy of instincts thus siphoned off attention from self-preservatory instincts. Motivation, psychopathology, and transferences were now infrequently traced back to thwarted self-preservative tendencies. The wishes generated by sexual and aggressive drives took centre stage, and the needs emanating from self-preservatory instincts were confined to the theoretical and clinical green room. Indeed, the entire concept of self-preservatory instincts became heuristically "repressed". Yet, like the repressed, which exerts a "continuous pressure in the direction of the conscious" (Freud, 1915d, p. 151), it kept seeking readmission into the main corpus of the psychoanalytic thought. Balint (1955) proposed the concept of a non-erotic "primary love" that was akin to the self-sustaining need for attachment. Winnicott (1960) spoke of "ego needs". Casement (1991) reformulated the concept as "growth needs", distinguishing them from libidinal demands. In North America, where until recently the works of Winnicott and Balint were rarely read, it became necessary to formulate the principles of self psychology (Kohut, 1977; Wolf, 1988).

Freud's going from his first dual-instinct theory to his second dual-instinct theory and not to a "triple-instinct theory" (sexual, aggressive, and self-preservatory instincts) resulted in this particular conundrum of having to rediscover self-preservatory instinct-like concepts ("psychic needs", "developmental needs", "ego needs", "growth needs", "self-object needs", etc.) over and over again.

The introduction of death as a fundamental content of the human mind

While wishful thinking on the part of many psychoanalysts has led to their viewing Freud's "death-instinct" concept as a proverbial red herring, the fact is that this notion is of profound significance. Having elucidated this multifaceted topic elsewhere in detail (Akhtar, 1995, 2009b, 2010, 2011), a brief mention of four areas that are deeply influenced by the acceptance of the "death-instinct" concept will suffice here.

First and foremost, it is to be noted that death instinct, like its counterpart, the life instinct, is present from the moment of birth until we die. Even though it operates silently (Freud, 1923b), its influence ensures that "the aim of all life is death" (Freud, 1920g, p. 38). The phrase "all life" can have two meanings: it can refer to the life of *all* people or to *all* the phases—childhood, adolescence, adulthood—of a single individual's life. Thinking along the latter path creates the possibility that a "developmental line" (A. Freud,

1963) of death-related concerns exists over the course of human life span. Freud's *Todesangst* (1923b, p. 58) might actually underlie, or, at least fuel, the anxieties of separateness and castration—rather than the other way around. It might appear in inverted form as counterphobic attitudes of adolescence and contribute to Jones' (1927) "aphanisis"—that is, the dread that one might lose sexual desire altogether and become separated from love objects forever. Such an unblinking look at the psychological vicissitudes of death throughout life has the potential of greatly enriching psychoanalytic theory.

Second, death instinct, far from being an unverifiable "biological speculation" (Hartmann, 1939, p. 11), is a clinically useful concept. While Melanie Klein (1933, 1935, 1952) championed the concept from its inception, her work remained focused on the externalized derivatives of the death instinct. This led to a deeper understanding of the creation of "bad" objects, cruel impulses, and paranoid anxieties. The contributions of her followers (Joseph, chapter 7 this volume; also Bion, 1957; Feldman, 2000; Rosenfeld, 1971) have extended the clinical utility of the death-instinct concept by demonstrating its impact upon mental operations. They emphasize the capacity of this instinct to unhinge mental links, oversimplify things, and reduce the tonus of psychic activity, ultimately to the point of its non-existence. From their perspective, the death instinct is directed not actually towards death but towards the destruction and distortion of the meaning and value of subjective and intersubjective life.

Third, while the potential origins of the death-instinct concept in Freud's personal life (e.g. the death of his daughter, Sophie; his own struggle with cancer) are well known, the intellectual sources for the death-instinct idea are not optimally noted. Freud acknowledged (1920g) borrowing the expression "Nirvana principle" from Barbara Low, a Sanskrit expert. The notion of the death instinct had, thus, from the beginning, an Eastern touch. Gustav Fechner, the renowned physicist whose "constancy principle" led Freud to the "Nirvana principle", was himself involved in Buddhism (Jones, 1957). And Romain Rolland, from whom Freud (1930a) obtained the related concept of "oceanic feeling", was an avid reader and biographer of the nineteenth-century Bengali mystics, Sri Rama-krishna Paramahansa and Swami Vivekananda. The Indian mystical tradition was thus a background conceptual source for Freud's death instinct. In this tradition, self was an illusion and an ever-changing process, rather than a clearly etched, sustained structure. The ultimate purpose of life was to be rid of the cycles of birth and death, to become one with the Creator. Loss of self, instead of being terrifying, was regarded as the supreme relief, or Nirvana. Such Eastern foundations of the death-instinct concept might have contributed to the unease felt by Western psychoanalysts regarding this concept. This resistance parallels the slowness that the West displayed in embracing the mathematical concept of zero. The idea of zero was, incidentally, also developed by the Hindus in India, who were without fear of either the void or the infinite as it exists in the cosmos (Seife, 2000). Regardless of such correlations, as far as the death instinct is concerned, time has come to explicitly acknowledge its Eastern origins. Such acknowledgment would give further credence to the fact that Freud's fear that psychoanalysis might be reduced to a "Jewish national concern" (letter to Karl Abraham, 3 May 1908, in Falzeder, 2002 was ill-founded. It would also open up vistas for exploring other potential East–West links (e.g. Bion's [1965] "O") in the development of psychoanalytic theory.

Finally, the acknowledgment of death's psychic existence from the beginning of life until its end has an impact upon how the analyst understands certain material that emerges during clinical work. For instance, he might put aside the customary inclination to view the funereal atmosphere during the termination phase as merely metaphorical. He might take it as the patient's desperate plea to be helped in talking about his actual mortality, which concerns him greatly, even though at an unconscious level. Exploring patients' feelings and attitudes about their mortality and helping them to gain a more active role in their post-death destiny are other ways in which the acceptance of death as an important psychic variable becomes evident in working with patients (Akhtar, 2011). This novel perspective does not put the usual analytic scepticism about the manifest content aside, nor does it recommend that the analyst introduce the topic of the patient's mortality. It only emphasizes the need to discern the ubiquitous though derivative presence of death-related concerns in the patient's associations.

Concluding remarks

Before closing, I want to make one more point: one that pertains to the fact that Freud often used the term "death instinct" in its plural form. On at least eight occasions in *Beyond the Pleasure Principle* (pp. 47, 49, 53 twice, 57, 60, 61, 63), in a letter to Max Eitingon (20 February 1920, cited in Strachey, 1955, p. 4), in *The Ego and the Id* (1923b, pp. 46, 54, 59), in his succinct version of the libido theory (Freud, 1923a, p. 258), and in "The Economic Problem of Masochism" (1924c, p. 160), Freud talks of "death instincts" rather than "death instinct". This linguistic usage has been given little attention, though it certainly appears curious. What could he have meant by death instincts? Are there many of them? I do not know. However, four possible explanations of Freud's use of the plural denomination are:

▷ *It is an aesthetic and formal accommodation to the designation "life instincts"* (which subsumed sexual and self-preservatory instincts and could, therefore, legitimately be rendered in the plural form), an expression Freud also uses. But, it is difficult to swallow that a writer of his great excellence and rigor would succumb to a phonetic gimmick of such variety.

▷ *It is an anomaly produced by the English translation of Freud's original work in German.* This idea falls flat when one finds that the rendition of death instinct in its plural form is as frequent in the original German as in its translated form (Peter Hoffer, personal communication, January 2010).

▷ *It is a manifestation of the defence that has come to be known as "denial by exaggeration"* (Fenichel, 1945; Sperling, 1963). This mechanism rests upon making a threatening id derivative or superego command into a gross caricature. By overstating the issue at hand, an air of mockery or maudlin sentimentality is injected, which helps to minimize the threat to the ego posed by the situation. Extrapolating this idea to the issue under consideration makes one wonder whether referring to "death instincts" helped Freud ward off the anxiety produced by his dark discovery of the death instinct.

▷ *It is an indicator that there might be more than one type of death instinct.* Varieties of death instinct might exist along the lines of intensity (mild versus strong), energic regulation (bound versus un-bound), libidinal admixture (eroticized versus non-eroticized), age-specificity (developmentally appropriate versus anachronistic), and even, its aim (malignant versus benign).

The last possibility is especially intriguing, since it can help to explain the divergent perspectives on death itself: death as a threat to life versus death as a welcome relief from life (Akhtar, 2010). Here again, the West–East cultural difference comes into play. But matters are perhaps larger than that. The view of death as fundamentally unacceptable might be a manifestation of "malignant death instinct". The view of death as acceptable and, past a certain age, even desirable might be the product of "benign" death instinct. The "malignant" variety of death instinct might be responsible for attacks on linking, black holes in the mind, autoimmune disorders, and intense sadomasochism. The "benign" variety of death instinct might be responsible for positive emptiness, dreamless sleep, fallow states of mind, and the psychic pause that often precedes a creative act. If the distinction along these lines holds, then the phenomenological scene involving the two death instincts would appear quite different. It would be evident that the "malignant" variety marches to the drumbeat of impending self-implosion while the "benign" variety sings soothing lullabies for eternal rest. Conceptualization along such lines would open up new vistas not only for psychoanalytic technique, but also for psychoanalytic theory at large.

Talking of theory brings us full circle back to the beginning of our discourse. We remind ourselves that Freud's (1920g) *Beyond the Pleasure Principle* resulted in altered perspectives on a number of concepts. These included:

1. sexual and self-preservatory instincts, which became subsumed under the "life instinct";
2. the resulting loss of the pride of place for the self-preservatory instinct;
3. the proposal of death instinct;
4. the elevation of aggression in the hierarchy of instincts;
5. the shift of aggression from self-preservatory to the death instinct;

6. the reversal in the primacy of sadism and masochism;
7. an instinctual foundation to the phenomenon of repetition;
8. enrichment of the theory of dreams;
9. the postulate that death was psychologically present from the inception of life and, in fact, was the latter's ultimate aim.

All these ideas are thoroughly addressed in the pages of our book. The contributions contained here pertain to teaching (Tomlinson) of *Beyond the Pleasure Principle,* Freud's revised instinct theory and its implications for the understanding of aggression (Parens, Caro-preso, and Simanke), technical implications of the death-instinct concept (Joseph, Feldman, Kernberg), a revised and enriched perspective on dreams (Levy) and on the repetition compulsion (Brenner), an Eastern perspective on death (Nagpal), and a final overview of what was missed (Young-Bruehl). This is a rich menu indeed. While the authors of these essays occasionally disagree both with Freud's views and with those of each other, their lively and wide-ranging discourse on the proposals he made in 1920 would have delighted Freud. It would have been a source of happiness for him or, dare I say, a joy that is beyond pleasure?

PART I

Beyond the Pleasure Principle
(1920g)

Sigmund Freud

BEYOND THE PLEASURE PRINCIPLE

I

In the theory of psycho-analysis we have no hesitation in assuming that the course taken by mental events is automatically regulated by the pleasure principle. We believe, that is to say, that the course of those events is invariably set in motion by an unpleasurable tension, and that it takes a direction such that its final outcome coincides with a lowering of that tension—that is, with an avoidance of unpleasure or a production of pleasure. In taking that course into account in our consideration of the mental processes which are the subject of our study, we are introducing an 'economic' point of view into our work; and if, in describing those processes, we try to estimate this 'economic' factor in addition to the 'topographical' and 'dynamic' ones, we shall, I think, be giving the most complete description of them of which we can at present conceive, and one which deserves to be distinguished by the term 'metapsychological'.[1]

It is of no concern to us in this connection to enquire how far, with this hypothesis of the pleasure principle, we have approached or adopted any particular, historically established, philosophical system. We have arrived at these speculative assumptions in an attempt to describe and to account for the facts of daily observation in our field of study. Priority and originality are not among the aims that psycho-analytic work sets itself; and the impressions that underlie the hypothesis of the pleasure principle are so obvious that they can scarcely be overlooked. On the other hand we would readily express our gratitude to any philosophical or psychological theory which was able to inform us of the meaning of the feelings of pleasure and unpleasure which act so imperatively upon us. But on this point we are, alas, offered nothing to our purpose. This is the most obscure and inaccessible region of the mind, and, since we cannot avoid contact with it, the least rigid hypothesis, it seems to me, will be the best. We have decided to relate

[1] [See Section IV of 'The Unconscious' (1915e).]

7

pleasure and unpleasure to the quantity of excitation that is present in the mind but is not in any way 'bound'; [1] and to relate them in such a manner that unpleasure corresponds to an *increase* in the quantity of excitation and pleasure to a *diminution*. What we are implying by this is not a simple relation between the strength of the feelings of pleasure and unpleasure and the corresponding modifications in the quantity of excitation; least of all—in view of all we have been taught by psychophysiology—are we suggesting any directly proportional ratio: the factor that determines the feeling is probably the amount of increase or diminution in the quantity of excitation *in a given period of time*. Experiment might possibly play a part here; but it is not advisable for us analysts to go into the problem further so long as our way is not pointed by quite definite observations. [2]

We cannot, however, remain indifferent to the discovery that an investigator of such penetration as G. T. Fechner held a view on the subject of pleasure and unpleasure which coincides in all essentials with the one that has been forced upon us by psycho-analytic work. Fechner's statement is to be found contained in a small work, *Einige Ideen zur Schöpfungs- und Entwicklungsgeschichte der Organismen*, 1873 (Part XI, Supplement, 94), and reads as follows: 'In so far as conscious impulses always have some relation to pleasure or unpleasure, pleasure and unpleasure too can be regarded as having a psycho-physical relation to conditions of stability and instability. This provides a basis for a hypothesis into which I propose to enter in greater detail elsewhere. According to this hypothesis, every psychophysical motion rising above the threshold of consciousness is attended by pleasure in proportion as, beyond a certain limit, it approximates to complete stability, and is attended by unpleasure in proportion as, beyond a certain limit, it deviates from complete stability; while between the two limits, which may be described as qualitative thresholds of pleasure and

---

[1] [The concepts of 'quantity' and of 'bound' excitation, which run through the whole of Freud's writings, found what is perhaps their most detailed discussion in the early 'Project' (1950a [1895]). See in particular the long discussion of the term 'bound' near the end of Section 1 of Part III of that work. See also p. 34 f. below.]

[2] [This point is again mentioned below on p. 63 and further developed in 'The Economic Problem of Masochism' (1924c).]

unpleasure, there is a certain margin of aesthetic indiffer-ence. . . .' [1]

The facts which have caused us to believe in the dominance of the pleasure principle in mental life also find expression in the hypothesis that the mental apparatus endeavours to keep the quantity of excitation present in it as low as possible or at least to keep it constant. This latter hypothesis is only another way of stating the pleasure principle; for if the work of the mental apparatus is directed towards keeping the quantity of excitation low, then anything that is calculated to increase that quantity is bound to be felt as adverse to the functioning of the apparatus, that is as unpleasurable. The pleasure principle follows from the principle of constancy: actually the latter principle was inferred from the facts which forced us to adopt the pleasure principle.[2] Moreover, a more detailed discussion will show that the tendency which we thus attribute to the mental apparatus is subsumed as a special case under Fechner's principle of the 'tendency towards stability', to which he has brought the feelings of pleasure and unpleasure into relation.

It must be pointed out, however, that strictly speaking it is incorrect to talk of the dominance of the pleasure principle over the course of mental processes. If such a dominance existed, the immense majority of our mental processes would have to be accompanied by pleasure or to lead to pleasure, whereas universal experience completely contradicts any such con-clusion. The most that can be said, therefore, is that there exists in the mind a strong *tendency* towards the pleasure principle, but that that tendency is opposed by certain other forces or circum-stances, so that the final outcome cannot always be in harmony

---

[1] [Cf. 'Project', end of Section 8 of Part I.—'Aesthetic' is here used in the old sense of 'relating to sensation or perception'.]

[2] [The 'principle of constancy' dates back to the very beginning of Freud's psychological studies. The first published discussion of it of any length was by Breuer (in semi-physiological terms) towards the end of Section 2(A) of his theoretical part of the *Studies on Hysteria* (Breuer and Freud, 1895). He there defines it as 'the tendency to keep intracerebral excitation constant'. In the same passage he attributes this principle to Freud and there in fact exist one or two earlier very brief references to it by Freud himself, though these were not published until after his death. (See Freud, 1941a [1892] and Breuer and Freud, 1940 [1892].) The subject is also discussed at length at the beginning of Freud's 'Project', under the name of 'neuronic inertia'.]

with the tendency towards pleasure. We may compare what Fechner (1873, 90) remarks on a similar point: 'Since however a tendency towards an aim does not imply that the aim is attained, and since in general the aim is attainable only by approximations. . . .'

If we turn now to the question of what circumstances are able to prevent the pleasure principle from being carried into effect, we find ourselves once more on secure and well-trodden ground and, in framing our answer, we have at our disposal a rich fund of analytic experience.

The first example of the pleasure principle being inhibited in this way is a familiar one which occurs with regularity. We know that the pleasure principle is proper to a *primary* method of working on the part of the mental apparatus, but that, from the point of view of the self-preservation of the organism among the difficulties of the external world, it is from the very outset inefficient and even highly dangerous. Under the influence of the ego's instincts of self-preservation, the pleasure principle is replaced by the *reality principle*.[1] This latter principle does not abandon the intention of ultimately obtaining pleasure, but it nevertheless demands and carries into effect the postponement of satisfaction, the abandonment of a number of possibilities of gaining satisfaction and the temporary toleration of unpleasure as a step on the long indirect road to pleasure. The pleasure principle long persists, however, as the method of working employed by the sexual instincts, which are so hard to 'educate', and, starting from those instincts, or in the ego itself, it often succeeds in overcoming the reality principle, to the detriment of the organism as a whole.

There can be no doubt, however, that the replacement of the pleasure principle by the reality principle can only be made responsible for a small number, and by no means the most intense, of unpleasurable experiences. Another occasion of the release of unpleasure, which occurs with no less regularity, is to be found in the conflicts and dissensions that take place in the mental apparatus while the ego is passing through its development into more highly composite organizations. Almost all the energy with which the apparatus is filled arises from its innate instinctual impulses. But these are not all allowed to reach

[1] [See 'Formulations on the Two Principles of Mental Functioning', Freud 1911*b*.]

the same phases of development. In the course of things it happens again and again that individual instincts or parts of instincts turn out to be incompatible in their aims or demands with the remaining ones, which are able to combine into the inclusive unity of the ego. The former are then split off from this unity by the process of repression, held back at lower levels of psychical development and cut off, to begin with, from the possibility of satisfaction. If they succeed subsequently, as can so easily happen with repressed sexual instincts, in struggling through, by roundabout paths, to a direct or to a substitutive satisfaction, that event, which would in other cases have been an opportunity for pleasure, is felt by the ego as unpleasure. As a consequence of the old conflict which ended in repression, a new breach has occurred in the pleasure principle at the very time when certain instincts were endeavouring, in accordance with the principle, to obtain fresh pleasure. The details of the process by which repression turns a possibility of pleasure into a source of unpleasure are not yet clearly understood or cannot be clearly represented; but there is no doubt that all neurotic unpleasure is of that kind—pleasure that cannot be felt as such.[1]

The two sources of unpleasure which I have just indicated are very far from covering the majority of our unpleasurable experiences. But as regards the remainder it can be asserted with some show of justification that their presence does not contradict the dominance of the pleasure principle. Most of the unpleasure that we experience is *perceptual* unpleasure. It may be perception of pressure by unsatisfied instincts; or it may be external perception which is either distressing in itself or which excites unpleasurable expectations in the mental apparatus—that is, which is recognized by it as a 'danger'. The reaction to these instinctual demands and threats of danger, a reaction which constitutes the proper activity of the mental apparatus, can then be directed in a correct manner by the pleasure principle or the reality principle by which the former is modified. This does not seem to necessitate any far-reaching limitation of the pleasure principle. Nevertheless the investigation of the mental reaction to external danger is precisely in a position to produce new material and raise fresh questions bearing upon our present problem.

[1] [*Footnote added* 1925:] No doubt the essential point is that pleasure and unpleasure, being conscious feelings, are attached to the ego.

S.F. XVIII—B

II

A CONDITION has long been known and described which occurs after severe mechanical concussions, railway disasters and other accidents involving a risk to life; it has been given the name of 'traumatic neurosis'. The terrible war which has just ended gave rise to a great number of illnesses of this kind, but it at least put an end to the temptation to attribute the cause of the disorder to organic lesions of the nervous system brought about by mechanical force.[1] The symptomatic picture presented by traumatic neurosis approaches that of hysteria in the wealth of its similar motor symptoms, but surpasses it as a rule in its strongly marked signs of subjective ailment (in which it resembles hypochondria or melancholia) as well as in the evidence it gives of a far more comprehensive general enfeeblement and disturbance of the mental capacities. No complete explanation has yet been reached either of war neuroses or of the traumatic neuroses of peace. In the case of the war neuroses, the fact that the same symptoms sometimes came about without the intervention of any gross mechanical force seemed at once enlightening and bewildering. In the case of the ordinary traumatic neuroses two characteristics emerge prominently: first, that the chief weight in their causation seems to rest upon the factor of surprise, of fright; and secondly, that a wound or injury inflicted simultaneously works as a rule against the development of a neurosis. 'Fright', 'fear' and 'anxiety'[2] are improperly used as synonymous expressions; they are in fact capable of clear distinction in their relation to danger. 'Anxiety' describes a particular state of expecting the danger or preparing for it, even though it may be an unknown one. 'Fear' requires a definite object of which to be afraid. 'Fright', however, is the name we give to the state a person gets into when he has run into danger without being prepared for it; it emphasizes the factor of surprise. I do not believe anxiety can produce a traumatic neuro-

[1] Cf. the discussion on the psycho-analysis of war neuroses by Freud, Ferenczi, Abraham, Simmel and Jones (1919) [to which Freud provided the introduction (1919d). See also his posthumously published 'Report on the Electrical Treatment of War Neuroses' (1955c [1920]).]

[2] [In German, 'Schreck', 'Furcht' and 'Angst'.]

12

sis. There is something about anxiety that protects its subject against fright and so against fright-neuroses. We shall return to this point later [p. 31 f.].[1]

The study of dreams may be considered the most trustworthy method of investigating deep mental processes. Now dreams occurring in traumatic neuroses have the characteristic of repeatedly bringing the patient back into the situation of his accident, a situation from which he wakes up in another fright. This astonishes people far too little. They think the fact that the traumatic experience is constantly forcing itself upon the patient even in his sleep is a proof of the strength of that experience: the patient is, as one might say, fixated to his trauma. Fixations to the experience which started the illness have long been familiar to us in hysteria. Breuer and Freud declared in 1893 [2] that 'hysterics suffer mainly from reminiscences'. In the war neuroses, too, observers like Ferenczi and Simmel have been able to explain certain motor symptoms by fixation to the moment at which the trauma occurred.

I am not aware, however, that patients suffering from traumatic neurosis are much occupied in their waking lives with memories of their accident. Perhaps they are more concerned with *not* thinking of it. Anyone who accepts it as something self-evident that their dreams should put them back at night into the situation that caused them to fall ill has misunderstood the nature of dreams. It would be more in harmony with their nature if they showed the patient pictures from his healthy past or of the cure for which he hopes. If we are not to be shaken in our belief in the wish-fulfilling tenor of dreams by the dreams of traumatic neurotics, we still have one resource open to us: we may argue that the function of dreaming, like so much else, is upset in this condition and diverted from its purposes, or we

[1] [Freud is very far indeed from always carrying out the distinction he makes here. More often than not he uses the word '*Angst*' to denote a state of fear without any reference to the future. It seems not unlikely that in this passage he is beginning to adumbrate the distinction drawn in *Inhibitions, Symptoms and Anxiety* (1926d) between anxiety as a reaction to a traumatic situation—probably equivalent to what is here called *Schreck*—and anxiety as a warning signal of the approach of such an event. See also his use of the phrase 'preparedness for anxiety' on p. 31.]

[2] ['On the Psychical Mechanism of Hysterical Phenomena', end of Section I.]

may be driven to reflect on the mysterious masochistic trends of the ego.[1]

At this point I propose to leave the dark and dismal subject of the traumatic neurosis and pass on to examine the method of working employed by the mental apparatus in one of its earliest *normal* activities—I mean in children's play.

The different theories of children's play have only recently been summarized and discussed from the psycho-analytic point of view by Pfeifer (1919), to whose paper I would refer my readers. These theories attempt to discover the motives which lead children to play, but they fail to bring into the foreground the *economic* motive, the consideration of the yield of pleasure involved. Without wishing to include the whole field covered by these phenomena, I have been able, through a chance opportunity which presented itself, to throw some light upon the first game played by a little boy of one and a half and invented by himself. It was more than a mere fleeting observation, for I lived under the same roof as the child and his parents for some weeks, and it was some time before I discovered the meaning of the puzzling activity which he constantly repeated.

The child was not at all precocious in his intellectual development. At the age of one and a half he could say only a few comprehensible words; he could also make use of a number of sounds which expressed a meaning intelligible to those around him. He was, however, on good terms with his parents and their one servant-girl, and tributes were paid to his being a 'good boy'. He did not disturb his parents at night, he conscientiously obeyed orders not to touch certain things or go into certain rooms, and above all he never cried when his mother left him for a few hours. At the same time, he was greatly attached to his mother, who had not only fed him herself but had also looked after him without any outside help. This good little boy, however, had an occasional disturbing habit of taking any small objects he could get hold of and throwing them away from him into a corner, under the bed, and so on, so that hunting for his toys and picking them up was often quite a business. As he did this he gave vent to a loud, long-drawn-out 'o-o-o-o', accompanied by an expression of interest and satisfaction. His mother

[1] [The last 15 words of this sentence were added in 1921. For all this see *The Interpretation of Dreams* (1900a), *Standard Ed.*, 5, 550 ff.]

and the writer of the present account were agreed in thinking that this was not a mere interjection but represented the German word '*fort*' ['gone']. I eventually realized that it was a game and that the only use he made of any of his toys was to play 'gone' with them. One day I made an observation which confirmed my view. The child had a wooden reel with a piece of string tied round it. It never occurred to him to pull it along the floor behind him, for instance, and play at its being a carriage. What he did was to hold the reel by the string and very skilfully throw it over the edge of his curtained cot, so that it disappeared into it, at the same time uttering his expressive 'o-o-o-o'. He then pulled the reel out of the cot again by the string and hailed its reappearance with a joyful '*da*' ['there']. This, then, was the complete game—disappearance and return. As a rule one only witnessed its first act, which was repeated untiringly as a game in itself, though there is no doubt that the greater pleasure was attached to the second act.[1]

The interpretation of the game then became obvious. It was related to the child's great cultural achievement—the instinctual renunciation (that is, the renunciation of instinctual satisfaction) which he had made in allowing his mother to go away without protesting. He compensated himself for this, as it were, by himself staging the disappearance and return of the objects within his reach. It is of course a matter of indifference from the point of view of judging the effective nature of the game whether the child invented it himself or took it over on some outside suggestion. Our interest is directed to another point. The child cannot possibly have felt his mother's departure as something agreeable or even indifferent. How then does his repetition of this distressing experience as a game fit in with the pleasure principle? It may perhaps be said in reply that her departure had to be enacted as a necessary preliminary to her joyful return, and that it was in the latter that lay the true purpose

[1] A further observation subsequently confirmed this interpretation fully. One day the child's mother had been away for several hours and on her return was met with the words 'Baby o-o-o-o!' which was at first incomprehensible. It soon turned out, however, that during this long period of solitude the child had found a method of making *himself* disappear. He had discovered his reflection in a full-length mirror which did not quite reach to the ground, so that by crouching down he could make his mirror-image 'gone'. [A further reference to this story will be found in *The Interpretation of Dreams*, Standard Ed., 5, 461n.]

of the game. But against this must be counted the observed fact that the first act, that of departure, was staged as a game in itself and far more frequently than the episode in its entirety, with its pleasurable ending.

No certain decision can be reached from the analysis of a single case like this. On an unprejudiced view one gets an impression that the child turned his experience into a game from another motive. At the outset he was in a *passive* situation—he was overpowered by the experience; but, by repeating it, unpleasurable though it was, as a game, he took on an *active* part. These efforts might be put down to an instinct for mastery that was acting independently of whether the memory was in itself pleasurable or not. But still another interpretation may be attempted. Throwing away the object so that it was 'gone' might satisfy an impulse of the child's, which was suppressed in his actual life, to revenge himself on his mother for going away from him. In that case it would have a defiant meaning: 'All right, then, go away! I don't need you. I'm sending you away myself.' A year later, the same boy whom I had observed at his first game used to take a toy, if he was angry with it, and throw it on the floor, exclaiming: 'Go to the fwont!' He had heard at that time that his absent father was 'at the front', and was far from regretting his absence; on the contrary he made it quite clear that he had no desire to be disturbed in his sole possession of his mother.[1] We know of other children who liked to express similar hostile impulses by throwing away objects instead of persons.[2] We are therefore left in doubt as to whether the impulse to work over in the mind some overpowering experience so as to make oneself master of it can find expression as a primary event, and independently of the pleasure principle. For, in the case we have been discussing, the child may, after all, only have been able to repeat his unpleasant experience in play because the repetition carried along with it a yield of pleasure of another sort but none the less a direct one.

Nor shall we be helped in our hesitation between these two views by further considering children's play. It is clear that in

---

[1] When this child was five and three-quarters, his mother died. Now that she was really 'gone' ('o-o-o'), the little boy showed no signs of grief. It is true that in the interval a second child had been born and had roused him to violent jealousy.

[2] Cf. my note on a childhood memory of Goethe's (1917*b*).

their play children repeat everything that has made a great impression on them in real life, and that in doing so they abreact the strength of the impression and, as one might put it, make themselves master of the situation. But on the other hand it is obvious that all their play is influenced by a wish that dominates them the whole time—the wish to be grown-up and to be able to do what grown-up people do. It can also be observed that the unpleasurable nature of an experience does not always unsuit it for play. If the doctor looks down a child's throat or carries out some small operation on him, we may be quite sure that these frightening experiences will be the subject of the next game; but we must not in that connection overlook the fact that there is a yield of pleasure from another source. As the child passes over from the passivity of the experience to the activity of the game, he hands on the disagreeable experience to one of his playmates and in this way revenges himself on a substitute.

Nevertheless, it emerges from this discussion that there is no need to assume the existence of a special imitative instinct in order to provide a motive for play. Finally, a reminder may be added that the artistic play and artistic imitation carried out by adults, which, unlike children's, are aimed at an audience, do not spare the spectators (for instance, in tragedy) the most painful experiences and can yet be felt by them as highly enjoyable.[1] This is convincing proof that, even under the dominance of the pleasure principle, there are ways and means enough of making what is in itself unpleasurable into a subject to be recollected and worked over in the mind. The consideration of these cases and situations, which have a yield of pleasure as their final outcome, should be undertaken by some system of aesthetics with an economic approach to its subject-matter. They are of no use for *our* purposes, since they presuppose the existence and dominance of the pleasure principle; they give no evidence of the operation of tendencies *beyond* the pleasure principle, that is, of tendencies more primitive than it and independent of it.

[1] [Freud had made a tentative study of this point in his posthumously published paper on 'Psychopathic Characters on the Stage' (1942a) which was probably written in 1905 or 1906.]

III

Twenty-five years of intense work have had as their result
that the immediate aims of psycho-analytic technique are quite
other to-day than they were at the outset. At first the analysing
physician could do no more than discover the unconscious
material that was concealed from the patient, put it together,
and, at the right moment, communicate it to him. Psychoanalysis was then first and foremost an art of interpreting.
Since this did not solve the therapeutic problem, a further aim
quickly came in view: to oblige the patient to confirm the
analyst's construction from his own memory. In that endeavour
the chief emphasis lay upon the patient's resistances: the art
consisted now in uncovering these as quickly as possible, in
pointing them out to the patient and in inducing him by human
influence—this was where suggestion operating as 'transference'
played its part—to abandon his resistances.

But it became ever clearer that the aim which had been set
up—the aim that what was unconscious should become conscious—is not completely attainable by that method. The
patient cannot remember the whole of what is repressed in him,
and what he cannot remember may be precisely the essential
part of it. Thus he acquires no sense of conviction of the cor-
rectness of the construction that has been communicated to
him. He is obliged to *repeat* the repressed material as a contemporary experience instead of, as the physician would prefer
to see, *remembering* it as something belonging to the past.[1] These
reproductions, which emerge with such unwished-for exacti-
tude, always have as their subject some portion of infantile
sexual life—of the Oedipus complex, that is, and its derivatives;
and they are invariably acted out in the sphere of the transference, of the patient's relation to the physician. When things
have reached this stage, it may be said that the earlier neurosis
has now been replaced by a fresh, 'transference neurosis'. It has

[1] See my paper on 'Recollecting, Repeating and Working Through'
(1914g). [An early reference will be found in this same paper to the
'compulsion to repeat', which is one of the principle topics discussed in
the present work. (See also the Editor's Note above, p. 5.)—The term
'transference neurosis' in the special sense in which it is used a few lines
lower down also appears in that paper.]

18

been the physician's endeavour to keep this transference neurosis within the narrowest limits: to force as much as possible into
the channel of memory and to allow as little as possible to
emerge as repetition. The ratio between what is remembered
and what is reproduced varies from case to case. The physician
cannot as a rule spare his patient this phase of the treatment.
He must get him to re-experience some portion of his forgotten
life, but must see to it, on the other hand, that the patient
retains some degree of aloofness, which will enable him, in spite
of everything, to recognize that what appears to be reality is in
fact only a reflection of a forgotten past. If this can be successfully achieved, the patient's sense of conviction is won, together
with the therapeutic success that is dependent on it.

In order to make it easier to understand this 'compulsion to
repeat', which emerges during the psycho-analytic treatment
of neurotics, we must above all get rid of the mistaken notion
that what we are dealing with in our struggle against resistances
is resistance on the part of the *unconscious*. The unconscious—
that is to say, the 'repressed'—offers no resistance whatever to
the efforts of the treatment. Indeed, it itself has no other endeavour than to break through the pressure weighing down on
it and force its way either to consciousness or to a discharge
through some real action. Resistance during treatment arises
from the same higher strata and systems of the mind which
originally carried out repression. But the fact that, as we know
from experience, the motives of the resistances, and indeed the
resistances themselves, are unconscious at first during the treatment, is a hint to us that we should correct a shortcoming in
our terminology. We shall avoid a lack of clarity if we make
our contrast not between the conscious and the unconscious but
between the coherent *ego*[1] and the *repressed*. It is certain that
much of the ego is itself unconscious, and notably what we may
describe as its nucleus; only a small part of it is covered by the
term 'preconscious'.[2] Having replaced a purely descriptive

[1] [The view of the ego as a coherent structure performing certain
functions seem to go back to Freud's 'Project'. See, for instance
Section 14 of Part I of that work (Freud 1950a). The subject was taken
up and developed in *The Ego and the Id*, 1923b. Cf. in particular the
end of Chapter I and Chapter II.

[2] [In its present form this sentence dates from 1921. In the first edition
(1920) it ran: 'It may be that much of the ego is itself unconscious; only
a part of it, probably, is covered by the term "preconscious".']

terminology by one which is systematic or dynamic, we can say that the patient's resistance arises from his ego,[1] and we then at once perceive that the compulsion to repeat must be ascribed to the unconscious repressed. It seems probable that the compulsion can only express itself after the work of treatment has gone half-way to meet it and has loosened the repression.[2]

There is no doubt that the resistance of the conscious and unconscious ego operates under the sway of the pleasure principle: it seeks to avoid the unpleasure which would be produced by the liberation of the repressed. *Our* efforts, on the other hand, are directed towards procuring the toleration of that unpleasure by an appeal to the reality principle. But how is the compulsion to repeat—the manifestation of the power of the repressed— related to the pleasure principle? It is clear that the greater part of what is re-experienced under the compulsion to repeat must cause the ego unpleasure, since it brings to light activities of repressed instinctual impulses. That, however, is unpleasure of a kind we have already considered and does not contradict the pleasure principle: unpleasure for one system and simultaneously satisfaction for the other.[3] But we come now to a new and remarkable fact, namely that the compulsion to repeat also recalls from the past experiences which include no possibility of pleasure, and which can never, even long ago, have brought satisfaction even to instinctual impulses which have since been repressed.

The early efflorescence of infantile sexual life is doomed to extinction because its wishes are incompatible with reality and with the inadequate stage of development which the child has reached. That efflorescence comes to an end in the most distressing circumstances and to the accompaniment of the most painful feelings. Loss of love and failure leave behind them a permanent injury to self-regard in the form of a narcissistic scar, which in my opinion, as well as in Marcinowski's (1918), contributes more than anything to the 'sense of inferiority'

---

[1] [A fuller and somewhat different account of the sources of resistance will be found in Chap. XI of *Inhibitions, Symptoms and Anxiety* (1926*d*).]

[2] [*Footnote added* 1923:] I have argued elsewhere [1923*c*] that what thus comes to the help of the compulsion to repeat is the factor of 'suggestion' in the treatment—that is, the patient's submissiveness to the physician, which has its roots deep in his unconscious parental complex.

[3] [Cf. Freud's allegorical use of the fairy tale of the 'Three Wishes' at the beginning of Lecture XIV of his *Introductory Lectures* (1916–17).]

which is so common in neurotics. The child's sexual researches, on which limits are imposed by his physical development, lead to no satisfactory conclusion; hence such later complaints as 'I can't accomplish anything; I can't succeed in anything'. The tie of affection, which binds the child as a rule to the parent of the opposite sex, succumbs to disappointment, to a vain expectation of satisfaction or to jealousy over the birth of a new baby—unmistakable proof of the infidelity of the object of the child's affections. His own attempt to make a baby himself, carried out with tragic seriousness, fails shamefully. The lessening amount of affection he receives, the increasing demands of education, hard words and an occasional punishment—these show him at last the full extent to which he has been scorned. These are a few typical and constantly recurring instances of the ways in which the love characteristic of the age of childhood is brought to a conclusion.

Patients repeat all of these unwanted situations and painful emotions in the transference and revive them with the greatest ingenuity. They seek to bring about the interruption of the treatment while it is still incomplete; they contrive once more to feel themselves scorned, to oblige the physician to speak severely to them and treat them coldly; they discover appropriate objects for their jealousy; instead of the passionately desired baby of their childhood, they produce a plan or a promise of some grand present—which turns out as a rule to be no less unreal. None of these things can have produced pleasure in the past, and it might be supposed that they would cause less unpleasure to-day if they emerged as memories or dreams instead of taking the form of fresh experiences. They are of course the activities of instincts intended to lead to satisfaction; but no lesson has been learnt from the old experience of these activities having led instead only to unpleasure.[1] In spite of that, they are repeated, under pressure of a compulsion.

What psycho-analysis reveals in the transference phenomena of neurotics can also be observed in the lives of some normal people. The impression they give is of being pursued by a malignant fate or possessed by some 'daemonic' power; but psycho-analysis has always taken the view that their fate is for the most part arranged by themselves and determined by early infantile influences. The compulsion which is here in evidence differs in

[1] [This sentence was added in 1921.]

no way from the compulsion to repeat which we have found in neurotics, even though the people we are now considering have never shown any signs of dealing with a neurotic conflict by producing symptoms. Thus we have come across people all of whose human relationships have the same outcome: such as the benefactor who is abandoned in anger after a time by each of his *protégés,* however much they may otherwise differ from one another, and who thus seems doomed to taste all the bitterness of ingratitude; or the man whose friendships all end in betrayal by his friend; or the man who time after time in the course of his life raises someone else into a position of great private or public authority and then, after a certain interval, himself upsets that authority and replaces him by a new one; or, again, the lover each of whose love affairs with a woman passes through the same phases and reaches the same conclusion. This 'perpetual recurrence of the same thing' causes us no astonishment when it relates to *active* behaviour on the part of the person concerned and when we can discern in him an essential character-trait which always remains the same and which is compelled to find expression in a repetition of the same experiences. We are much more impressed by cases where the subject appears to have a *passive* experience, over which he has no influence, but in which he meets with a repetition of the same fatality. There is the case, for instance, of the woman who married three successive husbands each of whom fell ill soon afterwards and had to be nursed by her on their death-beds.[1] The most moving poetic picture of a fate such as this is given by Tasso in his romantic epic *Gerusalemme Liberata.* Its hero, Tancred, unwittingly kills his beloved Clorinda in a duel while she is disguised in the armour of an enemy knight. After her burial he makes his way into a strange magic forest which strikes the Crusaders' army with terror. He slashes with his sword at a tall tree; but blood streams from the cut and the voice of Clorinda, whose soul is imprisoned in the tree, is heard complaining that he has wounded his beloved once again.

If we take into account observations such as these, based upon behaviour in the transference and upon the life-histories of men and women, we shall find courage to assume that there really does exist in the mind a compulsion to repeat which overrides the pleasure principle. Now too we shall be inclined to

[1] Cf. the apt remarks on this subject by C. G. Jung (1909).

relate to this compulsion the dreams which occur in traumatic neuroses and the impulse which leads children to play.

But it is to be noted that only in rare instances can we observe the pure effects of the compulsion to repeat, unsupported by other motives. In the case of children's play we have already laid stress on the other ways in which the emergence of the compulsion may be interpreted; the compulsion to repeat and instinctual satisfaction which is immediately pleasurable seem to converge here into an intimate partnership. The phenomena of transference are obviously exploited by the resistance which the ego maintains in its pertinacious insistence upon repression; the compulsion to repeat, which the treatment tries to bring into its service is, as it were, drawn over by the ego to *its* side (clinging as the ego does to the pleasure principle).[1] A great deal of what might be described as the compulsion of destiny seems intelligible on a rational basis; so that we are under no necessity to call in a new and mysterious motive force to explain it.

The least dubious instance [of such a motive force] is perhaps that of traumatic dreams. But on maturer reflection we shall be forced to admit that even in the other instances the whole ground is not covered by the operation of the familiar motive forces. Enough is left unexplained to justify the hypothesis of a compulsion to repeat—something that seems more primitive, more elementary, more instinctual than the pleasure principle which it over-rides. But if a compulsion to repeat *does* operate in the mind, we should be glad to know something about it, to learn what function it corresponds to, under what conditions it can emerge and what its relation is to the pleasure principle —to which, after all, we have hitherto ascribed dominance over the course of the processes of excitation in mental life.

---

[1] [Before 1923 the last clause read: 'the compulsion to repeat is as it were called to its help by the ego, clinging as it does to the pleasure principle.']

IV

WHAT follows is speculation, often far-fetched speculation, which the reader will consider or dismiss according to his individual predilection. It is further an attempt to follow out an idea consistently, out of curiosity to see where it will lead.

Psycho-analytic speculation takes as its point of departure the impression, derived from examining unconscious processes, that consciousness may be, not the most universal attribute of mental processes, but only a particular function of them. Speaking in metapsychological terms, it asserts that consciousness is a function of a particular system which it describes as *Cs.*[1] What consciousness yields consists essentially of perceptions of excitations coming from the external world and of feelings of pleasure and unpleasure which can only arise from within the mental apparatus; it is therefore possible to assign to the system *Pcpt.-Cs.*[2] a position in space. It must lie on the borderline between outside and inside; it must be turned towards the external world and must envelop the other psychical systems. It will be seen that there is nothing daringly new in these assumptions; we have merely adopted the views on localization held by cerebral anatomy, which locates the 'seat' of consciousness in the cerebral cortex—the outermost, enveloping layer of the central organ. Cerebral anatomy has no need to consider why, speaking anatomically, consciousness should be lodged on the surface of the brain instead of being safely housed somewhere in its inmost interior. Perhaps *we* shall be more successful in accounting for this situation in the case of our system *Pcpt.-Cs.*

Consciousness is not the only distinctive character which we ascribe to the processes in that system. On the basis of impressions derived from our psycho-analytic experience, we assume that all excitatory processes that occur in the *other* systems leave

---

[1] [See Freud, *The Interpretation of Dreams* (1900a), *Standard Ed.*, **5**, 610 ff., and 'The Unconscious' (1915e), Section II.]

[2] [The system *Pcpt.* (the perceptual system) was first described by Freud in *The Interpretation of Dreams, Standard Ed.*, **5**, 536 ff. In a later paper (1917d) he argued that the system *Pcpt.* coincided with the system *Cs.*]

24

permanent traces behind in them which form the foundation of memory. Such memory-traces, then, have nothing to do with the fact of becoming conscious; indeed they are often most powerful and most enduring when the process which left them behind was one which never entered consciousness. We find it hard to believe, however, that permanent traces of excitation such as these are also left in the system *Pcpt.-Cs.* If they remained constantly conscious, they would very soon set limits to the system's aptitude for receiving fresh excitations.[1] If, on the other hand, they were unconscious, we should be faced with the problem of explaining the existence of unconscious processes in a system whose functioning was otherwise accompanied by the phenomenon of consciousness. We should, so to say, have altered nothing and gained nothing by our hypothesis relegating the process of becoming conscious to a special system. Though this consideration is not absolutely conclusive, it nevertheless leads us to suspect that becoming conscious and leaving behind a memory-trace are processes incompatible with each other within one and the same system. Thus we should be able to say that the excitatory process becomes conscious in the system *Cs.* but leaves no permanent trace behind there; but that the excitation is transmitted to the systems lying next within and that it is in *them* that its traces are left. I followed these same lines in the schematic picture which I included in the speculative section of my *Interpretation of Dreams*.[2] It must be borne in mind that little enough is known from other sources of the origin of consciousness; when, therefore, we lay down the proposition that *consciousness arises instead of a memory-trace*, the assertion deserves consideration, at all events on the ground of its being framed in fairly precise terms.

If this is so, then, the system *Cs.* is characterized by the peculiarity that in it (in contrast to what happens in the other psychical systems) excitatory processes do not leave behind any permanent change in its elements but expire, as it were, in the phenomenon of becoming conscious. An exception of this sort

[1] What follows is based throughout on Breuer's views in [the second section of his theoretical contribution to] *Studies on Hysteria* (Breuer and Freud, 1895). [Freud himself discussed the subject in *The Interpretation of Dreams, Standard Ed.*, 5, 538 and it had previously been fully considered in his 'Project' of 1895 (1950a), Part I, Section 3. He returned to the topic later in his paper on the 'Mystic Writing-Pad' (1925a).]

[2] [*Standard Ed.*, 5, 538.]

to the general rule requires to be explained by some factor that applies exclusively to that one system. Such a factor, which is absent in the other systems, might well be the exposed situation of the system *Cs.*, immediately abutting as it does on the external world.

Let us picture a living organism in its most simplified possible form as an undifferentiated vesicle of a substance that is susceptible to stimulation. Then the surface turned towards the external world will from its very situation be differentiated and will serve as an organ for receiving stimuli. Indeed embryology, in its capacity as a recapitulation of developmental history, actually shows us that the central nervous system originates from the ectoderm; the grey matter of the cortex remains a derivative of the primitive superficial layer of the organism and may have inherited some of its essential properties. It would be easy to suppose, then, that as a result of the ceaseless impact of external stimuli on the surface of the vesicle, its substance to a certain depth may have become permanently modified, so that excitatory processes run a different course in it from what they run in the deeper layers. A crust would thus be formed which would at last have been so thoroughly 'baked through' by stimulation that it would present the most favourable possible conditions for the reception of stimuli and become incapable of any further modification. In terms of the system *Cs.*, this would mean that its elements could undergo no further permanent modification from the passage of excitation, because they had already been modified in the respect in question to the greatest possible extent: now, however, they would have become capable of giving rise to consciousness. Various ideas may be formed which cannot at present be verified as to the nature of this modification of the substance and of the excitatory process. It may be supposed that, in passing from one element to another, an excitation has to overcome a resistance, and that the diminution of resistance thus effected is what lays down a permanent trace of the excitation, that is, a facilitation. In the system *Cs.*, then, resistance of this kind to passage from one element to another would no longer exist.[1] This picture can be brought into relation with Breuer's distinction between quiescent (or bound) and mobile cathectic energy in the elements

[1] [This passage is foreshadowed in the later half of Section 3 of Part I of the 'Project'.]

of the psychical systems;[1] the elements of the system *Cs.* would carry no bound energy but only energy capable of free discharge. It seems best, however, to express oneself as cautiously as possible on these points. None the less, this speculation will have enabled us to bring the origin of consciousness into some sort of connection with the situation of the system *Cs.* and with the peculiarities that must be ascribed to the excitatory processes taking place in it.

But we have more to say of the living vesicle with its receptive cortical layer. This little fragment of living substance is suspended in the middle of an external world charged with the most powerful energies; and it would be killed by the stimulation emanating from these if it were not provided with a protective shield against stimuli. It acquires the shield in this way: its outermost surface ceases to have the structure proper to living matter, becomes to some degree inorganic and thenceforward functions as a special envelope or membrane resistant to stimuli. In consequence, the energies of the external world are able to pass into the next underlying layers, which have remained living, with only a fragment of their original intensity; and these layers can devote themselves, behind the protective shield, to the reception of the amounts of stimulus which have been allowed through it. By its death, the outer layer has saved all the deeper ones from a similar fate—unless, that is to say, stimuli reach it which are so strong that they break through the protective shield. *Protection against* stimuli is an almost more important function for the living organism than *reception of* stimuli. The protective shield is supplied with its own store of energy and must above all endeavour to preserve the special modes of transformation of energy operating in it against the effects threatened by the enormous energies at work in the external world—effects which tend towards a levelling out of them and hence towards destruction. The main purpose of the *reception* of stimuli is to discover the direction and nature of the external stimuli; and for that it is enough to take small specimens of the external world, to sample it in small quantities. In highly developed organisms the receptive cortical layer of the former vesicle has long been withdrawn into the depths of

[1] Breuer and Freud, 1895. [See Section 2 of Breuer's theoretical contribution, and in particular the footnote at the beginning of that section. Cf. also footnote 1 on p. 8 above.]

s.f. xviii—c

the interior of the body, though portions of it have been left behind on the surface immediately beneath the general shield against stimuli. These are the sense organs, which consist essentially of apparatus for the reception of certain specific effects of stimulation, but which also include special arrangements for further protection against excessive amounts of stimulation and for excluding unsuitable kinds of stimuli.[1] It is characteristic of them that they deal only with very small quantities of external stimulation and only take in *samples* of the external world. They may perhaps be compared with feelers which are all the time making tentative advances towards the external world and then drawing back from it.

At this point I shall venture to touch for a moment upon a subject which would merit the most exhaustive treatment. As a result of certain psycho-analytic discoveries, we are to-day in a position to embark on a discussion of the Kantian theorem that time and space are 'necessary forms of thought'. We have learnt that unconscious mental processes are in themselves 'timeless'.[2] This means in the first place that they are not ordered temporally, that time does not change them in any way and that the idea of time cannot be applied to them. These are negative characteristics which can only be clearly understood if a comparison is made with *conscious* mental processes. On the other hand, our abstract idea of time seems to be wholly derived from the method of working of the system *Pcpt.-Cs.* and to correspond to a perception on its own part of that method of working. This mode of functioning may perhaps constitute another way of providing a shield against stimuli. I know that these remarks must sound very obscure, but I must limit myself to these hints.[3]

We have pointed out how the living vesicle is provided with a shield against stimuli from the external world; and we had previously shown that the cortical layer next to that shield must be differentiated as an organ for receiving stimuli from without. This sensitive cortex, however, which is later to become the system *Cs.*, also receives excitations from *within*. The situation of the system between the outside and the inside and the differ-

---

[1] [Cf. 'Project', Part I, Sections 5 and 9.]

[2] [See Section V of 'The Unconscious' (1915*e*).]

[3] [Freud recurs to the origin of the idea of time at the end of his paper on 'The Mystic Writing-Pad' (1925*a*). The same paper contains a further discussion of the 'shield against stimuli'.]

ence between the conditions governing the reception of excitations in the two cases have a decisive effect on the functioning of the system and of the whole mental apparatus. Towards the outside it is shielded against stimuli, and the amounts of excitation impinging on it have only a reduced effect. Towards the inside there can be no such shield; [1] the excitations in the deeper layers extend into the system directly and in undiminished amount, in so far as certain of their characteristics give rise to feelings in the pleasure-unpleasure series. The excitations coming from within are, however, in their intensity and in other, qualitative, respects—in their amplitude, perhaps—more commensurate with the system's method of working than the stimuli which stream in from the external world.[2] This state of things produces two definite results. First, the feelings of pleasure and unpleasure (which are an index to what is happening in the interior of the apparatus) predominate over all external stimuli. And secondly, a particular way is adopted of dealing with any internal excitations which produce too great an increase of unpleasure: there is a tendency to treat them as though they were acting, not from the inside, but from the outside, so that it may be possible to bring the shield against stimuli into operation as a means of defence against them. This is the origin of *projection*, which is destined to play such a large part in the causation of pathological processes.

I have an impression that these last considerations have brought us to a better understanding of the dominance of the pleasure principle; but no light has yet been thrown on the cases that contradict that dominance. Let us therefore go a step further. We describe as 'traumatic' any excitations from outside which are powerful enough to break through the protective shield. It seems to me that the concept of trauma necessarily implies a connection of this kind with a breach in an otherwise efficacious barrier against stimuli. Such an event as an external trauma is bound to provoke a disturbance on a large scale in the functioning of the organism's energy and to set in motion every possible defensive measure. At the same time, the pleasure principle is for the moment put out of action. There is no longer any possibility of preventing the mental apparatus from being flooded with large amounts of stimulus, and another

[1] [Cf. 'Project', beginning of Section 10 of Part I.]
[2] [Cf. 'Project', later part of Section 4 of Part I.]

problem arises instead—the problem of mastering the amounts of stimulus which have broken in and of binding them, in the psychical sense, so that they can then be disposed of.

The specific unpleasure of physical pain is probably the result of the protective shield having been broken through in a limited area. There is then a continuous stream of excitations from the part of the periphery concerned to the central apparatus of the mind, such as could normally arise only from *within* the apparatus.[1] And how shall we expect the mind to react to this invasion? Cathectic energy is summoned from all sides to provide sufficiently high cathexes of energy in the environs of the breach. An 'anticathexis' on a grand scale is set up, for whose benefit all the other psychical systems are impoverished, so that the remaining psychical functions are extensively paralysed or reduced. We must endeavour to draw a lesson from examples such as this and use them as a basis for our metapsychological speculations. From the present case, then, we infer that a system which is itself highly cathected is capable of taking up an additional stream of fresh inflowing energy and of converting it into quiescent cathexis, that is of binding it psychically. The higher the system's own quiescent cathexis, the greater seems to be its binding force; conversely, therefore, the lower its cathexis, the less capacity will it have for taking up inflowing energy[2] and the more violent must be the consequences of such a breach in the protective shield against stimuli. To this view it cannot be justly objected that the increase of cathexis round the breach can be explained far more simply as the direct result of the inflowing masses of excitation. If that were so, the mental apparatus would merely receive an increase in its cathexes of energy, and the paralysing character of pain and the impoverishment of all the other systems would remain unexplained. Nor do the very violent phenomena of discharge to which pain gives rise affect our explanation, for they occur in a reflex manner—that is, they follow without the intervention of the mental apparatus. The indefiniteness of all our discussions on what we describe as metapsychology is of course due to the fact that we know nothing of the nature of the excitatory process that takes place in the elements of the

[1] Cf. 'Instincts and their Vicissitudes' (1915c), [and 'Project', Part I, Sections 6].

[2] [Cf. the 'principle of the insusceptibility to excitation of uncathected systems' in a footnote near the end of Freud, 1917d.]

psychical systems, and that we do not feel justified in framing any hypothesis on the subject. We are consequently operating all the time with a large unknown factor, which we are obliged to carry over into every new formula. It may be reasonably supposed that this excitatory process can be carried out with energies that vary *quantitatively*; it may also seem probable that it has more than one *quality* (in the nature of amplitude, for instance). As a new factor we have taken into consideration Breuer's hypothesis that charges of energy occur in two forms [see pp. 20–1]; so that we have to distinguish between two kinds of cathexis of the psychical systems or their elements—a freely flowing cathexis that presses on towards discharge and a quiescent cathexis. We may perhaps suspect that the binding of the energy that streams into the mental apparatus consists in its change from a freely flowing into a quiescent state.

We may, I think, tentatively venture to regard the common traumatic neurosis as a consequence of an extensive breach being made in the protective shield against stimuli. This would seem to reinstate the old, naive theory of shock, in apparent contrast to the later and psychologically more ambitious theory which attributes aetiological importance not to the effects of mechanical violence but to fright and the threat to life. These opposing views are not, however, irreconcilable; nor is the psycho-analytic view of the traumatic neurosis identical with the shock theory in its crudest form. The latter regards the essence of the shock as being the direct damage to the molecular structure or even to the histological structure of the elements of the nervous system; whereas what *we* seek to understand are the effects produced on the organ of the mind by the breach in the shield against stimuli and by the problems that follow in its train. And we still attribute importance to the element of fright. It is caused by lack of any preparedness for anxiety,[1] including lack of hypercathexis of the systems that would be the first to receive the stimulus. Owing to their low cathexis those systems are not in a good position for binding the inflowing amounts of excitation and the consequences of the breach in the protective shield follow all the more easily. It will be seen, then, that preparedness for anxiety and the hypercathexis of the receptive systems constitute the last line of defence of the shield against stimuli. In the case of quite a number of traumas, the

[1] [Cf. the note on p. 13 above.]

difference between systems that are unprepared and systems that are well prepared through being hypercathected may be a decisive factor in determining the outcome; though where the strength of a trauma exceeds a certain limit this factor will no doubt cease to carry weight. The fulfilment of wishes is, as we know, brought about in a hallucinatory manner by dreams, and under the dominance of the pleasure principle this has become their function. But it is not in the service of that principle that the dreams of patients suffering from traumatic neuroses lead them back with such regularity to the situation in which the trauma occurred. We may assume, rather, that dreams are here helping to carry out another task, which must be accomplished before the dominance of the pleasure principle can even begin. These dreams are endeavouring to master the stimulus retrospectively, by developing the anxiety whose omission was the cause of the traumatic neurosis. They thus afford us a view of a function of the mental apparatus which, though it does not contradict the pleasure principle, is nevertheless independent of it and seems to be more primitive than the purpose of gaining pleasure and avoiding unpleasure.

This would seem to be the place, then, at which to admit for the first time an exception to the proposition that dreams are fulfilments of wishes. Anxiety dreams, as I have shown repeatedly and in detail, offer no such exception. Nor do 'punishment dreams', for they merely replace the forbidden wish-fulfilment by the appropriate punishment for it; that is to say, they fulfil the wish of the sense of guilt which is the reaction to the repudiated impulse.[1] But it is impossible to classify as wish-fulfilments the dreams we have been discussing which occur in traumatic neuroses, or the dreams during psycho-analyses which bring to memory the psychical traumas of child-hood. They arise, rather, in obedience to the compulsion to repeat, though it is true that in analysis that compulsion is supported by the wish (which is encouraged by 'suggestion')[2] to conjure up what has been forgotten and repressed. Thus it would seem that the function of dreams, which consists in

[1] [See *The Interpretation of Dreams* (1900a), *Standard Ed.*, 5, 557, and Section 9 of Freud's 'Remarks on the Theory and Practice of Dream-Interpretation' (1923c).]

[2] [The clause in brackets was substituted in 1923 for the words 'which is not unconscious' which appeared in the earlier editions.]

setting aside any motives that might interrupt sleep, by fulfilling the wishes of the disturbing impulses, is not their *original* function. It would not be possible for them to perform that function until the whole of mental life had accepted the dominance of the pleasure principle. If there is a 'beyond the pleasure principle', it is only consistent to grant that there was also a time before the purpose of dreams was the fulfilment of wishes. This would imply no denial of their later function. But if once this general rule has been broken, a further question arises. May not dreams which, with a view to the psychical binding of traumatic impressions, obey the compulsion to repeat—may not such dreams occur *outside* analysis as well? And the reply can only be a decided affirmative.

I have argued elsewhere [1] that 'war neuroses' (in so far as that term implies something more than a reference to the circumstances of the illness's onset) may very well be traumatic neuroses which have been facilitated by a conflict in the ego. The fact to which I have referred on page 6, that a gross physical injury caused simultaneously by the trauma diminishes the chances that a neurosis will develop, becomes intelligible if one bears in mind two facts which have been stressed by psycho-analytic research: firstly, that mechanical agitation must be recognized as one of the sources of sexual excitation,[2] and secondly, that painful and feverish illnesses exercise a powerful effect, so long as they last, on the distribution of libido. Thus, on the one hand, the mechanical violence of the trauma would liberate a quantity of sexual excitation which, owing to the lack of preparation for anxiety, would have a traumatic effect; but, on the other hand, the simultaneous physical injury, by calling for a narcissistic hypercathexis of the injured organ,[3] would bind the excess of excitation. It is also well known, though the libido theory has not yet made sufficient use of the fact, that such severe disorders in the distribution of libido as melancholia are temporarily brought to an end by intercurrent organic illness, and indeed that even a fully developed condition of dementia praecox is capable of a temporary remission in these same circumstances.

[1] See my introduction (1919*d*) to *Psycho-Analysis and the War Neuroses.*
[2] Cf. my remarks elsewhere (*Three Essays* [*Standard Ed.*, 7, 201–2]) on the effect of swinging and railway-travel.
[3] See my paper on narcissism (1914*c*) [Beginning of Section II].

V

THE fact that the cortical layer which receives stimuli is without
any protective shield against excitations from within must have
as its result that these latter transmissions of stimulus have a
preponderance in economic importance and often occasion
economic disturbances comparable with traumatic neuroses.
The most abundant sources of this internal excitation are what
are described as the organism's 'instincts'—the representatives
of all the forces originating in the interior of the body and transmitted to the mental apparatus—at once the most important
and the most obscure element of psychological research.

It will perhaps not be thought too rash to suppose that the
impulses arising from the instincts do not belong to the type of
bound nervous processes but of *freely mobile* processes which
press towards discharge. The best part of what we know of these
processes is derived from our study of the dream-work. We there
discovered that the processes in the unconscious systems were
fundamentally different from those in the preconscious (or conscious) systems. In the unconscious, cathexes can easily be
completely transferred, displaced and condensed. Such treatment, however, could produce only invalid results if it were
applied to preconscious material; and this accounts for the
familiar peculiarities exhibited by manifest dreams after the
preconscious residues of the preceding day have been worked
over in accordance with the laws operating in the unconscious.
I described the type of process found in the unconscious as the
'primary' psychical process, in contradistinction to the 'secondary' process which is the one obtaining in our normal waking
life. Since all instinctual impulses have the unconscious systems
as their point of impact, it is hardly an innovation to say that
they obey the primary process. Again, it is easy to identify
the primary psychical process with Breuer's freely mobile
cathexis and the secondary process with changes in his bound or
tonic cathexis.[1] If so, it would be the task of the higher strata of
the mental apparatus to bind the instinctual excitation reaching

---

[1] Cf. my *Interpretation of Dreams*, Chapter VII [*Standard Ed.*, **5**, 588 ff.
Cf. also Breuer and Freud, 1895 (Section 2 of Breuer's theoretical contribution)].

34

the primary process. A failure to effect this binding would provoke a disturbance analogous to a traumatic neurosis; and only after the binding has been accomplished would it be possible for the dominance of the pleasure principle (and of its modification, the reality principle) to proceed unhindered. Till then the other task of the mental apparatus, the task of mastering or binding excitations, would have precedence—not, indeed, in *opposition* to the pleasure principle, but independently of it and to some extent in disregard of it.

The manifestations of a compulsion to repeat (which we have described as occurring in the early activities of infantile mental life as well as among the events of psycho-analytic treatment) exhibit to a high degree an instinctual [1] character and, when they act in opposition to the pleasure principle, give the appearance of some 'daemonic' force at work. In the case of children's play we seemed to see that children repeat unpleasurable experiences for the additional reason that they can master a powerful impression far more thoroughly by being active than they could by merely experiencing it passively. Each fresh repetition seems to strengthen the mastery they are in search of. Nor can children have their *pleasurable* experiences repeated often enough, and they are inexorable in their insistence that the repetition shall be an identical one. This character trait disappears later on. If a joke is heard for a second time it produces almost no effect; a theatrical production never creates so great an impression the second time as the first; indeed, it is hardly possible to persuade an adult who has very much enjoyed reading a book to re-read it immediately. Novelty is always the condition of enjoyment. But children will never tire of asking an adult to repeat a game that he has shown them or played with them, till he is too exhausted to go on. And if a child has been told a nice story, he will insist on hearing it over and over again rather than a new one; and he will remorselessly stipulate that the repetition shall be an identical one and will correct any alterations of which the narrator may be guilty—though they may actually have been made in the hope of gaining fresh approval.[2]

[1] ['*Triebhaft*' here and at the beginning of the next paragraph. The word '*Trieb*' bears much more of a feeling of urgency than the English 'instinct'.]

[2] [Cf. some remarks on this towards the end of the sixth section of Chapter VII of Freud's book on jokes (1905c).]

None of this contradicts the pleasure principle; repetition, the re-experiencing of something identical, is clearly in itself a source of pleasure. In the case of a person in analysis, on the contrary, the compulsion to repeat the events of his childhood in the transference evidently disregards the pleasure principle in every way. The patient behaves in a purely infantile fashion and thus shows us that the repressed memory-traces of his primaeval experiences are not present in him in a bound state and are indeed in a sense incapable of obeying the secondary process. It is to this fact of not being bound, moreover, that they owe their capacity for forming, in conjunction with the residues of the previous day, a wishful phantasy that emerges in a dream. This same compulsion to repeat frequently meets us as an obstacle to our treatment when at the end of an analysis we try to induce the patient to detach himself completely from his physician. It may be presumed, too, that when people unfamiliar with analysis feel an obscure fear—a dread of rousing something that, so they feel, is better left sleeping—what they are afraid of at bottom is the emergence of this compulsion with its hint of possession by some 'daemonic' power.

But how is the predicate of being 'instinctual' [1] related to the compulsion to repeat? At this point we cannot escape a suspicion that we may have come upon the track of a universal attribute of instincts and perhaps of organic life in general which has not hitherto been clearly recognized or at least not explicitly stressed. [2] *It seems, then, that an instinct is an urge inherent in organic life to restore an earlier state of things* which the living entity has been obliged to abandon under the pressure of external disturbing forces; that is, it is a kind of organic elasticity, or, to put it another way, the expression of the inertia inherent in organic life. [3]

This view of instincts strikes us as strange because we have become used to see in them a factor impelling towards change and development, whereas we are now asked to recognize in them the precise contrary—an expression of the *conservative* nature of living substance. On the other hand we soon call to mind examples from animal life which seem to confirm the

[1] [See the last footnote but one.]
[2] [The last six words were added in 1921.]
[3] I have no doubt that similar notions as to the nature of 'instincts' have already been put forward repeatedly.

view that instincts are historically determined. Certain fishes, for instance, undertake laborious migrations at spawning-time in order to deposit their spawn in particular waters far removed from their customary haunts. In the opinion of many biologists what they are doing is merely to seek out the localities in which their species formerly resided but which in the course of time they have exchanged for others. The same explanation is believed to apply to the migratory flights of birds of passage— but we are quickly relieved of the necessity for seeking for further examples by the reflection that the most impressive proofs of there being an organic compulsion to repeat lie in the phenomena of heredity and the facts of embryology. We see how the germ of a living animal is obliged in the course of its development to recapitulate (even if only in a transient and abbreviated fashion) the structures of all the forms from which it is sprung, instead of proceeding quickly by the shortest path to its final shape. This behaviour is only to a very slight degree attributable to mechanical causes, and the historical explanation cannot accordingly be neglected. So too the power of regenerating a lost organ by growing afresh a precisely similar one extends far up into the animal kingdom.

We shall be met by the plausible objection that it may very well be that, in addition to the conservative instincts which impel towards repetition, there may be others which push forward towards progress and the production of new forms. This argument must certainly not be overlooked, and it will be taken into account at a later stage.[1] But for the moment it is tempting to pursue to its logical conclusion the hypothesis that all instincts tend towards the restoration of an earlier state of things. The outcome may give an impression of mysticism or of sham profundity; but we can feel quite innocent of having had any such purpose in view. We seek only for the sober results of research or of reflection based on it; and we have no wish to find in those results any quality other than certainty.[2]

Let us suppose, then, that all the organic instincts are conservative, are acquired historically and tend towards the

[1] [The last half of this sentence was added in 1921.]
[2] [*Footnote added* 1925:] The reader should not overlook the fact that what follows is the development of an extreme line of thought. Later on, when account is taken of the sexual instincts, it will be found that the necessary limitations and corrections are applied to it.

43

restoration of an earlier state of things. It follows that the phenomena of organic development must be attributed to external
disturbing and diverting influences. The elementary living
entity would from its very beginning have had no wish to
change; if conditions remained the same, it would do no more
than constantly repeat the same course of life. In the last resort,
what has left its mark on the development of organisms must be
the history of the earth we live in and of its relation to the sun.
Every modification which is thus imposed upon the course of
the organism's life is accepted by the conservative organic
instincts and stored up for further repetition. Those instincts are
therefore bound to give a deceptive appearance of being forces
tending towards change and progress, whilst in fact they are
merely seeking to reach an ancient goal by paths alike old and
new. Moreover it is possible to specify this final goal of all
organic striving. It would be in contradiction to the conservative nature of the instincts if the goal of life were a state of
things which had never yet been attained. On the contrary, it
must be an *old* state of things, an initial state from which the
living entity has at one time or other departed and to which
it is striving to return by the circuitous paths along which its
development leads. If we are to take it as a truth that knows no
exception that everything living dies for *internal* reasons—
becomes inorganic once again—then we shall be compelled to
say that *'the aim of all life is death'* and, looking backwards, that
'inanimate things existed before living ones'.

The attributes of life were at some time evoked in inanimate
matter by the action of a force of whose nature we can form no
conception. It may perhaps have been a process similar in type
to that which later caused the development of consciousness in a
particular stratum of living matter. The tension which then
arose in what had hitherto been an inanimate substance endeavoured to cancel itself out. In this way the first instinct came into
being: the instinct to return to the inanimate state. It was still
an easy matter at that time for a living substance to die; the
course of its life was probably only a brief one, whose direction
was determined by the chemical structure of the young life.
For a long time, perhaps, living substance was thus being constantly created afresh and easily dying, till decisive external
influences altered in such a way as to oblige the still surviving
substance to diverge ever more widely from its original course

of life and to make ever more complicated *détours* before reaching its aim of death. These circuitous paths to death, faithfully kept to by the conservative instincts, would thus present us to-day with the picture of the phenomena of life. If we firmly maintain the exclusively conservative nature of instincts, we cannot arrive at any other notions as to the origin and aim of life.

The implications in regard to the great groups of instincts which, as we believe, lie behind the phenomena of life in organisms must appear no less bewildering. The hypothesis of self-preservative instincts, such as we attribute to all living beings, stands in marked opposition to the idea that instinctual life as a whole serves to bring about death. Seen in this light, the theoretical importance of the instincts of self-preservation, of self-assertion and of mastery greatly diminishes. They are component instincts whose function it is to assure that the organism shall follow its own path to death, and to ward off any possible ways of returning to inorganic existence other than those which are immanent in the organism itself. We have no longer to reckon with the organism's puzzling determination (so hard to fit into any context) to maintain its own existence in the face of every obstacle. What we are left with is the fact that the organism wishes to die only in its own fashion. Thus these guardians of life, too, were originally the myrmidons of death. Hence arises the paradoxical situation that the living organism struggles most energetically against events (dangers, in fact) which might help it to attain its life's aim rapidly—by a kind of short-circuit. Such behaviour is, however, precisely what characterizes purely instinctual as contrasted with intelligent efforts.[1]

But let us pause for a moment and reflect. It cannot be so. The sexual instincts, to which the theory of the neuroses gives a quite special place, appear under a very different aspect.

The external pressure which provokes a constantly increasing extent of development has not imposed itself upon *every* organism. Many have succeeded in remaining up to the present time at their lowly level. Many, though not all, such creatures, which must resemble the earliest stages of the higher animals

[1] [In the editions before 1925 the following footnote appeared at this point. 'A correction of this extreme view of the self-preservative instincts follows.']

and plants, are, indeed, living to-day. In the same way, the whole path of development to natural death is not trodden by *all* the elementary entities which compose the complicated body of one of the higher organisms. Some of them, the germ-cells, probably retain the original structure of living matter and, after a certain time, with their full complement of inherited and freshly acquired instinctual dispositions, separate themselves from the organism as a whole. These two characteristics may be precisely what enables them to have an independent existence. Under favourable conditions, they begin to develop—that is, to repeat the performance to which they owe their existence; and in the end once again one portion of their substance pursues its development to a finish, while another portion harks back once again as a fresh residual germ to the beginning of the process of development. These germ-cells, therefore, work against the death of the living substance and succeed in winning for it what we can only regard as potential immortality, though that may mean no more than a lengthening of the road to death. We must regard as in the highest degree significant the fact that this function of the germ-cell is reinforced, or only made possible, if it coalesces with another cell similar to itself and yet differing from it.

The instincts which watch over the destinies of these elementary organisms that survive the whole individual, which provide them with a safe shelter while they are defenceless against the stimuli of the external world, which bring about their meeting with other germ-cells, and so on—these constitute the group of the sexual instincts. They are conservative in the same sense as the other instincts in that they bring back earlier states of living substance; but they are conservative to a higher degree in that they are peculiarly resistant to external influences; and they are conservative too in another sense in that they preserve life itself for a comparatively long period.[1] They are the true life instincts. They operate against the purpose of the other instincts, which leads, by reason of their function, to death; and this fact indicates that there is an opposition between them and the other instincts, an opposition whose importance was long ago recognized by the theory of the neuroses. It is as though the

[1] [*Footnote added* 1923:] Yet it is to them alone that we can attribute an internal impulse towards 'progress' and towards higher development! (See below [pp. 42–3].)

life of the organism moved with a vacillating rhythm. One group of instincts rushes forward so as to reach the final aim of life as swiftly as possible; but when a particular stage in the advance has been reached, the other group jerks back to a certain point to make a fresh start and so prolong the journey. And even though it is certain that sexuality and the distinction between the sexes did not exist when life began, the possibility remains that the instincts which were later to be described as sexual may have been in operation from the very first, and it may not be true that it was only at a later time that they started upon their work of opposing the activities of the 'ego-instincts'.[1]

Let us now hark back for a moment ourselves and consider whether there is any basis at all for these speculations. Is it really the case that, *apart from the sexual instincts,*[2] there are no instincts that do not seek to restore an earlier state of things? that there are none that aim at a state of things which has never yet been attained? I know of no certain example from the organic world that would contradict the characterization I have thus proposed. There is unquestionably no universal instinct towards higher development observable in the animal or plant world, even though it is undeniable that development does in fact occur in that direction. But on the one hand it is often merely a matter of opinion when we declare that one stage of development is higher than another, and on the other hand biology teaches us that higher development in one respect is very frequently balanced or outweighed by involution in another. Moreover there are plenty of animal forms from whose early stages we can infer that their development has, on the contrary, assumed a retrograde character. Both higher development and involution might well be the consequences of adaptation to the pressure of external forces; and in both cases the part played by instincts might be limited to the retention (in the form of an internal source of pleasure) of an obligatory modification.[3]

[1] [*Footnote added* 1925:] It should be understood from the context that the term 'ego-instincts' is used here as a provisional description and derives from the earliest psycho-analytical terminology. [See below, pp. 50–1 and 61.]

[2] [These five words were italicized from 1921 onwards.]

[3] Ferenczi (1913, 137) has reached the same conclusion along different lines: 'If this thought is pursued to its logical conclusion, one must make oneself familiar with the idea of a tendency to perseveration or

It may be difficult, too, for many of us, to abandon the belief that there is an instinct towards perfection at work in human beings, which has brought them to their present high level of intellectual achievement and ethical sublimation and which may be expected to watch over their development into super-men. I have no faith, however, in the existence of any such internal instinct and I cannot see how this benevolent illusion is to be preserved. The present development of human beings requires, as it seems to me, no different explanation from that of animals. What appears in a minority of human individuals as an untiring impulsion towards further perfection can easily be understood as a result of the instinctual repression upon which is based all that is most precious in human civilization. The repressed instinct never ceases to strive for complete satisfaction, which would consist in the repetition of a primary experience of satisfaction. No substitutive or reactive formations and no sublimations will suffice to remove the repressed instinct's persisting tension; and it is the difference in amount between the pleasure of satisfaction which is *demanded* and that which is actually *achieved* that provides the driving factor which will permit of no halting at any position attained, but, in the poet's words, '*ungebändigt immer vorwärts dringt*'.[1] The backward path that leads to complete satisfaction is as a rule obstructed by the resistances which maintain the repressions. So there is no alternative but to advance in the direction in which growth is still free—though with no prospect of bringing the process to a conclusion or of being able to reach the goal. The processes involved in the formation of a neurotic phobia, which is nothing else than an attempt at flight from the satisfaction of an instinct, present us with a model of the manner of origin of this sup-posititious 'instinct towards perfection'—an instinct which can-not possibly be attributed to *every* human being. The *dynamic* conditions for its development are, indeed, universally present; but it is only in rare cases that the *economic* situation appears to favour the production of the phenomenon.

I will add only a word to suggest that the efforts of Eros to

regression dominating organic life as well, while the tendency to further development, to adaptation, etc., would become active only as a result of external stimuli.'

[1] ['Presses ever forward unsubdued.'] Mephistopheles in *Faust*, Part I [Scene 4].

combine organic substances into ever larger unities probably provide a substitute for this 'instinct towards perfection' whose existence we cannot admit. The phenomena that are attributed to it seem capable of explanation by these efforts of Eros taken in conjunction with the results of repression.[1]

[1] [This paragraph, which was added in 1923, anticipates the account of Eros that is to follow in the next chapter, p. 50 ff.]

VI

THE upshot of our enquiry so far has been the drawing of a sharp distinction between the 'ego-instincts' and the sexual instincts, and the view that the former exercise pressure towards death and the latter towards a prolongation of life. But this conclusion is bound to be unsatisfactory in many respects even to ourselves. Moreover, it is actually only of the former group of instincts that we can predicate a conservative, or rather retrograde, character corresponding to a compulsion to repeat. For on our hypothesis the ego-instincts arise from the coming to life of inanimate matter and seek to restore the inanimate state; whereas as regards the sexual instincts, though it is true that they reproduce primitive states of the organism, what they are clearly aiming at by every possible means is the coalescence of two germ-cells which are differentiated in a particular way. If this union is not effected, the germ-cell dies along with all the other elements of the multicellular organism. It is only on this condition that the sexual function can prolong the cell's life and lend it the appearance of immortality. But what is the important event in the development of living substance which is being repeated in sexual reproduction, or in its fore-runner, the conjugation of two protista? [1] We cannot say; and we should consequently feel relieved if the whole structure of our argument turned out to be mistaken. The opposition between the ego or death instincts [2] and the sexual or life instincts would then cease to hold and the compulsion to repeat would no longer possess the importance we have ascribed to it.

Let us turn back, then, to one of the assumptions that we have already made, with the expectation that we shall be able to give it a categorical denial. We have drawn far-reaching conclusions from the hypothesis that all living substance is bound to die from internal causes. We made this assumption thus carelessly because it does not seem to us to *be* an assumption. We are accustomed to think that such is the fact, and we

---

[1] [In what follows Freud appears to use the terms 'protista' and 'protozoa' indifferently to signify unicellular organisms. The translation follows the original.]

[2] [The first published appearance of the term.]

44

are strengthened in our thought by the writings of our poets. Perhaps we have adopted the belief because there is some comfort in it. If we are to die ourselves, and first to lose in death those who are dearest to us, it is easier to submit to a remorseless law of nature, to the sublime *'Aνáγκη* [Necessity], than to a chance which might perhaps have been escaped. It may be, however, that this belief in the internal necessity of dying is only another of those illusions which we have created '*um die Schwere des Daseins zu ertragen*'.[1] It is certainly not a primaeval belief. The notion of 'natural death' is quite foreign to primitive races; they attribute every death that occurs among them to the influence of an enemy or of an evil spirit. We must therefore turn to biology in order to test the validity of the belief.

If we do so, we may be astonished to find how little agreement there is among biologists on the subject of natural death and in fact that the whole concept of death melts away under their hands. The fact that there is a fixed average duration of life at least among the higher animals naturally argues in favour of there being such a thing as death from natural causes. But this impression is countered when we consider that certain large animals and certain gigantic arboreal growths reach a very advanced age and one which cannot at present be computed. According to the large conception of Wilhelm Fliess [1906], all the phenomena of life exhibited by organism —and also, no doubt, their death—are linked with the completion of fixed periods, which express the dependence of two kinds of living substance (one male and the other female) upon the solar year. When we see, however, how easily and how extensively the influence of external forces is able to modify the date of the appearance of vital phenomena (especially in the plant world) —to precipitate them or hold them back—doubts must be cast upon the rigidity of Fliess's formulas or at least upon whether the laws laid down by him are the sole determining factors.

The greatest interest attaches from our point of view to the treatment given to the subject of the duration of life and the death of organisms in the writings of Weismann (1882, 1884, 1892, etc.) It was he who introduced the division of living substance into mortal and immortal parts. The mortal part is

---

[1] ['To bear the burden of existence.' (Schiller, *Die Braut von Messina*, I, 8.]

the body in the narrower sense—the 'soma'—which alone is subject to natural death. The germ-cells, on the other hand, are potentially immortal, in so far as they are able, under certain favourable conditions, to develop into a new individual, or, in other words, to surround themselves with a new soma. (Weismann, 1884.)

What strikes us in this is the unexpected analogy with our own view, which was arrived at along such a different path. Weismann, regarding living substance morphologically, sees in it one portion which is destined to die—the soma, the body apart from the substance concerned with sex and inheritance—and an immortal portion—the germ-plasm, which is concerned with the survival of the species, with reproduction. We, on the other hand, dealing not with the living substance but with the forces operating in it, have been led to distinguish two kinds of instincts: those which seek to lead what is living to death, and others, the sexual instincts, which are perpetually attempting and achieving a renewal of life. This sounds like a dynamic corollary to Weismann's morphological theory.

But the appearance of a significant correspondence is dissipated as soon as we discover Weismann's views on the problem of death. For he only relates the distinction between the mortal soma and the immortal germ-plasm to *multicellular* organisms; in unicellular organisms the individual and the reproductive cell are still one and the same (Weismann, 1882, 38). Thus he considers that unicellular organisms are potentially immortal, and that death only makes its appearance with the multicellular metazoa. It is true that this death of the higher organisms is a natural one, a death from internal causes; but it is not founded on any primal characteristic of living substance (Weismann, 1884, 84) and cannot be regarded as an absolute necessity with its basis in the very nature of life (Weismann, 1882, 33). Death is rather a matter of expediency, a manifestation of adaptation to the external conditions of life; for, when once the cells of the body have been divided into soma and germ-plasm, an unlimited duration of individual life would become a quite pointless luxury. When this differentiation had been made in the multicellular organisms, death became possible and expedient. Since then, the soma of the higher organisms has died at fixed periods for internal reasons, while the protista have remained immortal. It is not the case, on the other hand, that reproduction was only introduced at the same time as death. On the contrary, it is a primal characteristic of living matter, like growth (from which it originated), and life has been continuous from its first beginning upon earth. (Weismann, 1884, 84 f.)

It will be seen at once that to concede in this way that higher organisms have a natural death is of very little help to us. For if death is a *late* acquisition of organisms, then there can be no question of there having been death instincts from the very beginning of life on this earth. Multicellular organisms may die for internal reasons, owing to defective differentiation or to imperfections in their metabolism, but the matter is of no interest from the point of view of our problem. An account of the origin of death such as this is moreover far less at variance with our habitual modes of thought than the strange assumption of 'death instincts'.

The discussion which followed upon Weismann's suggestions led, so far as I can see, to no conclusive results in any direction.[1] Some writers returned to the views of Goette (1883), who regarded death as a direct result of reproduction. Hartmann (1906, 29) does not regard the appearance of a 'dead body'—a dead portion of the living substance—as the criterion of death, but defines death as 'the termination of individual development'. In this sense protozoa too are mortal; in their case death always coincides with reproduction, but is to some extent obscured by it, since the whole substance of the parent animal may be transmitted directly into the young offspring.

Soon afterwards research was directed to the experimental testing on unicellular organisms of the alleged immortality of living substance. An American biologist, Woodruff, experimenting with a ciliate infusorian, the 'slipper-animalcule', which reproduces by fission into two individuals, persisted until the 3029th generation (at which point he broke off the experiment), isolating one of the part-products on each occasion and placing it in fresh water. This remote descendent of the first slipper-animalcule was just as lively as its ancestor and showed no signs of ageing or degeneration. Thus, in so far as figures of this kind prove anything, the immortality of the protista seemed to be experimentally demonstrable.[2]

Other experimenters arrived at different results. Maupas,

[1] Cf. Hartmann (1906), Lipschütz (1914) and Doflein (1919).
[2] For this and what follows see Lipschütz (1914, 26 and 52 ff.).

Calkins and others, in contrast to Woodruff, found that after a certain number of divisions these infusoria become weaker, diminish in size, suffer the loss of some part of their organization and eventually die, unless certain recuperative measures are applied to them. If this is so, protozoa would appear to die after a phase of senescence exactly like the higher animals—thus completely contradicting Weismann's assertion that death is a late acquisition of living organisms.

From the aggregate of these experiments two facts emerge which seem to offer us a firm footing.

First: If two of the animalculae, at the moment before they show signs of senescence, are able to coalesce with each other, that is to 'conjugate' (soon after which they once more separate), they are saved from growing old and become 're-juvenated'. Conjugation is no doubt the fore-runner of the sexual reproduction of higher creatures; it is as yet unconnected with propagation and is limited to the mixing of the substances of the two individuals. (Weismann's 'amphimixis'.) The re-cuperative effects of conjugation can, however, be replaced by certain stimulating agents, by alterations in the composition of the fluid which provides their nourishment, by raising their temperature or by shaking them. We are reminded of the celebrated experiment made by J. Loeb, in which, by means of certain chemical stimuli, he induced segmentation in sea-urchins' eggs—a process which can normally occur only after fertilization.

Secondly: It is probable nevertheless that infusoria die a natural death as a result of their own vital processes. For the contradiction between Woodruff's findings and the others is due to his having provided each generation with fresh nutrient fluid. If he omitted to do so, he observed the same signs of senescence as the other experimenters. He concluded that the animalculae were injured by the products of metabolism which they ex-truded into the surrounding fluid. He was then able to prove conclusively that it was only the products of its *own* metabolism which had fatal results for the particular kind of animalcule. For the same animalculae which inevitably perished if they were crowded together in their own nutrient fluid flourished in a solution which was over-saturated with the waste products of a distantly related species. An infusorian, therefore, if it is left to itself, dies a natural death owing to its incomplete voidance of the products of its own metabolism. (It may be that the same incapacity is the ultimate cause of the death of all higher animals as well.)

At this point the question may well arise in our minds whether any object whatever is served by trying to solve the problem of natural death from a study of the protozoa. The primitive organization of these creatures may conceal from our eyes important conditions which, though in fact present in them too, only become *visible* in higher animals where they are able to find morphological expression. And if we abandon the morphological point of view and adopt the dynamic one, it becomes a matter of complete indifference to us whether natural death can be shown to occur in protozoa or not. The substance which is later recognized as being immortal has not yet become separated in them from the mortal one. The instinctual forces which seek to conduct life into death may also be operating in protozoa from the first, and yet their effects may be so completely concealed by the life-preserving forces that it may be very hard to find any direct evidence of their presence. We have seen, moreover, that the observations made by biologists allow us to assume that internal processes of this kind leading to death do occur also in protista. But even if protista turned out to be immortal in Weismann's sense, his assertion that death is a late acquisition would apply only to its *manifest* phenomena and would not make impossible the assumption of processes *tending* towards it.

Thus our expectation that biology would flatly contradict the recognition of death instincts has not been fulfilled. We are at liberty to continue concerning ourselves with their possibility, if we have other reasons for doing so. The striking similarity between Weismann's distinction of soma and germ-plasm and our separation of the death instincts from the life instincts persists and retains its significance.

We may pause for a moment over this pre-eminently dualistic view of instinctual life. According to E. Hering's theory, two kinds of processes are constantly at work in living substance, operating in contrary directions, one constructive or assimilatory and the other destructive or dissimilatory. May we venture to recognize in these two directions taken by the vital processes the activity of our two instinctual impulses, the life instincts and the death instincts? There is something else, at any rate, that we cannot remain blind to. We have unwittingly

steered our course into the harbour of Schopenhauer's philosophy. For him death is the 'true result and to that extent the
purpose of life',[1] while the sexual instinct is the embodiment of
the will to live.

Let us make a bold attempt at another step forward. It is
generally considered that the union of a number of cells into
a vital association—the multicellular character of organisms—
has become a means of prolonging their life. One cell helps to
preserve the life of another, and the community of cells can
survive even if individual cells have to die. We have already
heard that conjugation, too, the temporary coalescence of two
unicellular organisms, has a life-preserving and rejuvenating
effect on both of them. Accordingly, we might attempt to apply
the libido theory which has been arrived at in psycho-analysis to
the mutual relationship of cells. We might suppose that the life
instincts or sexual instincts which are active in each cell take the
other cells as their object, that they partly neutralize the death
instincts (that is, the processes set up by them) in those cells
and thus preserve their life; while the other cells do the same for
them, and still others sacrifice themselves in the performance of
this libidinal function. The germ-cells themselves would behave
in a completely 'narcissistic' fashion—to use the phrase that we
are accustomed to use in the theory of the neuroses to describe
a whole individual who retains his libido in his ego and pays
none of it out in object-cathexes. The germ-cells require their
libido, the activity of their life instincts, for themselves, as a
reserve against their later momentous constructive activity.
(The cells of the malignant neoplasms which destroy the
organism should also perhaps be described as narcissistic in this
same sense: pathology is prepared to regard their germs as
innate and to ascribe embryonic attributes to them.)[2] In this way
the libido of our sexual instincts would coincide with the Eros of
the poets and philosophers which holds all living things together.

Here then is an opportunity for looking back over the slow
development of our libido theory. In the first instance the
analysis of the transference neuroses forced upon our notice the
opposition between the 'sexual instincts', which are directed
towards an object, and certain other instincts, with which we
were very insufficiently acquainted and which we described

[1] Schopenhauer (1851; *Sämtliche Werke*, ed. Hübscher, 1938, **5**, 236).
[2] [This sentence was added in 1921.]

provisionally as the 'ego-instincts'.[1] A foremost place among these was necessarily given to the instincts serving the self-preservation of the individual. It was impossible to say what other distinctions were to be drawn among them. No knowledge would have been more valuable as a foundation for true psychological science than an approximate grasp of the common characteristics and possible distinctive features of the instincts. But in no region of psychology were we groping more in the dark. Everyone assumed the existence of as many instincts or 'basic instincts' as he chose, and juggled with them like the ancient Greek natural philosophers with their four elements—earth, air, fire and water. Psycho-analysis, which could not escape making *some* assumption about the instincts, kept at first to the popular division of instincts typified in the phrase 'hunger and love'. At least there was nothing arbitrary in this; and by its help the analysis of the psychoneuroses was carried forward quite a distance. The concept of 'sexuality', and at the same time of the sexual instinct, had, it is true, to be extended so as to cover many things which could not be classed under the reproductive function; and this caused no little hubbub in an austere, respectable or merely hypocritical world.

The next step was taken when psycho-analysis felt its way closer towards the psychological ego, which it had first come to know only as a repressive, censoring agency, capable of erecting protective structures and reactive formations. Critical and far-seeing minds had, it is true, long since objected to the concept of libido being restricted to the energy of the sexual instincts directed towards an object. But they failed to explain how they had arrived at their better knowledge or to derive from it anything of which analysis could make use. Advancing more cautiously, psycho-analysis observed the regularity with which libido is withdrawn from the object and directed on to the ego (the process of introversion); and, by studying the libidinal development of children in its earliest phases, came to the conclusion that the ego is the true and original reservoir of libido,[2]

---

[1] [So, for instance, in the account of this opposition given in Freud's paper on psychogenic disturbances of vision (1910*i*).]

[2] [This idea was fully stated by Freud in his paper on narcissism (1914*c*), Section I. See, however, his later footnote, near the beginning of Chapter III of *The Ego and the Id* (1923*b*), in which he corrects this statement and describes the *id* as 'the great reservoir of libido'.]

and that it is only from that reservoir that libido is extended on to objects. The ego now found its position among sexual objects and was at once given the foremost place among them. Libido which was in this way lodged in the ego was described as 'narcissistic'.[1] This narcissistic libido was of course also a manifestation of the force of the sexual instinct in the analytical sense of those words, and it had necessarily to be identified with the 'self-preservative instincts' whose existence had been recognized from the first. Thus the original opposition between the ego-instincts and the sexual instincts proved to be inadequate. A portion of the ego-instincts was seen to be libidinal; sexual instincts—probably alongside others—operated in the ego. Nevertheless we are justified in saying that the old formula which lays it down that psychoneuroses are based on a conflict between ego-instincts and sexual instincts contains nothing that we need reject to-day. It is merely that the distinction between the two kinds of instinct, which was originally regarded as in some sort of way *qualitative*, must now be characterized differently—namely as being *topographical*. And in particular it is still true that the transference neuroses, the essential subject of psycho-analytic study, are the result of a conflict between the ego and the libidinal cathexis of objects.

But it is all the more necessary for us to lay stress upon the libidinal character of the self-preservative instincts now that we are venturing upon the further step of recognizing the sexual instinct as Eros, the preserver of all things, and of deriving the narcissistic libido of the ego from the stores of libido by means of which the cells of the soma are attached to one another. But we now find ourselves suddenly faced by another question. If the self-preservative instincts too are of a libidinal nature, are there perhaps no other instincts whatever but the libidinal ones? At all events there are none other visible. But in that case we shall after all be driven to agree with the critics who suspected from the first that psycho-analysis explains *everything* by sexuality, or with innovators like Jung who, making a hasty judgement, have used the word 'libido' to mean instinctual force in general. Must not this be so?

It was not our *intention* at all events to produce such a result. Our argument had as its point of departure a sharp distinction between ego-instincts, which we equated with death instincts,

[1] See my paper on narcissism (1914c) [Section I].

and sexual instincts, which we equated with life instincts. (We were prepared at one stage [p. 39] to include the so-called self-preservative instincts of the ego among the death instincts; but we subsequently [p. 52] corrected ourselves on this point and withdrew it.) Our views have from the very first been *dualistic*, and to-day they are even more definitely dualistic than before— now that we describe the opposition as being, not between ego-instincts and sexual instincts but between life instincts and death instincts. Jung's libido theory is on the contrary *monistic*; the fact that he has called his one instinctual force 'libido' is bound to cause confusion, but need not affect us otherwise.[1] We suspect that instincts other than those of self-preservation operate in the ego, and it ought to be possible for us to point to them. Unfortunately, however, the analysis of the ego has made so little headway that it is very difficult for us to do so. It is possible, indeed, that the libidinal instincts in the ego may be linked in a peculiar manner [2] with these other ego-instincts which are still strange to us. Even before we had any clear understanding of narcissism, psycho-analysts had a suspicion that the 'ego-instincts' had libidinal components attached to them. But these are very uncertain possibilities, to which our opponents will pay very little attention. The difficulty remains that psycho-analysis has not enabled us hitherto to point to any [ego-] instincts other than the libidinal ones. That, however, is no reason for our falling in with the conclusion that no others in fact exist.

In the obscurity that reigns at present in the theory of the instincts, it would be unwise to reject any idea that promises to throw light on it. We started out from the great opposition between the life and death instincts. Now object-love itself presents us with a second example of a similar polarity—that between love (or affection) and hate (or aggressiveness). If only we could succeed in relating these two polarities to each other and in deriving one from the other! From the very first we recognized the presence of a sadistic component in the sexual instinct.[3] As we know, it can make itself independent and can, in the form of a perversion, dominate an individual's entire

[1] [The two preceding sentences were added in 1921.]
[2] [In the first edition only: '—by instinctual "confluence", to borrow a term used by Adler [1908]—'.]
[3] This was already so in the first edition of *Three Essays on the Theory of Sexuality* in 1905 [*Standard Ed.*, 7, 157 ff.].

sexual activity. It also emerges as a predominant component instinct in one of the 'pregenital organizations', as I have named them. But how can the sadistic instinct, whose aim it is to injure the object, be derived from Eros, the preserver of life? Is it not plausible to suppose that this sadism is in fact a death instinct which, under the influence of the narcissistic libido, has been forced away from the ego and has consequently only emerged in relation to the object? It now enters the service of the sexual function. During the oral stage of organization of the libido, the act of obtaining erotic mastery over an object coincides with that object's destruction; later, the sadistic instinct separates off, and finally, at the stage of genital primacy, it takes on, for the purposes of reproduction, the function of overpowering the sexual object to the extent necessary for carrying out the sexual act. It might indeed be said that the sadism which has been forced out of the ego has pointed the way for the libidinal components of the sexual instinct, and that these follow after it to the object. Wherever the original sadism has undergone no mitigation or intermixture, we find the familiar ambivalence of love and hate in erotic life.[1]

If such an assumption as this is permissible, then we have met the demand that we should produce an example of a death instinct—though, it is true, a displaced one. But this way of looking at things is very far from being easy to grasp and creates a positively mystical impression. It looks suspiciously as though we were trying to find a way out of a highly embarrassing situation at any price. We may recall, however, that there is nothing new in an assumption of this kind. We put one forward on an earlier occasion, before there was any question of an embarrassing situation. Clinical observations led us at that time to the view that masochism, the component instinct which is complementary to sadism, must be regarded as sadism that has been turned round upon the subject's own ego.[2] But there is no difference in principle between an instinct turning from an object to the ego and its turning from the ego to an object—which is the new point now under discussion. Masochism, the turning round of the instinct upon the subject's own ego, would

---

[1] [This foreshadows Freud's discussion of instinctual 'fusion' in Chap. IV of *The Ego and the Id* (1923b).]

[2] See my *Three Essays* (1905d) [*Standard Ed.*, **7**, 158]; and 'Instincts and their Vicissitudes' (1915c).

in that case be a return to an earlier phase of the instinct's history, a regression. The account that was formerly given of masochism requires emendation as being too sweeping in one respect: there *might* be such a thing as primary masochism— a possibility which I had contested at that time.[1]

Let us, however, return to the self-preservative sexual instincts. The experiments upon protista have already shown us that conjugation—that is, the coalescence of two individuals which separate soon afterwards without any subsequent cell-division occurring—has a strengthening and rejuvenating effect upon both of them.[2] In later generations they show no signs of degenerating and seem able to put up a longer resistance to the injurious effects of their own metabolism. This single observation may, I think, be taken as typical of the effect produced by sexual union as well. But how is it that the coalescence of two only slightly different cells can bring about this renewal of life? The experiment which replaces the conjugation of protozoa by the application of chemical or even of mechanical stimuli (cf. Lipschütz, 1914) enables us to give what is no doubt a conclusive reply to this question. The result is brought about by the influx of fresh amounts of stimulus. This tallies well with the hypothesis that the life process of the individual leads for internal reasons to an abolition of chemical tensions, that is to say, to death, whereas union with the living substance of a different individual increases those tensions, introducing what may be described as fresh 'vital differences' which must then be lived off. As regards this dissimilarity there must of course be one or more optima. The dominating tendency of mental life, and perhaps of nervous life in general, is the effort to reduce, to keep constant or to remove internal tension due to

---

[1] A considerable portion of these speculations have been anticipated by Sabina Spielrein (1912) in an instructive and interesting paper which, however, is unfortunately not entirely clear to me. She there describes the sadistic components of the sexual instinct as 'destructive'. A. Stärke (1914), again, has attempted to identify the concept of libido itself with the biological concept (assumed on theoretical grounds) of an impetus towards death. See also Rank (1907). All these discussions, like that in the text, give evidence of the demand for a clarification of the theory of the instincts such as has not yet been achieved.—[A later discussion of the destructive instinct by Freud himself occupies Chapter VI of *Civilization and its Discontents* (1930a).]

[2] See the account quoted above, p. 48 from Lipschütz (1914).

stimuli (the 'Nirvana principle', to borrow a term from Barbara Low [1920, 73])—a tendency which finds expression in the pleasure principle; [1] and our recognition of that fact is one of our strongest reasons for believing in the existence of death instincts.

But we still feel our line of thought appreciably hampered by the fact that we cannot ascribe to the sexual instinct the characteristic of a compulsion to repeat which first put us on the track of the death instincts. The sphere of embryonic developmental processes is no doubt extremely rich in such phenomena of repetition; the two germ-cells that are involved in sexual reproduction and their life history are themselves only repetitions of the beginnings of organic life. But the essence of the processes to which sexual life is directed is the coalescence of two cell-bodies. That alone is what guarantees the immortality of the living substance in the higher organisms.

In other words, we need more information on the origin of sexual reproduction and of the sexual instincts in general. This is a problem which is calculated to daunt an outsider and which the specialists themselves have not yet been able to solve. We shall therefore give only the briefest summary of whatever seems relevant to our line of thought from among the many discordant assertions and opinions.

One of these views deprives the problem of reproduction of its mysterious fascination by representing it as a part manifestation of growth. (Cf. multiplication by fission, sprouting or gemmation.) The origin of reproduction by sexually differentiated germ-cells might be pictured along sober Darwinian lines by supposing that the advantage of amphimixis, arrived at on some occasion by the chance conjugation of two protista, was retained and further exploited in later development.[2] On this view 'sex' would not be anything very ancient; and the extraordinarily violent instincts whose aim it is to bring about

[1] [Cf. p. 7 ff. The whole topic is further considered in 'The Economic Problem of Masochism' (1924c).]

[2] Though Weismann (1892) denies this advantage as well: 'In no case does fertilization correspond to a rejuvenescence or renewal of life, nor is its occurrence necessary in order that life may endure: it is merely an arrangement which renders possible the intermingling of two different hereditary tendencies.' [English translation, 1893, 231.] He nevertheless believes that an intermingling of this kind leads to an increase in the variability of the organism concerned.

sexual union would be repeating something that had once occurred by chance and had since become established as being advantageous.

The question arises here, as in the case of death [p. 49], whether we do right in ascribing to protista those characteristics alone which they actually exhibit, and whether it is correct to assume that forces and processes which become visible only in the higher organisms originated in those organisms for the first time. The view of sexuality we have just mentioned is of little help for our purposes. The objection may be raised against it that it postulates the existence of life instincts already operating in the simplest organisms; for otherwise conjugation, which works counter to the course of life and makes the task of ceasing to live more difficult, would not be retained and elaborated but would be avoided. If, therefore, we are not to abandon the hypothesis of death instincts, we must suppose them to be associated from the very first with life instincts. But it must be admitted that in that case we shall be working upon an equation with two unknown quantities.

Apart from this, science has so little to tell us about the origin of sexuality that we can liken the problem to a darkness into which not so much as a ray of a hypothesis has penetrated. In quite a different region, it is true, we *do* meet with such a hypothesis; but it is of so fantastic a kind—a myth rather than a scientific explanation—that I should not venture to produce it here, were it not that it fulfils precisely the one condition whose fulfilment we desire. For it traces the origin of an instinct to *a need to restore an earlier state of things.*

What I have in mind is, of course, the theory which Plato put into the mouth of Aristophanes in the *Symposium*, and which deals not only with the *origin* of the sexual instinct but also with the most important of its variations in relation to its object. 'The original human nature was not like the present, but different. In the first place, the sexes were originally three in number, not two as they are now; there was man, woman, and the union of the two. . . .' Everything about these primaeval men was double: they had four hands and four feet, two faces, two privy parts, and so on. Eventually Zeus decided to cut these men in two, 'like a sorb-apple which is halved for pickling'. After the division had been made, 'the two parts of man, each desiring his other half, came together, and threw their arms about one another eager to grow into one'.[1]

Shall we follow the hint given us by the poet-philosopher, and venture upon the hypothesis that living substance at the time of its coming to life was torn apart into small particles, which have ever since endeavoured to reunite through the sexual instincts? that these instincts, in which the chemical affinity of inanimate matter persisted, gradually succeeded, as they developed through the kingdom of the protista, in overcoming the difficulties put in the way of that endeavour by an environment charged with dangerous stimuli—stimuli which compelled them to form a protective cortical layer? that these splintered fragments of living substance in this way attained a multicellular condition and finally transferred the instinct for reuniting, in the most highly concentrated form, to the germ-cells?—But here, I think, the moment has come for breaking off.

[1] [Jowett's translation. *Footnote added* 1921:] I have to thank Professor Heinrich Gomperz, of Vienna, for the following discussion on the origin of the Platonic myth, which I give partly in his own words. It is to be remarked that what is essentially the same theory is already to be found in the Upanishads. For we find the following passage in the *Brihadâran-yaka-upanishad*, 1, 4, 3 [Max-Müller's translation, **2**, 85 f.], where the origin of the world from the Atman (the Self or Ego) is described: 'But he felt no delight. Therefore a man who is lonely feels no delight. He wished for a second. He was so large as man and wife together. He then made this his Self to fall in two, and then arose husband and wife. Therefore Yagñavalkya said: "We two are thus (each of us) like half a shell." Therefore the void which was there, is filled by the wife.'

The *Brihadâranyaka-upanishad* is the most ancient of all the Upanishads, and no competent authority dates it later than about the year 800 B.C. In contradiction to the prevailing opinion, I should hesitate to give an unqualified denial to the possibility of Plato's myth being derived, even if it were only indirectly, from the Indian source, since a similar possibility cannot be excluded in the case of the doctrine of transmigration. But even if a derivation of this kind (through the Pythagoreans in the first instance) were established, the significance of the coincidence between the two trains of thought would scarcely be diminished. For Plato would not have adopted a story of this kind which had somehow reached him through some oriental tradition—to say nothing of giving it so important a place—unless it had struck him as containing an element of truth.

In a paper devoted to a systematic examination of this line of thought before the time of Plato, Ziegler (1913) traces it back to Babylonian origins.

[Freud had already alluded to Plato's myth in his *Three Essays, Standard Ed.*, **7**, 136.]

Not, however, without the addition of a few words of critical reflection. It may be asked whether and how far I am myself convinced of the truth of the hypotheses that have been set out in these pages. My answer would be that I am not convinced myself and that I do not seek to persuade other people to believe in them. Or, more precisely, that I do not know how far I believe in them. There is no reason, as it seems to me, why the emotional factor of conviction should enter into this question at all. It is surely possible to throw oneself into a line of thought and to follow it wherever it leads out of simple scientific curiosity, or, if the reader prefers, as an *advocatus diaboli*, who is not on that account himself sold to the devil. I do not dispute the fact that the third step in the theory of the instincts, which I have taken here, cannot lay claim to the same degree of certainty as the two earlier ones—the extension of the concept of sexuality and the hypothesis of narcissism. These two innovations were a direct translation of observation into theory and were no more open to sources of error than is inevitable in all such cases. It is true that my assertion of the regressive character of instincts also rests upon observed material—namely on the facts of the compulsion to repeat. It may be, however, that I have over-estimated their significance. And in any case it is impossible to pursue an idea of this kind except by repeatedly combining factual material with what is purely speculative and thus diverging widely from empirical observation. The more frequently this is done in the course of constructing a theory, the more untrustworthy, as we know, must be the final result. But the degree of uncertainty is not assignable. One may have made a lucky hit or one may have gone shamefully astray. I do not think a large part is played by what is called 'intuition' in work of this kind. From what I have seen of intuition, it seems to me to be the product of a kind of intellectual impartiality. Unfortunately, however, people are seldom impartial where ultimate things, the great problems of science and life, are concerned. Each of us is governed in such cases by deep-rooted internal prejudices, into whose hands our speculation unwittingly plays. Since we have such good grounds for being distrustful, our attitude towards the results of our own deliberations cannot well be other than one of cool benevolence. I hasten to add, however, that self-criticism such as this is far from binding one to any special tolerance towards dissentient opinions. It is

S.F. XVIII—E

perfectly legitimate to reject remorselessly theories which are contradicted by the very first steps in the analysis of observed facts, while yet being aware at the same time that the validity of one's own theory is only a provisional one.

We need not feel greatly disturbed in judging our speculation upon the life and death instincts by the fact that so many bewildering and obscure processes occur in it—such as one instinct being driven out by another or an instinct turning from the ego to an object, and so on. This is merely due to our being obliged to operate with the scientific terms, that is to say with the figurative language, peculiar to psychology (or, more precisely, to depth psychology). We could not otherwise describe the processes in question at all, and indeed we could not have become aware of them. The deficiencies in our description would probably vanish if we were already in a position to replace the psychological terms by physiological or chemical ones. It is true that they too are only part of a figurative language; but it is one with which we have long been familiar and which is perhaps a simpler one as well.

On the other hand it should be made quite clear that the uncertainty of our speculation has been greatly increased by the necessity for borrowing from the science of biology. Biology is truly a land of unlimited possibilities. We may expect it to give us the most surprising information and we cannot guess what answers it will return in a few dozen years to the questions we have put to it. They may be of a kind which will blow away the whole of our artificial structure of hypotheses. If so, it may be asked why I have embarked upon such a line of thought as the present one, and in particular why I have decided to make it public. Well—I cannot deny that some of the analogies, correlations and connections which it contains seemed to me to deserve consideration.[1]

---

[1] I will add a few words to clarify our terminology, which has undergone some development in the course of the present work. We came to know what the 'sexual instincts' were from their relation to the sexes and to the reproductive function. We retained this name after we had been obliged by the findings of psycho-analysis to connect them less closely with reproduction. With the hypothesis of narcissistic libido and the extension of the concept of libido to the individual cells, the sexual instinct was transformed for us into Eros, which seeks to force together and hold together the portions of living substance. What are commonly called the sexual instincts are looked upon by us as the part of Eros

which is directed towards objects. Our speculations have suggested that Eros operates from the beginning of life and appears as a 'life instinct' in opposition to the 'death instinct' which was brought into being by the coming to life of inorganic substance. These speculations seek to solve the riddle of life by supposing that these two instincts were struggling with each other from the very first. [*Added* 1921:] It is not so easy, perhaps, to follow the transformations through which the concept of the 'ego-instincts' has passed. To begin with we applied that name to all the instinctual trends (of which we had no closer knowledge) which could be distinguished from the sexual instincts directed towards an object; and we opposed the ego-instincts to the sexual instincts of which the libido is the manifestation. Subsequently we came to closer grips with the analysis of the ego and recognized that a portion of the 'ego-instincts' is also of a libidinal character and has taken the subject's own ego as its object. These narcissistic self-preservative instincts had thenceforward to be counted among the libidinal sexual instincts. The opposition between the ego-instincts and the sexual instincts was transformed into one between the ego-instincts and the object-instincts, both of a libidinal nature. But in its place a fresh opposition appeared between the libidinal (ego- and object-) instincts and others, which must be presumed to be present in the ego and which may perhaps actually be observed in the destructive instincts. Our speculations have transformed this opposition into one between the life instincts (Eros) and the death instincts.

VII

If it is really the case that seeking to restore an earlier state of things is such a universal characteristic of instincts, we need not be surprised that so many processes take place in mental life independently of the pleasure principle. This characteristic would be shared by all the component instincts and in their case would aim at returning once more to a particular stage in the course of development. These are matters over which the pleasure principle has as yet no control; but it does not follow that any of them are necessarily opposed to it, and we have still to solve the problem of the relation of the instinctual processes of repetition to the dominance of the pleasure principle.

We have found that one of the earliest and most important functions of the mental apparatus is to bind the instinctual impulses which impinge on it, to replace the primary process prevailing in them by the secondary process and convert their freely mobile cathectic energy into a mainly quiescent (tonic) cathexis. While this transformation is taking place no attention can be paid to the development of unpleasure; but this does not imply the suspension of the pleasure principle. On the contrary, the transformation occurs on *behalf* of the pleasure principle; the binding is a preparatory act which introduces and assures the dominance of the pleasure principle.

Let us make a sharper distinction than we have hitherto made between function and tendency. The pleasure principle, then, is a tendency operating in the service of a function whose business it is to free the mental apparatus entirely from excitation or to keep the amount of excitation in it constant or to keep it as low as possible. We cannot yet decide with certainty in favour of any of these ways of putting it; but it is clear that the function thus described would be concerned with the most universal endeavour of all living substance—namely to return to the quiescence of the inorganic world. We have all experienced how the greatest pleasure attainable by us, that of the sexual act, is associated with a momentary extinction of a highly intensified excitation. The binding of an instinctual impulse would be a preliminary function designed to prepare the excitation for its final elimination in the pleasure of discharge.

This raises the question of whether feelings of pleasure and unpleasure can be produced equally from bound and from unbound excitatory processes. And there seems to be no doubt whatever that the unbound or primary processes give rise to far more intense feelings in both directions than the bound or secondary ones. Moreover the primary processes are the earlier in time; at the beginning of mental life there are no others, and we may infer that if the pleasure principle had not already been operative in *them* it could never have been established for the later ones. We thus reach what is at bottom no very simple conclusion, namely that at the beginning of mental life the struggle for pleasure was far more intense than later but not so unrestricted: it had to submit to frequent interruptions. In later times the dominance of the pleasure principle is very much more secure, but it itself has no more escaped the process of taming than the other instincts in general. In any case, whatever it is that causes the appearance of feelings of pleasure and unpleasure in processes of excitation must be present in the secondary process just as it is in the primary one.

Here might be the starting-point for fresh investigations. Our consciousness communicates to us feelings from within not only of pleasure and unpleasure but also of a peculiar tension which in its turn can be either pleasurable or unpleasurable. Should the difference between these feelings enable us to distinguish between bound and unbound processes of energy? or is the feeling of tension to be related to the absolute magnitude, or perhaps to the level, of the cathexis, while the pleasure and unpleasure series indicates a change in the magnitude of the cathexis *within a given unit of time*?[1] Another striking fact is that the life instincts have so much more contact with our internal perception—emerging as breakers of the peace and constantly producing tensions whose release is felt as pleasure—while the death instincts seem to do their work unobtrusively. The pleasure principle seems actually to serve the death instincts. It is true that it keeps watch upon stimuli from without, which are regarded as dangers by both kinds of instincts; but it is more especially on guard against increases of stimulation from within, which would make the task of living more difficult. This in turn raises a host of other questions to which we can at

[1] [Cf. above, p. 8. These questions had already been touched on by Freud in his 'Project', e.g. in Part I, Section 8 and Part III, Section 1.]

present find no answer. We must be patient and await fresh methods and occasions of research. We must be ready, too, to abandon a path that we have followed for a time, if it seems to be leading to no good end. Only believers, who demand that science shall be a substitute for the catechism they have given up, will blame an investigator for developing or even transforming his views. We may take comfort, too, for the slow advances of our scientific knowledge in the words of the poet:

Was man nicht erfliegen kann, muss man erhinken.

. . . .

Die Schrift sagt, es ist keine Sünde zu hinken.[1]

[1] ['What we cannot reach flying we must reach limping. . . . The Book tells us it is no sin to limp.' The last lines of 'Die beiden Gulden', a version by Rückert of one of the *Maqâmât* of al-Hariri. Freud also quoted these lines in a letter to Fliess of Oct. 20, 1895 (Freud 1950a, Letter 32).]

PART **II**

Discussion of
Beyond the Pleasure Principle

1

Jenseits and beyond:
teaching Freud's late work

W. Craig Tomlinson

The title of this chapter addresses my experience teaching *Beyond the Pleasure Principle* (1920g) not only in isolation, but also in context, in particular as a gateway to all of Freud's writing after that date. There are several reasons for this approach.

First, of all of Freud's texts, this watershed work ranks as an equal among firsts on the list of the classics of psychoanalytic literature. Just as *The Ego and the Id* (1923b) and *Civilization and Its Discontents* (1930a) would be unthinkable without the second dual instinct theory which Freud introduces in *Beyond the Pleasure Principle*, any student of psychoanalysis who had never read those later texts would be left with a sorry appraisal of the earlier work, among other deficits. The implications of *Beyond the Pleasure Principle* as delineated first by Freud in the 1920s and then by others were, in fact, monumental.

Second, *Beyond the Pleasure Principle* was as important within the nascent psychoanalytic community of Freud's time as it was pivotal in Freud's own development as a thinker. Thus to teach it requires far more than the usual emphasis on the afterlife of a written text. We study all classic works of psychoanalysis from a particular historical vantage point, with biases informed by past and current debates, controversies, and allegiances. Recent Freud scholarship has made us more aware than ever of how important the social, clinical, and scientific context of the early psychoanalytic community was in the development of Freud's theory (see, among others, Grosskurth, 1991; Jacobi, 1983; Makari, 2008; Roazen, 1975), particularly in its later decades. The monolithic image of Freud as a thinker who evolved in splendid isolation has undergone serious and much needed modification. To appreciate his achievement fully, we need to understand the context in which his contributions were written.

Third, *Beyond the Pleasure Principle* has proved to be an important branch point in the divergent social and intellectual history of psychoanalysis. Perhaps no other work of Freud has had such influence on organizational tensions within the international community of psychoanalysis—a tension that was already evident at the time it was published and that has continued for almost a century because of the work's potential to highlight differences among mainstream psychoanalysts from Europe and North and South America. Much psychoanalytic social history can be traced to how different analysts received, debated, and quarrelled over the ideas in this work in the decades after it was written. Many of the schisms in international psychoanalysis—between ego psychologists and Kleinians, between fundamentalists and reformers, between Europe and the Americas—have important roots in this text. It would not be much of an overstatement to say that much of the richness and diversity of psychoanalytic contributions stemming from differing approaches to psychoanalysis can be traced to *Beyond the Pleasure Principle.*

Finally, irrelevant to Freud or the history of psychoanalysis but relevant to me, a quirk of fate and scheduling has meant that I have spent considerable time as a teacher with an assignment to teach all of Freud *after* this work. Thus my teaching has been quite literally beyond *Jenseits des Lustprinzips.* This assignment to teach late Freud naturally focuses on a detailed examination of two broad areas in which Freud's second dual instinct theory, as elaborated in *Beyond the Pleasure Principle,* is crucial: first, the evolution and development of Freud's structural theory, its implications and ramifications; and, second, Freud's elaborations of his theory into a wider social theory and cultural context, which emanate from his considerations of group process and identification in *Group Psychology and the Analysis of the Ego* (1921c) and move towards his later speculations about social structures in *Civilization and its Discontents* and *The Future of an Illusion* (1927c). For both of these projects, *Beyond the Pleasure Principle* is always something of a silent, crucial text in the background, to which one constantly returns. Add to this a third task of introducing Freud's highly tentative and fragmentary but path-breaking re-orientation of the relation between drive and affect in *Inhibitions, Symptoms, and Anxiety* (1926d)—a text whose importance is often underrepresented in psychoanalytic curricula, owing in part to its difficulty and awkwardness—and one has quite a psychoanalytic legacy stemming from this 1920 text that looks beyond, into the *Jenseits* of psychoanalytic theory, as it were.

Who is the audience?

A critical but often underrated charge of any teacher is to gauge his audience and modify his approach accordingly. As it happens, I have spent most of my time teaching practicing psychiatrists and clinical psychologists at a psychoanalytic institute affiliated with an American university. These students thus have a background that tends, on the whole, to be more clinical than scholarly or academic, although this is not always the case. (I am made very aware of how prior background shapes my classroom approach—for example, when a professor of literature, a historian, or a scientist visits, and I am reminded that there are so many perspectives from which to view these later works). The most helpful adaptations are not always predictable. For example, one might expect that for such students, to intersperse clinical examples and discuss the rich and varied clinical afterlife of *Beyond the Pleasure Principle* would be most welcome. I find, however, that this group often appreciates hearing about non-clinical approaches with which they are less familiar, including literary or philosophical readings of Freud's texts. Moreover, when talking in clinical terms—and sometimes especially then—they crave integration of theory, to which they have been amply exposed but which they still struggle to apply in everyday practice. Conversely, I might be more inclined to emphasize the clinical implications of Freud's work with undergraduates or academic scholars who might otherwise miss the important context of clinical work, rather than engage with them solely on the theoretical terrain with which they are most familiar. For example, the central problem of repetition compulsion in *Beyond the Pleasure Principle* loses an essential resonance for anyone who has not experienced the emotional intensity of trying to help a human being suffering from the recurrent nightmares, vivid flashbacks, waking daydreams, and autonomic hyperarousal of post-traumatic stress—or, for that matter, the patience required when working through the memories and endless repetitions encountered in people with especially prominent obsessional character problems. Similarly, the immediate experience of another central theme of *Beyond the Pleasure Principle,* the notion of a powerful innate destructive drive, loses its intensity without the background of immediate clinical and personal experience of the unconscious.

One tries, of course, to convey to students some of the immediate intensity of the psychoanalytic situation by example and judicious storytelling. Yet conversely, one of these clinical problems—post-traumatic stress—just happens to be an area in which clinicians today have been bombarded with innumerable theories, treatment paradigms, and viewpoints. To integrate Freud's new and modified theory of trauma and repetition here with clinical experience is perhaps one of the most important things with which one can hope to help students. Typically, the result of such theoretical overload is that students maintain separate and even contradictory theoretical and treatment paradigms in a kind of parallel circuitry, abandoning one for the other as they feel pulled in different directions by clinical, peer consensus, intellectual, financial, or other concerns. If one can help students incorporate some of these competing paradigms within a psychoanalytic model, one has helped to overcome a very powerful de facto resistance to psychoanalysis within mental health training.

Brief clinical vignettes are helpful here and offer a ready opportunity to present some of the challenges of thinking simultaneously in terms of both of Freud's dual instinct theories, as well as from other perspectives, like object relations, affect theory, or self psychology. I might present, for example, a female patient with a history of sexual acting out, a series of unstable relationships with men, alcohol abuse, and poor affect regulation. After outlining a background history of early trauma involving poor parental boundaries, an unavailable father, and adolescent sexual abuse, we can explore current behaviour and object relations from a multiplicity of perspectives: topographic (are early unconscious memories being recreated?), drive theory (defusion of aggressive and libidinal drives, repetition compulsion?), affect theory (what signal affects trigger such behaviours?), re-enactment of unstable original part self and object relations, or failure to integrate stable self-representations and identity. *Beyond the Pleasure Principle,* used in this way, can also serve as a gateway to a current everyday clinical problem: how do we work with a multiplicity of alternative theories at once in a clinical setting?

A further practical consideration might be described as more pedestrian: one has to determine not only the students' background and orientation, but also their availability. I have found as a teacher that the ability of students to read widely varies with their current life situation—a fact that might seem banal but overwhelmingly informs the classroom approach. Graduate students in history or philosophy might easily have eight or ten times the hours available to read each week than do practicing clinicians. While I might wish to teach this work with extensive forays into related literature, for example, this luxury is not always available: young physicians in the early phases of their careers, often with young families to support and attending what is essentially a costly night-school for specialized training and education, are making heroic sacrifices to begin with, particularly in a world in which psychoanalysis is anything but a reliable way of earning a living. Nor do the external constraints of my students' lives make it possible to require more active engagement, such as presenting short, topical seminar papers in addition to completing the reading each week—which I would dearly love to do for pedagogical reasons. Here one has a further obligation as a teacher: I lecture more than I might do otherwise, highlight relevant commentary and disputes, and summarize complex arguments from the literature, while making the prospect of engaging with it directly enticing in the hope that some will be inspired to read more on their own. It is better to inspire a lifelong student than painfully force-feed volumes of commentary.

Another different challenge in teaching this work to practicing clinicians engaged not only in a personal analysis but also learning psychoanalytic technique emerges: What are the implications of

Freud's late works, both as understood throughout the evolution of clinical psychoanalysis and today? How have analysts differed over the years in the clinical implications and applications of such concepts as repetition compulsion and a death drive? As a teacher within a mainstream American psychoanalytic institute, I view with scepticism Freud's phylogenetic excursions in this work. From a scientific viewpoint, such speculations as that all life strives towards death, imbued with their nineteenth-century philosophical aura, are products of the era in which they were conceived. We have to remind ourselves that when Freud made his grand speculations in this work, the discovery of DNA was still decades in the future. The remarkably fertile fields of modern evolutionary biology and genetics have shown little interest in such speculations because they have additional knowledge and real tools with which to work.

The death-instinct controversy

There is, of course, the central problem in this text related to the controversy over the very notion of a death instinct. Like most American analysts today, I view Freud's explorations here as a very early attempt to grapple with problems of aggression, problems that were later taken up by theoreticians like Hartmann, C. Brenner, and Kernberg. Brenner's characteristically succinct summary is useful in focusing a debate (C. Brenner, 1982). Brenner notes that: (1) Freud's original view was that aggression is beyond the pleasure principle, a formulation in which aggression leads to pleasure only when fused with libido (eroticized) and directed outwards; (2) since Hartmann and colleagues, aggression bears the same relation to pleasure/unpleasure as does libido, so that discharge of aggression leads to pleasure, while lack of discharge of and accumulation leads to unpleasure and, therefore, (3) there is thus no need to assume a repetition compulsion or death drive (C. Brenner, 1982, pp. 30–31). But as a teacher one wants to convey the diversity of viewpoints on this subject and recognize the differing reception of this work among theoreticians of diverse theoretical perspectives in Europe, South America, and other parts of the world. In addition, one has to convey the important tradition of clinical and theoretical work carried out by several generations of past and modern Kleinians who, inspired by Freud's notion of a death drive, took aggression and primitive aggression seriously in psychoanalytic work and extended our clinical understanding of its manifestations. American students of psychoanalysis usually have a ready access point into this tradition via the work of Kernberg. It is a pleasure to see them connect Freud's early struggles with incorporating aggression into psychoanalytic theory to Kernberg's achievements over a half century later. It is then possible for them to integrate ego psychological and Kleinian notions about aggression into a psychoanalytic understanding of borderline and narcissistic psychopathology and primitive defences.

Despite Freud's attempts at explanation in chapter V of *Beyond the Pleasure Principle* that the repetition compulsion only "gives the impression" of being some demonic force, his complaint in chapter III that any notion of a "demonic power" in the compulsion of normal people to repeat is a false notion (to cover what is prearranged by childhood experience) has arguably gone somewhat overlooked—perhaps both in Freud's metaphysical excursions about the death instinct itself as well as in the afterlife of this work. I use this example to drive home the point that students should take Freud seriously when he acknowledges that his ideas in this work are provisional, not fully worked out, and intended to generate, not resolve, debate. It is important to stress the self-acknowledged tentativeness of Freud's explorations in this work (most clearly in chapter VI). As with all great works of art, in reading—and teaching—a work that is an established classic it is easy to forget that in 1920 it was understood by its author as a preliminary and tentative work: the beginnings of a "third step" (59ff) that followed upon Freud's elaborations of the concept of sexuality in the first decade of the twentieth century and his hypotheses about the role of narcissism in the second.

As can be gleaned from this discussion, I find that even with beginning students a historical perspective is an absolute necessity in teaching Freud. By historical I mean not just understanding Freud in history, or how one appraises this text after ninety years of scientific and psychoanalytic evolution, but also the particular importance of history—both internally in Freud's own chronology and externally in the influences of his own increasingly creative but fractious burgeoning psychoanalytic movement. Teaching with a historiographic mindset and a historical frame of reference not only helps to avoid teaching Freud as psychoanalytic gospel, but is a broader intellectual and historiographic principle illustrating to students that classics are nevertheless shaped and formed by the particular era in which they were written. We understand them as well from a particular and conditioned historical vantage point of our own. We cannot afford to read otherwise.

With *Beyond the Pleasure Principle*, there is an added historical enticement: the social history of this work, as compellingly detailed by Makari (2008), represents a crucial moment in the social and organizational history of psychoanalysis. This text turns out to be importantly rooted in critiques dating to the early teens by Adler, Stekel, and Spielrein, which, focusing on aggression, were incorporated by Freud with varying degrees of acknowledgement. The opposition of *Eros* with the death drive had an immediate psychoanalytic source: namely, presentations at the Vienna Psychoanalytic Society by Wilhelm Stekel and Wilhelm Reik as early as 1911 (Nunberg & Federn, 1962–1975, Vol. 1, p. 175, and Vol. 3, p. 312—see Makari, 2008, pp. 311ff, 547) and papers conceived by Spielrein even earlier and finally published in 1912 (Makari, 2008). It is interesting to remind students that Freud never used the now familiar psychoanalytic term *Thanatos* in print, though his predecessors at the Vienna Psychoanalytic did. Freud conspicuously left the death drive as a "drive without a name" (see Land, 1991). Such sources are a more important part of the genesis of *Beyond the Pleasure Principle* than Freud's borrowing from Groddeck and Nietzsche in the adoption of the term "*das Es*" in *The Ego and the Id,* which is more commonly cited. They are so because they document an active discussion in Freud's inner circle of the role of aggression in instinct theory almost a decade before *Beyond the Pleasure Principle* was published. That discussion was actively squelched, as the *Minutes of the Vienna Psychoanalytic Society* (Nunberg & Federn, 1962–1975) document. The codification of a heroic myth of the evolution of psychoanalytic ideas during the era in which the *Standard Edition* came into being is visible in this work, and is itself a crucial part of the afterlife of *Beyond the Pleasure Principle.* That heroic myth was used to consolidate theoretical and institutionalized power within psychoanalytic organizations. This era of psychoanalytic history, with its orthodoxies and counter-rebellions, is still very much present in the multiple intellectual, clinical, and personal pressures felt by candidates in psychoanalytic institutes. I try to convey as much of this social history as possible when teaching, because when one does so the text comes alive in an exciting, immediate, and provocative way. Written texts are not all, perhaps not even usually, produced in isolation in a library, and the background makes a real difference with *Beyond the Pleasure Principle*. I am reminded here—and have used the analogy—that it matters when we read Homer to know that scholars have reconstructed from internal evidence that these stories are the product of a long non-written tradition of oral poetry with multiple orders of formulaic diction serving partly to buttress the storyteller's memory, and not composed quietly in some ancient Greek version of a Victorian study.

Issues related to translation

Perhaps in contrast to tradition in American institutes, and sometimes at the risk of being accused of teaching basic concepts with too much complexity, I have found that some discussion of translation issues, as well as what I would label tempero-cultural ones, are useful and even crucial with Freud's texts, in particular his late works. The language of the *Standard Edition* has acquired such authority among English-speaking psychoanalysts, and become so fixed in their oral traditions, that for all practical purposes students are unaware that they are even reading works in translation. Thus, to invite reflection on this topic is itself an educational imperative, and no less important than it would be to remind an introductory religion class that the Bible was not in fact originally written in Elizabethan English.

But there are more specific challenges in the translation of Freud's terms in his late works as well: The first and most obvious example in *Beyond the Pleasure Principle* has to do with the translation of *Trieb* as "instinct", a choice that is in my opinion one of the *Standard Edition*'s more outright, and perhaps most consequential, errors. Not only is "drive" literally more correct and readily available, but the terms *Trieb* and *Instinkt* are—and were well before Freud's time—both available and used quite distinctly in German.

Thus choosing the wrong term here is doubly misleading. I have argued elsewhere that a second consequence of this error is to cut off an essential context of an entire lively tradition of literary and philosophical discussion dating to at least the eighteenth century (Tomlinson, 1992). Of course, the mistranslation of "drive" is just as pertinent when teaching the *Three Essays* (1905d) as it is here, and this very fact offers an opportunity to enliven a discussion of Freud's two instinct theories. It also provides a window into the afterlife of Freud's first and second dual instinct theories in the history of psychoanalysis in America, with its metapsychological reification (one is tempted to say deification) of the concept of drive, along with the wholesale privileging of instinct over affect in motivation, over object relations, and self in post-war psychoanalysis, complete with a new translation and somewhat cumbersome re-coinage of Freud's term as "instinctual drive" in the era of Hartmann.

There are other problems of translation in Freud's late works that I also try to make students aware of, some subtle and some not. The manifold problems created by the coinage of "id", "ego", and "superego" (for *Es, Ich,* and *Überich*) are, of course, now well known, but since the terms have become an essential part of the oral traditions of teaching in American psychoanalytic institutes and remain in near universal usage, one has a more subtle problem in inviting students to reconsider the terms as thought of in their most original, everyday usage as they try to comprehend Freud's structural theory. The same challenge is of course encountered with *Group Psychology and the Analysis of the Ego*, as well as a further one engendered by the misleading rendering of *Masse* in English as "group". This term not only understates the size of the crowd and misses its pejorative connotations, but cannot help but evoke for today's students and clinicians almost irrelevant associations to their experiences with contemporary group psychotherapy. More subtle issues of translation can often be used to help students grasp difficult concepts: the simple kinship of "*Verdrängung, Urverdrängung,* and *Nachverdrängung*" is lost if all one has to go on is "repression", "primal repression", and "after-pressure" (in addition, obviously, to the well-known problems engendered by the rendition of "*Verdrängung*" as "repression" and "*Abwehr*" as "defence").

How much of this is important? I think a lot of it is. I wish I had more time to digress into the important poetic and intellectual reference in Freud's coinage of the term "*Urverdrängung*" to the extraordinarily influential preoccupation of German intellectuals in the era of Herder and Goethe with the search for *Urphänomene.* But there are practical benefits as well. The clumsiness of the *Standard Edition* version of Freud's crucial definition of a symptom in *Inhibitions, Symptoms, and Anxiety*" as "a sign of, and a substitute for, an instinctual satisfaction which has remained in abeyance" mystifies the whole process in a way that the original, quite simple formulation "*unterbliebene Triebbefriedigung*" does not (the adjective *unterbliebene* in German having the more simple meaning of "not happened", among other nuances here). I have found that explaining the difference sometimes helps students with a crucial concept. (To some relief I have occasionally invoked the Rolling Stones here, suggesting that it might be easier to remember a symptom as a something that arises when a drive "just can't get no satisfaction".)

Obviously, these are only a few issues of translation and concept definition that one could discuss in Freud's late works, and there are many more, but I do find one additional reference helpful to mention: "*Jenseits*", the very first word in the title of this text, might just as correctly be rendered into English as "the other side"—or, for that matter, even "the far side". Freud's title contains an allusion to a long tradition in German philosophy and theology of contrasting "*diesseits*" and "*jenseits*" for "this-worldly" and "other-worldly", the latter implying a direct reference to a religious afterlife. The term is thus rife with important allusions not only to religion but also to the German Romanticism of the era of Novalis, Hölderlin, and even Goethe (one of Freud's great heroes). These associations are not as far-fetched as they sound, for while instantaneously conjured up to any educated German reader of Freud's title, they are altogether lost to students who have available only the blander English equivalent, "beyond" and little familiarity with the considerable influence and power of this tradition in nineteenth-century German thought and culture. Did Freud intend a subtle jab at religion here? Or perhaps a very subtle acknowledgement that metapsychology and the psychoanalytic theory of the instincts run the risk of shading into mythology, as he elsewhere acknowledged? It seems to me that students should at least be given the invitation and the tools to ponder such questions for themselves.

A few thoughts in closing

There are significant scientific issues to grapple with in Freud's *Jenseits des Lustprinzips*. Chapter IV, for example, is perhaps even more problematic in light of contemporary neuroscience than the notion of a death instinct. What are we to do, for example, with Freud's argument that the dura mater, the tough protective covering of the brain, has an important psychic function? The assertion is ridiculous except at the level of metaphor—but, then, why not the skull, for that matter, or even a thick head of hair? And why the sudden need on Freud's part for such literalism to deal with our age-old unease with the interface and interconnection between our minds, our subjective mental experience with all its varied mental representations, and the inescapability of the physical universe that includes the bodies, brains, neurons, synapses, and the neurotransmitting chemicals upon which all that subjective experience depends? Similarly, Freud's assertion at the outset of chapter V that the "cortical layer which receives stimuli is without any protective shield against excitations from within must have as its result that these latter transmissions have a preponderance in economic importance and often occasion economic disturbances comparable with traumatic neuroses" (p. 34) sounds like neuroscience but is not to a twenty-first-century ear. In fact, one might ask if it is even a consistent metaphor. For what are unconscious processes and defences if not "projections from within"? Does Freud mean to locate the unconscious specifically within the cerebral cortex (what about the limbic system, a modern reader might ask)? What does it mean that Freud, with an illustrious and sophisticated background at least in the neuroscience of the late nineteenth century, veers so strongly into metaphor here? If one does not invite students to wrestle with such questions as they read *Beyond the Pleasure Principle*, I believe one reinforces in them the tendency to learn psychoanalysis as more mythology or even theology than as a science of the mind.

Similarly, how does one teach Freud's protracted arguments about protozoa, adduced as reasoning leading from evolutionary biology to the necessity of a "death drive" and a "life drive", within the context of twenty-first-century evolutionary biology? The momentous discoveries of twentieth-century biology about DNA and heredity were decades away in 1920, and while some of Freud's speculations strike us as no more current than Ptolemaic theories of the universe, we can appreciate the breathtaking integration of metaphor and the great sweep of evolution when Freud speculates here about what is mortal (the soma) and immortal (from a modern perspective, DNA) in life. What a grand use of metaphor to describe the germ cells or the cells of malignant neoplasms as "narcissistic" (p. 50) because they resemble a narcissistic individual who "retains libido in his ego and pays none of it out in object cathexes" (p. 50). One need not accept the details of Freud's speculations here as scientifically credible in the twenty-first century, in either their content, their presumptions about what constitutes biological evidence, or their conclusions to share in a sense of wonder at the scope of Freud's thinking about the human condition as he self-consciously veers into the territory of philosophy once covered by Schopenhauer (p. 50), Plato (p. 57), and the Upanishads (p. 58). If students are able to share in the wonderment of such speculation without abandoning reason and the principles of scientific evidence altogether, they will have an intellectual accomplishment that will stay with them for a lifetime.

2

Life and death in Freudian metapsychology: a reappraisal of the second instinctual dualism

Fátima Caropreso & Richard Theisen Simanke

In *Beyond the Pleasure Principle*, Freud (1920g) introduced his second instinctual dualism hypothesis. Until then he had argued for the existence of a duality of self-preservation and sexual instincts. This duality had been challenged for some time, mainly since he articulated the concept of narcissism. In 1920, sexual and self-preservation instincts once and for all become part of the same type of instinct—the life instinct. And then Freud established another opposition—the life instinct and the death instinct.

Ernest Jones (1957) maintains that, in spite of Freud's tremendous prestige among psychoanalysts, few readily accepted the new theses presented in *Beyond the Pleasure Principle*. Indeed, the concept of a death instinct unleashed a great many polemics among psychoanalysts. Monzani (1989) observes that "the reactions to this paper were disparate, however the majority had one point in common: a sort of 'theoretical shudder', an uneasiness, and a frank negativity" (p. 147). In addition to Fenichel, Reich, Brun, and others, even Ernest Jones appeared among those who declared themselves to be clearly against the notion of a death instinct. Such a reaction to this concept from these psychoanalysts shows that they regarded it as something entirely new on Freud's part. It did not seem to be clearly consistent with the rest of Freud's theorization. Indeed, it seemed both unjustified and unnecessary. It could have been, as Monzani (1989) says, a slip-up, one of Freud's idiosyncrasies or philosophical or metaphysical inclinations that, in essence, would have nothing to do with psychoanalysis. Similar positions can be found in the work of more recent authors.

Laplanche (1970) maintains that the death instinct is one of the most compelling ideas to emerge from Freud's work and that it is basic to Freudian thought. For Laplanche, it was an entirely new development, impossible to anticipate from Freud's earlier work, beyond his metapsychological considerations in 1915 as well as his system that was on the verge of reform. Laplanche also feels that the notion of the death instinct diverges from his examination of narcissism since it was proposed not to fortify that notion but to weaken it.

Our intention in this chapter is to take up the arguments Freud developed in *Beyond the Pleasure Principle*, specifically arguments concerning the notions of the life- and death instincts. We then examine some ideas developed in subsequent metapsychological texts. We argue that, if one keeps in mind the development of Freud's metapsychological theory beginning with his "Project for a Scientific Psychology" (Freud, 1950 [1895]), the death instinct, rather than being a new and extra-theoretical idea, given Freud's work up to then, seems to be something that, one way or another, makes explicit what was implicit in all his previous theoretical work. Put another way, the death instinct is a concept that fulfils an internal need in psychoanalytic metapsychology as it had been presented from the beginning. One of the few authors to recognize this connection is Sulloway, who links it to the biological foundation Freud proposed for his psychological theses. Sulloway (1979) says that Freud's "theory of the death instinct has a perfectly rational logic in his own psychobiological terms" (p. 395). Indeed, the Eros concept or life instinct has rarely been subject to strenuous objections, nor has it received near as much attention from Freud's commentators as has the death instinct.

However, when one considers in detail the theorization begun in 1920, the hypothesis that there would be life instincts that oppose

death instincts does not seem to lie in easy harmony with the ideas
Freud developed at this point. And this suggests that there may not
be a guaranteed place for the life instinct in Freudian psychology.
To put it another way: when one thinks about the theses developed in *Beyond the Pleasure Principle* and in other metapsychological
works, it is hard to avoid the impression that for Freud a tendency
towards death lies behind all vital phenomena, including those that
seem to work to preserve life. Given this connection that emerges
between the death instinct and the foundations of psychoanalytic
thought, as Freud conceived it, one could not, with any consistency,
reject this concept and remain part of the Freudian framework. In
other words, rejection of the death instinct as not essential to the
Freudian framework was the first reaction to this concept and has
continued to be so in later discussions pertaining to this matter
(e.g. Yorke, 1986).

The death instinct

In *Beyond the Pleasure Principle*, Freud (1920g) formulated the hypothesis that there could be a function in one's psychic apparatus
that would antedate the one controlled by the pleasure principle.
This function was the "repetition compulsion", which would work
to link whatever stimulation there may be to one's psychic apparatus. This, in turn, allowed the pleasure principle to become
dominant. As he pondered the relationship between repetition
compulsion and instinctual activity, Freud hit upon the concept of
the death instinct. He concluded that repetition compulsion must
be an overriding element of all instincts:

> *It seems, then, that an instinct is an urge inherent in organic life to
> restore an earlier state of things* which the living entity has been
> obliged to abandon under the pressure of external disturbing
> forces; that is, it is a kind of organic elasticity, or to put it an-
> other way, the expression of the inertia inherent in organic life.
> [Freud, 1920g, p. 36]

At this point Freud seems to expand his notion of instinct vis-à-vis
his earlier positions. Up to that point instinct had been thought
of as the psychic expression of endogenous stimulation or as en-

dogenous stimulation itself—to the extent that the latter found expression in the psyche. In his metapsychological articles published between the years of 1915 and 1917, Freud defines instinct both ways, wavering between the two concepts (Strachey, 1957). Be that as it may, instinct was repeatedly characterized as a concept dealing exclusively with the psychic apparatus. However, in *Beyond the Pleasure Principle* instinct becomes a more encompassing concept no longer limited to the psyche, but instead inherent in the totality of the living being. In the above quote, Freud defines it as an urge "inherent in organic life" to return to an earlier state of affairs. Thus instinct becomes an exigency or inherent tendency of the living entity, and this tendency is, essentially, a repetition compulsion. This compulsion is no longer just a process or mechanism exclusive to mental life; it is, rather, held to be a phenomenon that antedated mental life. It is the urge present in life itself, the urge to reproduce a prior condition, further back in time and more primordial.

But in *Beyond the Pleasure Principle* Freud wonders what could be this prior, original state to which all instinct would inevitably aspire to return? In other words, what would be all life's final goal? Freud's answer is "that the aim of all life is death and, looking backwards, that inanimate things existed before living ones" (Freud, 1920g, p. 38). From its origin, then, life was held to contain the tendency to return to an inorganic state. In this case, to return to an inorganic state means to free oneself of all stimulation and of all tension—that is, to achieve death. Extending this principle to the psychic apparatus, we arrive at the hypothesis that the primordial tendency that governs this framework is an inclination to eliminate all stimulation. Having reached this point, Freud appears to rescue the "inertia principle" he advanced in his ""Project for a Scientific Psychology"" (Freud, 1950 [1895]). In this work Freud had proposed that the primary tendency of the psychic apparatus would be to free itself from all stimulation, and thus all stimulation that may have reached the psychic apparatus would be eliminated by the most direct route—reflex discharge. Still, the impossibility of suppressing stimulation coming from within the body through reflex movements, such as, for example, hunger (where a specific action to obtain food would have to be performed on the world), would impose a first modification on the constancy principle. The neural framework would have to retain a modicum of stimulation so that the actions necessary for the satisfaction of the need for food and of other bodily needs could be carried out. Thus the inertia principle would give way to a "tendency towards constancy". This tendency would not be opposed to the inertia principle; rather, it would act on its behalf, creating the conditions to enable an endogenous stimulation to be efficiently discharged.

In chapter VII of *The Interpretation of Dreams* (1900a), even though Freud said nothing explicit about the inertia principle, he clearly took up the idea that the psychic apparatus originally contained a tendency to discharge stimulation in the most direct manner possible, but he maintained that this tendency would end up being modified owing to the need to annul endogenous stimulation as well:

> at first the apparatus's efforts were directed toward keeping itself so far as possible free from stimuli; consequently its first structure followed the plan of a reflex apparatus, so that any sensory excitation impinging on it could be promptly discharged along a motor path. But the exigencies of life interfere with this simple function, and it is to them, too, that the apparatus owes the impetus to further development. [Freud, 1900a, p. 565]

In his 1915 metapsychological articles Freud once more takes up this hypothesis concerning the apparatus's original tendency. In "Instincts and Their Vicissitudes" (Freud, 1915c), for example, he affirms:

> the nervous system is an apparatus which has the function of getting rid of the stimuli that reach it, or of reducing them to the lowest possible level; or which, if it were feasible, would maintain itself in an altogether unstimulated condition. [p. 120]

Thus, beginning with the "Project for a Scientific Psychology" (1950 [1895]), Freud's postulation of a primordial tendency that would govern the psychic apparatus became an integral part of his psychic apparatus theory. And this tendency would work to eliminate all stimulation and to nullify any increase in stimulation. However, in *Beyond the Pleasure Principle* Freud makes explicit something that had up to that point been merely implicit: the primordial tendency to discharge stimulation as much as possible is the expression of an inclination to die. As Monzani (1989) observes, once he introduced the death instinct, Freud articulates something that was more or less implicitly present in all his theorizations, beginning with "Project for a Scientific Psychology".

In the "Project", nonetheless, the tendency for inertia was held to be a principle that regulated only nervous and psychic activity. In 1920 Freud considered this bent to be a totality inherent in life itself. When life began, simultaneously there began a tendency to return to the earlier state of total absence of stimulation, or, in other words, to an inanimate state. To put it another way, when life's properties came forth from inanimate matter, the first instinct must have emerged—that of returning to the inanimate state. In the beginning, Freud speculates, to die must have been easy: merely a short life route would have to be travelled and, for this reason, life must have been created and recreated countless times. However, the alterations in external conditions would have imposed greater and greater detours on living matter's original path. And these external stimuli would thus be responsible for life's processes becoming progressively more complex. The hypotheses presented up to this point lead, therefore, to the idea that death is life's primordial tendency and that the preservation of life would have come about due to factors external to life itself. In this sense it would be legitimate to postulate the existence of a death instinct, but there would still be nothing to allow one to speak of a life instinct. Given all the above, at this point there would be nothing to suggest that there was an urge inherent in organic matter to keep itself in an animate state, or, let us say, there would be no internal impulse to preserve life.

'But, Freud asked, do the instincts of self-preservation not counter the supposition that instinctual activity would only work for death? His answer is in the beginning negative: keeping in mind the death-instinct hypothesis, self-preservation instincts would only be partial instincts destined to safeguard each organism's peculiar route to death. To a certain extent, these ideas were also presupposed in the "Project". According to the theory developed there, there would be a basic tendency to eliminate all stimulation in the most direct manner—that is, through the use of reflex motor responses. But this primary form of coping would not be able to bring about the cessation of endogenous excitation. Eliminating endogenous excitation would only be possible through direct action on the outer world. The first condition for this action would be that the apparatus would learn to tolerate a certain level of stimulation so that it could engage in processes more complex than simple reflex responses. In this way, the entire process, after all is said and done, always aspired to nothing more than the most efficient discharge of stimulation, but would still end up preserving life. This life that goes on and evolves, nonetheless, would be no more than a subterfuge appearing as a life pursues a path whose final objective would be to lead to the greatest possible elimination of stimuli and to satisfy in that way the demand explicitly expressed from 1920 onwards by the concept of death instinct.

From this perspective, self-preservation instincts would only apparently have as their objective the preservation of life—they would also work to serve the death instinct. Since suppression of endogenous stimulation would not be possible as a reflex, an overriding postponement of discharge and the learning of other means of eliminating stimulation would end by causing the animate state to persist even longer. In the "Project" Freud asserts that an organism's initial helplessness is the "instinctive spring" of all psychic development. But this psychic development would only have come about because, owing to the original helpless state, the organism would not be able to attain its goal of total elimination of stimulation without specific inhibitions and new skills. In this sense, behind all psychic development, the primary objective to return to the original state of zero stimulation seems always to be present.

In *Beyond the Pleasure Principle*, Freud concludes early on that the picture of life's phenomena would consist merely of a detour in reaching each organism's particular death, and what appear to be urges to preserve life—that is, the life-preserving instincts' manifestations—would be nothing more than each organism's peculiar way of attaining death. Organisms want to die only in their special way, as Freud says, concluding that life-preserving manifestations can be reconciled with the death-instinct hypothesis. But there is a phenomenon in instinctive activity that appears to elude the tendency towards death—sexual drives. Freud attempted to use sexual instincts to justify his assertion that one may go on speaking of instinctual duality.

The life instinct

In the beginning, in *Beyond the Pleasure Principle*, Freud argues that it is not the activity associated with sex drive as a whole that eludes the general inclination towards death, death is only eluded on the cellular level of sexual activity. Thus, at least initially, only that part of sexual goings-on involved in reproduction—that is, only a tiny part of the activity propelled by sexual instincts—would counter the death instinct. Further on, nevertheless, he claims that there is something that permits one to conclude that the entirety of sexual instincts would favour life's preservation over the tendency to return to an inanimate state.

Freud maintained early on that sexual instincts would ensure the union between germ cells. These instincts would be, thus, the true life instincts countering the death instinct. Thus he says:

> It is as though the life of the organism moved with a vacillating rhythm. One group of instincts rushes forward so as to reach the final aim of life as swiftly as possible; but when a particular stage in the advance has been reached, the other group jerks back to a certain point to make a fresh start and so prolong the journey. [Freud, 1920g, pp. 40–41]

In this way Freud intended to restrict whatever might oppose the death instinct to the fusion of two germ cells produced through sexual instincts. Thus he could establish an opposition between death instincts—which up to this point seem to include instincts for self-preservation as well—and sexual instincts, which would be the actual life instincts. However, arriving at this juncture, the following challenge can be made. If instinct in general is defined as an urge to return to an earlier state that is inherent to life, repetition compulsion would be the pure manifestation of all instincts and not just the death instinct. But, if that is the case, one must clarify exactly what it is that sexual instincts repeat. In other words, what is the most primitive and original state which they aspire to attain?

Death instincts, as was seen, would work to return the organism to its original inanimate state—that is, within the very origin of life this impulse to return to the previous state of lifelessness would have formed. But what about the life instinct? To what prior state would it seek to return? In an attempt to find an answer to this question, Freud asks another. To what does sexual reproduction, or even copulation between two protists, its precursor, seek to return?

He tried to find a clue to solve this matter in his incursions into biology. There would be biological data to indicate that copulation between two protists, the precursor of sexual reproduction in the higher animals, would have a rejuvenating effect on both participants. In addition, other forms of stimulation would produce the same effect on organisms. If, for example, the composition of the nutritive liquid in which the organism lives is changed, this would have the same rejuvenating effect on the organism that copulation would. From another point of view, if the protists are left among their own waste, they undergo a progressive degeneration. From these observations it must have been possible to come to the following conclusion: that which in fact has the capacity to renew life is an increase in stimulation. And, thus, not only the fusion of two germ cells to produce a new life would counter the tendency to die, but so would the increased stimulation produced by the contact between two bodies, as well as other types of stimulation. From this perspective we could identify, not merely in the sexual activity that leads to the fusion between two germ cells, but also sexual manifestations in general as something that would counter death—that is, contact between two bodies would produce an increase in stimulation of the organism. In this vein Freud comes to the following conclusion:

> We might suppose that the life instincts or sexual instincts which are active in each cell take the other cells as their object, that they partly neutralize the death instincts (that is, the processes set up by them) in those cells and thus preserve their life. [Freud, 1920g, p. 50]

The assertion that an increase in stimulation strengthens life is entirely in accord with Freud's supposition that life's process leads, for internal reasons, to a levelling of chemical tensions. From this angle one can assume that death instinct would work towards weakening stimulation, and life instinct would favour an increase in stimulation. Still, we can pose the following questions. Wouldn't sexual instincts also ultimately lead to a discharge in stimulation? Wouldn't the contact between two bodies be nothing more than an intermediate goal of the sex drive—that is, a stage in the process caused by the sex drive, and whose final objective would continue to be a discharge of stimulation? Freud's definition of instinct offered in *Three Essays on the Theory of Sexuality* (1905d) and in his metapsychological article "Instincts and Their Vicissitudes" (1915c) seems to allow for these queries. In these works Freud argues that all instincts have a "goal", an "object", and a "source" and that "the aim [*Ziel*] of an instinct is in every instance satisfaction, which can only be obtained by removing the state of stimulation at the source of the instinct" (Freud, 1915c, p. 122). Thus the elimination of stimulation would be the true goal of all instinct. However, Freud argues that the paths to elimination could be extremely varied. In view of this, the contact between two bodies, a contact that would end up strengthening life, seems to be nothing more than a secondary consequence, after all is said and done, of a process impelled by the need to discharge stimulation. It is a side effect of a process whose ultimate goal would still be death.

These ideas can only be entertained here because, even though there are elements in Freud's writing that support them, he never actually articulated them as such. Still, in *Beyond the Pleasure Principle* the question seems to be open as to what original state the life instinct would seek to return. The biological data Freud invokes do not offer a definitive answer to this question, although they do suggest clues towards such an answer. If sexual instincts actually had the primordial goal of promoting contact between two bodies, the original state to which they seek to return should be the fusion of two bodies. Since this state must be every bit as primordial as that sought after by the death instinct, and if both instincts are held to be present from life's inception, as well as their being equally primordial, one can conclude that inanimate matter, once animate, divided into different parts, which, from that point on, yearned to reunite. With life a tendency must have emerged to return both to an inanimate state (the death instinct) and to a prior, undifferentiated state (the life instinct).

Even though this is what Freud's hypotheses suggest, there seems to be nothing in biology to support these suppositions adequately. In view of this, Freud says:

> Shall we follow the hint given us by the poet-philosopher, and venture upon the hypothesis that living substance at the time of its coming to life was torn apart into small particles, which have ever since endeavoured to reunite through the sexual instincts? That these instincts, in which the chemical affinity of inanimate matter persisted, gradually succeeded, as they developed through the kingdom of the protista, in overcoming the difficulties put in the way of that endeavour by an environment charged with dangerous stimuli—stimuli which compelled them to form a protective cortical layer? That these splintered fragments of living substance in this way attained a multicellular condition and finally transferred the instinct for reuniting, in the most highly concentrated form, to the germ-cells?—But here, we think, the moment has come for breaking off. [Freud, 1920g, p. 58]

Freud then brings up the myth that Plato has Aristophanes develop in *The Banquet*. This philosophical outlook sets forth ideas that Freud was grappling with—that is, ideas that allow him to derive the sexual instinct from the need to achieve an earlier, more primitive state. Still, these are only suggestions and metaphors that hardly carry the weight of scientific support for Freud's hypothesis. As far as *Beyond the Pleasure Principle* is concerned, one must recognize that the above matter, the question of what original state the life instinct would seek to recover, is only formulated, then left open, without a definite answer.

Beginning with these hypotheses developed by Freud, we can now pose the following questions: If the primary goal of the life instinct was to return to an original, fused state, wouldn't this original state be death, since this would be, simultaneously, an inanimate state? Would the sought-after state be bereft of tension—that is, of life? Even though contact between two bodies brings about an increase in stimulation, consequently fortifying life, wouldn't this be a secondary consequence, which would make the sexual instinct also after all the death instinct?

Beyond the Pleasure Principle leaves us with the impression that, no matter how hard Freud tried to accord the life instinct the same status as the death instinct, it seems difficult to avoid the conclusion that death lurks behind all life.

The first versus the second instinctual dualism

As we have maintained, in *Beyond the Pleasure Principle* Freud first puts life-preserving instincts among death instincts. He then proposes an opposition between life-preserving instincts and sexual instincts—the former work towards death, the latter towards further life. But phenomena related to narcissism had already demonstrated the difficulty of maintaining a clear distinction between life-preserving and sexual instincts. For some time prior to this point, Freud had understood that the ego would have to be the libido's true and original reservoir. The ego would thus be one of many sexual objects, and this makes it necessary to recognize that part of the ego's instincts is libidinal in nature. Given this, in a second thought, but still within *Beyond the Pleasure Principle*, Freud tries to correct his first hypothesis, according to which life-preserving instincts would be death instincts:

> But it is all the more necessary for us to lay stress upon the libidinal character of the self-preservative instincts now that we are venturing upon the further step of recognizing the sexual instinct as Eros, the preserver of all things, and of deriving the narcissistic libido of the ego from the stores of libido by means of which the cells of the soma are attached to one another. But we now find ourselves suddenly faced by another question. If the self-preservative instincts too are of a libidinal nature, are there perhaps no other instincts whatever but the libidinal ones? [Freud, 1920g, p. 52]

If life-preserving instincts are also libidinal instincts, then what would be the place for death instincts? Should instinctual dualism be discarded? Freud, as is well known, could in no way accept this consequence. He argued for maintaining the hypothesis that within the ego there would be instincts other than the libidinal ones—even if these instincts could not be identified. He suggested that perhaps aggression could be considered a manifestation of the death instinct. In this way there would be an opposition between love and hate, which he had already proposed in 1915 as one of the great psychic polarities.

However, the hypothesis that aggression would be one of the death instinct's manifestations presents a series of complications, because among others, as Freud himself recognized, there is a close relationship between sexuality and aggression.

But let us examine another aspect of the problem. The concept of narcissism imposed an at least partial identification between self-preservation and sexual instincts, and, early on in *Beyond the Pleasure Principle*, Freud argues that self-preservation instincts are also death instincts. Indeed, since Freud's "Project" (1950 [1895]), it had been established that the organism's development and preservation derived from the impossibility of attaining an elimination of endogenous stimulation through reflexes. Thus, whatever occurs in the maintenance and progress of life would have always had the total elimination of psychic and vital tension as its final goal. Self-preservation instincts would exist to serve the death instinct. Life, as Freud saw it, would be a side trip or detour on the road to death.

But, as we have seen, the opposition between sexual and self-preserving instincts cannot be wholly sustained—at least some of the latter turned out to be libidinal instincts. So there are two factors to consider. On the one hand, self-preservative instincts are perfectly reconcilable with the death-instinct hypothesis and its goal. On top of which, the idea that self-preservative goings on would only secondarily end up saving life seems to be a necessary consequence of the hypothesis that there was a primordial and universal tendency for organisms to annul all tension. Thus the primary impulse behind self-preservative instincts would also be an impulse towards death. Nonetheless, on the other hand, one cannot sustain the opposition between sexual and self-preservative instincts since some of the latter would also be sexual.

Faced with this, Freud discarded the relationship he had posited between self-preservative and death instincts and proposed that self-preservative instincts should in fact be included among life instincts. But there is no way to ignore the fact that nothing seems to contradict the notion that self-preservative instincts also contribute to our tendency to die, that these instincts seek death through a longer and more tortuous route identified with the history of life itself. Given this, would it not be legitimate to conclude that at least some sexual instincts are also death instincts? In other words, is it not the case that to sexualize life-preserving instincts seems to contaminate sexual instincts with life-preserving instincts' ultimate goal—death?

The duality between life and death instincts is not at all easily justified. But Freud held on to this new instinctual dualism in spite of the difficulty in finding sufficient justification for his position. When he asked himself whether the death-instinct hypothesis should not be discarded, he replied:

> The dominating tendency of mental life, and perhaps of nervous life in general, is the effort to reduce, to keep constant or to remove internal tension due to stimuli (the "Nirvana principle", to borrow a term from Barbara Low [1920a, 73])—a tendency which finds expression in the pleasure principle; and our recognition of that fact is one of our strongest reasons for believing in the existence of death instincts. [Freud, 1920g, p. 56]

Death instinct would follow necessarily from Freud's hypothesis that this was psychic life's original tendency—that is, from this "Nirvana principle", as he called it in 1920. Remember what Freud claimed when he proposed the inertia principle in the "Project". There he says that clinical-pathological observations, especially those related to hysteria and compulsion, suggested to him that nervous excitation was a quantity in flux and that, beginning with this observation, it was possible to establish the inertia principle as fundamental to nervous activity. As we have argued, the death-instinct hypothesis seems to be implicated in the apparatus's original tendency to discharge all stimulation. If, according to what Freud says in the "Project", clinical data lead to the postulation of the nervous system's fundamental tendency, then the death-instinct notion would also be anchored in clinical data, and, thus, there was a reason to hold on to this idea.

Keeping in mind the most fundamental premises of Freud's theory, life instincts, even though they produce the more visible manifestations, seem more difficult to justify than death instincts. The only evidence of anything that seems to be clearly in opposition to death is the fusion of germ cells. Still, the relatively late development of sex-based reproduction compromises the primordial character one would attribute to life instincts. The supposition that the original goal of sexual instincts would be the tendency of two bodies to unite—and only after this would this tendency be transferred to germ cells—seems to attenuate somewhat the opposition between life and death instincts based on these considerations. As we have argued, one can suppose that the motivation for two bodies to make contact may, after all, be consequential to seeking discharge of sexual stimulation. This discharge would thus be the primary goal of sexual instincts, and this too would dilute the opposition Freud tried to establish between life and death instincts.

Freud recognizes in *Beyond the Pleasure Principle* that this new instinctual dualism does not offer the same degree of certainty as his earlier efforts in instinctual theory. Some hypotheses he developed in later writings seem to make the death and life instinct duality more problematic and to reinforce the impression that there is in fact no difference between these two types of instinct.

Instinctual dualism after *Beyond the Pleasure Principle*

In "The Economic Problem of Masochism", Freud (1924c) quite clearly establishes what the relationship would be among the various principles that govern psychic activity, as well as what the relationship would be among these principles and the two types of instincts he had proposed in 1920. In *Beyond the Pleasure Principle*, he had differentiated between the pleasure principle—which of necessity would be bound (Freud's *Bindung*) to stimulation—and the Nirvana principle, which would precede the former, since the pleasure principle would only be activated when attached to stimulation resulting from the processes determined by the repetition compulsion. That is, *Bindung* is a necessary condition of the pleasure principle, and the Nirvana principle precedes the pleasure principle, which only comes about through *Bindung*, which derives from the processes determined by the repetition compulsion.

Freud had also argued in 1920 that the pleasure principle would be a "tendency" serving a "function" (the Nirvana principle) and that both would participate in all living beings' most universal aspiration to return all the way to the repose of the inorganic world. To sum up, both principles would directly contribute to death instincts. In *The Ego and the Id* (1923b), however, Freud does not distinguish the pleasure principle from the Nirvana principle particularly clearly; indeed, he refers to them as if they were the same principle. In "The Economic Principle of Masochism" he nonetheless does argue that one must once more differentiate them, and he tries to clarify what their relationship would be:

> However this may be, we must perceive that the Nirvana principle, belonging as it does to the death instinct, has undergone a modification in living organisms through which it has become the pleasure principle; and we shall henceforward avoid regarding the two principles as one. It is not difficult, if we care to follow up this line of thought, to guess what power was the source of the modification. It can only be the life instinct, the libido, which has thus, alongside of the death instinct, seized upon a share in the regulation of the processes of life. In this way we obtain a small but interesting set of connections. The "Nirvana" principle expresses the trend of the death instinct; the "pleasure" principle represents the demands of the libido; and the modification of the latter principle, the "reality" principle, represents the influence of the external world. [Freud, 1924c, p. 160]

Thus a primordial principle, the Nirvana principle, would act on behalf of the death instincts. The life instinct would impose a modification of this principle, occasioning the pleasure principle's appearance, and the external world would impose a second modification, giving rise to the reality principle. Following this, Freud clarifies that none of these principles is totally undone by the others. All go on, sometimes peacefully, sometimes in conflict. But the relationship Freud established among the various principles he proposed and the instincts seems clearly to imply the death instinct's precedence over the life instinct. Psychic processes would be governed originally by the Nirvana principle, which would be directly at the service of the death instinct. The life instinct would get started later on, and this would have as its consequence a modification of the Nirvana principle and its transformation into the pleasure principle. If this is true, then the death instinct should be considered more primordial than the life instinct, which would mean that the symmetry between the two instincts can no longer be maintained. On top of this, in *Beyond the Pleasure Principle,* Freud had clearly asserted that the pleasure principle would, just like the Nirvana principle, contribute to the death instinct. In fact, for there to be an opposition between these two instincts, the pleasure principle should not be thought of in that way, since that would at best classify life instincts as death instincts' secondary modifications rather than as an equally primordial independent principle.

In *An Outline of Psychoanalysis* (1940a [1938]), Freud appears to strengthen even further the death instinct's anteriority to the life instinct. He does this when he rejects the hypothesis he had advanced in *Beyond the Pleasure Principle*—the hypothesis that all instinct would be regressive in nature. In the second part of *An Outline of Psychoanalysis*, he addresses this new instinctual dualism once more, but in this instance he ends up rejecting the possibility of attributing a conservative bent to life instincts. In the beginning, merely repeating what he had proposed in 1920, he seems once again to take up the hypothesis that all instinct would be conservative:

> The forces which we assume to exist behind the tensions caused by the needs of the id are called *instincts*. They represent the somatic demands upon the mind. Though they are the ultimate cause of all activity, they are of a conservative nature; the state, whatever it may be, which an organism has reached gives rise to a tendency to re-establish that state so soon as it has been abandoned. [Freud, 1940a (1938), p. 148]

Still, immediately after this Freud argues that this conservative nature may, in truth, be a characteristic of the death instincts. It would not be possible to attribute it to life instincts as well, since that would imply that living matter divided once life appeared, and that it began at that point to aspire to return to its anterior, unitary state:

> If we assume that living things came later than inanimate ones and arose from them, then the death instinct fits in with the formula we have proposed to the effect that instincts tend toward a return to an earlier state. In the case of Eros (or the love instinct) we cannot apply this formula. To do so would presuppose that living substance was once a unity which had later been torn apart and was now striving toward re-union. [Freud, 1940a (1938), pp. 148–149]

In the history of living matter, Freud admits that there is no knowledge of any such thing ever happening, and, thus, there would be no justification for attributing this conservative nature to life instincts as well. Given this conclusion, what are the implications for theory?

If it were only the death instincts that aimed to return to a prior state, the repetition compulsion would have to be a feature of death instincts and not, as Freud supposed in *Beyond the Pleasure Principle*, a universal characteristic of all instinct. And if that were so, then only the death instinct would be operative in that function controlled solely by the Nirvana principle, or the original psychic function—the repetition compulsion. In this case the death instinct would antedate the appearance of the life instinct, which would only emerge in the psychic apparatus's later stages of operation. And it is this hypothesis that Freud appears to defend in "The Economic Problem of Masochism" (1924c). There, as we have seen, he maintains that the Nirvana principle expresses death instincts' tendencies whereas the pleasure principle, a "modification" of the Nirvana principle, represents the libido's demands. According to this viewpoint, one would suppose that the death instinct begins first, propelled by the Nirvana principle, and that only afterwards would the life instinct emerge, bringing with it the pleasure principle. All this seems to lead to the hypothesis that the death instinct underlies all psychic processes and leads us then to the problem of why life would have sprung forth, despite this primordial tendency to die, without there being a primordial principle that opposed the death instinct.

Still, Freud was reluctant to concede the death instinct's precedence over the life instinct. In *An Outline of Psychoanalysis* (1940a [1938]), in spite of his denying the life instinct's conservative nature, he tries to hold on to the hypothesis that both instincts would be equally primordial:

> We may picture an initial state as one in which the total available energy of Eros, which henceforward we shall speak of as "libido", is present in the still undifferentiated ego-id and serves to neutralize the destructive tendencies which are simultaneously present. [Freud, 1940a [1938], pp. 149–150]

Even so, there seems to be a basic impasse in the theory. The Nirvana principle would be primordial and would be propelled into being by the death instinct. Repetition compulsion would only be a manifestation of the death instinct and would precede the pleasure principle's effect. And the pleasure principle would begin to operate owing to propulsion from the life instinct. But if the pleasure principle derives from the life instinct's action and if the life instinct originates as a modification of the Nirvana principle, then necessarily the death instinct appears in the psychic apparatus before the life instinct. Still, Freud maintained the parity hypothesis for both instincts, which would be equally primordial, notwithstanding all his argumentation that points in the opposite direction. And this contradiction was left unresolved in Freud's psychoanalytic theory.

Final considerations

Since Freud maintains, for example, in "The Economic Problem of Masochism" (1924c), that the pleasure principle is a modification of the Nirvana principle, it becomes difficult to maintain a clear opposition between both types of instincts. This is because in *Beyond the Pleasure Principle* Freud had argued that the pleasure principle would serve the death instinct, just as the Nirvana principle would. For there to be a total opposition between both instincts, Freud would need an equivalent opposition between the two principles we have discussed. And this would contradict Freud's hypotheses developed in the works examined above.

Freud advanced another hypothesis that seems to attenuate the theory that there is an opposition between life- and death instincts. Sexual instincts would promote contact between two bodies. Keeping in mind the earlier definitions of instinct and considering sexual instinct as their model, their goal would in fact be to promote discharge of sexual stimulation. The resulting increase in stimulation from the contact between bodies would be a secondary consequence of a process whose final objective would always be to eliminate tension, and for that reason it would, to a certain extent, be consonant with the goal attributed to the death instinct. Thus, to maintain the hypothesis that the primary purpose of sexual instincts would be to promote contact between bodies, which would make them "life" instincts, one would have to reformulate the notion of sexual instinct.

Another impasse in the theory derives from the fact that self-preservation instincts are, as Freud explicitly asserted, totally reconcilable with the death-instinct hypothesis. Indeed, at least in the paradigmatic case of hunger, life-preserving instincts seem to have a much greater affinity with death instincts than with life instincts. If what preserves life is an increase in stimulation, in the case of hunger, at least, as Freud established in the "Project" (1950 [1895]), the conservation of a stimulation constant is only a means to an end that, in this case, is the suppression of endogenous stimulation, which, carried to the extreme, would suppress life itself.

For these reasons we have attempted to argue that the second instinctual duality hypothesis, since its first formulation in 1920, does not seem to fit easily into Freudian metapsychology. Beginning with *Beyond the Pleasure Principle* and then in Freud's later works, one is left with the impression that, no matter how hard Freud tried to hold on to his opposition between life and death instincts, he was never able to base the opposition on anything solid nor to justify it in an entirely convincing manner. In spite of the reserved reception the death-instinct notion received and in spite of its being considered the most problematic point in the final period of Freudian metapsychology, this concept, the death instinct, seems to be an internal necessity to the theory. It is logically derivable from the theory's premises, whereas there seems to be no natural place for the life instinct, which seems to be a hypothesis Freud introduced and could not bear to discard but which seems, in fact, to be a sort of extra-theoretical accretion.

This asymmetry between the categories that form the second Freudian instinctual duality gives precedence to the death instinct over the life instinct or Eros, even though Eros encompasses those instincts that formed the earlier duality: the sexual and self-preserving instincts. The formulation of the concept of the death instinct seems to be more a "redefining" of these instincts than a proposing (or a discovery) of a third group of instincts that would oppose the original set now known as life instincts. This redefinition would emphasize instinct's deadly nature as a whole. And this emphasis, far from being a new idea, actually makes explicit one of instinct's fundamental properties, which, derived logically from the very concept of instinct, was only implicit in the theory before 1920. Caropreso and Simanke (2006) show that the same can be said of the repetition compulsion, which was implicit from the beginning of Freud's theorization but was made explicit only in 1920. Just as death instinct is, to a certain extent, "deduced" from the repetition compulsion, so it should not come as a shock that Freud should clarify with the death-instinct concept one more idea already present in his earlier thinking.

Two consequences of these considerations need to be emphasized. The first is that one must recognize that beneath this new instinctual dualism lies a sort of monism in which all instinct finally turns out to be death instinct. It is still somewhat surprising that Freud came to the same conclusion through biology that Lacan polemically proposed after a wide-reaching revision of Freudian theory. As is well known, this revision was based on theoretical concepts offered in the human sciences, anthropology and linguistics, as well as philosophy.

Lacan begins by conceiving the subject as something determined by a language's structure and, consequently, by a language's formal and combinatory aspects. This is condensed in his notion of "pure signifier" or "signifier as such". Using the dialectical principle that "the word is the item's death" allows him to consider neurotic symptoms, especially hysteria, to be the result of the fatal workings that the signifier or the "letter" performs on the body, which would make it penetrated with death from the beginning. And then his notion that the "letter" is mortal, even though its fatal character is only present in language itself, allows him to conclude that, virtually and after all, all instinct is death instinct (Lacan, 1966, p. 848).

The second consequence leads to the need to rethink Freud's new dualism. Various scholars (e.g. Figueiredo, 1999; Lifton, 1976; Sulloway, 1979) have already shown that the dualism problem is not the central problem in *Beyond the Pleasure Principle*, nor in Freud's second instinctual dualism hypothesis. Indeed, given the asymmetry and the death instinct's precedence, as well as how the repetition compulsion is considered instinctual exigency's defining characteristic, this dualism can only be constructed on the common foundation established by the conservative and ultimately deadly nature of all instincts.

Clearly, then, the instinctual duality proposed in 1920 cannot be the same as the former duality, where sexual and self-preserving instincts derived from different biological bases—species and individual preservation. From another point of view, the opposition between life and death instincts seems to typify two conflicting aspects of instinctual demands in general. These demands rest on life's inherent tensions: one tends towards complexity and organization, the other towards the elimination of tension and a return to the inanimate. It is, thus, possible to specify more clearly the thesis that "all instinct is a death instinct". Each individual instinct would be simultaneously life and death instinct according to how one regards it; however, some instincts may exhibit more clearly one or another aspect, such as the relationship between aggression and death instinct. Indeed, on various occasions Freud insisted that none of these instincts would surface as only one: they would always be part one, part another. Freud's second instinctual theory, then, would assign a duality inherent to instinct itself, and it would not, strictly speaking, posit a difference between two types of biologically different instincts.

Given the death instinct's commonality with the totality of the theory, it does not seem possible to accept Freudian metapsychology and reject death instinct. In his analysis of Freud's writing, Sulloway emphatically and with great rigour asserts that "his conception of the death instinct was a logical tour de force that has rarely been understood in its proper perspective" (1979, pp. 408–9). But what is the problem with this concept? Could it, in fact, be just a speculative fantasy and scientific foolishness contradicting all biological principles (Brun, 1953; Sulloway, 1979)? After all, the notion that there is an instinctive basis for aggression (Lorenz, 1963a) and that an organism's death is to an extent genetically programmed (Dawkins, 1976) are far from heterodoxy in contemporary biological research. These are matters that could not be developed here, but we mention them only to suggest that perhaps full appreciation of Freud's theorization on these matters, and on the death instinct in particular, needs to be based and oriented through a dialogue with and systematic interaction between biology and psychoanalysis. Indeed, as far as instinct is concerned, Freud repeatedly insisted on their integration.

Note

Chapter translated by Arthur Brakel.

3

An unusual manifestation of repetition compulsion in traumatized patients

Ira Brenner

> Only believers, who demand that science shall be a substitute
> for the catechism that they have given up, will blame an
> investigator for developing or even transforming his views.
>
> Freud, *Beyond the Pleasure Principle* (1920g), p. 63

Shaken by the Great War himself, Sigmund Freud's opening remarks to the Budapest Congress in 1919 addressed the incomplete-
ness of psychoanalytic knowledge as it related to the war neuroses.
Dissatisfied with attributing the unimaginable carnage to repressed
sexuality or anal sadism, he had to reconsider the ideas already put
forth by colleagues such as Adler (1910), Stekel (1911), Spielrein
(1912), and Reik (1911) about the role of aggression in the human
psyche. He needed to expand his theory so "Rather implausibly,
Freud also posited a 'war-like' 'I' that created a lust for destruction"
(Makari, 2008, p. 315). This line of thought evolved into the "third
step in the theory of the instincts, which . . . cannot lay claim to the
same degree of certainty as the two earlier ones—the extension of
the concept of sexuality and the hypothesis of narcissism" (Freud,
1920g, p. 59).

Having recently published his thoughts on sadomasochism as they pertained to the Wolf Man (Freud, 1918b [1914]) and nearing completion on his work on masochism in "A Child Is Being Beaten" (Freud, 1919e), Freud started a new essay with what he described to Ferenczi as a "mysterious" title: *Beyond the Pleasure Principle* (letter from Freud to Ferenczi, 17 March 1919, Falzeder & Brabant, 1996, p. 355). In so doing, he appeared to be reversing himself, and he greatly disturbed his loyal followers by undermining the primacy of libido theory and the pleasure principle. This radical shift was stimulated by what he described as a separate class of dreams that did not adhere to the theory of wish-fulfilment, the recurrent traumatic dreams of soldiers that revisited the horror of the battlefield. Seeking an explanation, he revisited Fechner's constancy principle and conceptualized that the quest for stability and constancy required a need for mastery of an overwhelming stimulus that was not only a valid aspect of motivation, "beyond" the pleasure principle. The major mental principle that he had previously described, known as the compulsion to repeat (Freud, 1914g, 1950 [1895]), was therefore fuelled by an innate drive for mastery, sameness, reduction of inner tension, and a movement towards ultimate peace: the eternal sleep of death. Thus, the "Nirvana Principle"—a term coined by Barbara Low (1920b)—could therefore explain how our species could wage war and bring about unspeakable destruction: it was now conjectured by Freud to be out of an unconscious drive towards permanent inner peace.

This theory appeared to be the ultimate paradox that many analysts, such as those espousing "modern conflict theory" (Abend, 2007), found, and continue to find, not only difficult to accept but also unnecessary for clinical work (I. Brenner, 2001). Notable exceptions are the Kleinians and a number of analysts working with traumatized individuals (Laub & Lee, 2003). However, even among those who endorse the concept it is not unusual to issue a disclaimer, such as downgrading it to a less than basic aspect of all psyches. For example, Kernberg has recently stated: "The death drive, I propose, is not a primary drive but represents a significant complication of aggression as a major motivational system, is central in the therapeutic work with severe psychopathology, and as such is imminently useful as a concept in the clinical realm (Kernberg, 2009, p. 1018—see chapter 6, this volume).

Almost a century later, contemporary analysts may not be able to fully appreciate the confusion and uproar over Freud's dismantling of his own orthodoxy. The faithful followers of libido theory were in a huge quandary. Perhaps we psychoanalysts practicing today experienced an echo of this phenomenon when the late Charles Brenner questioned the value of the structural theory after devoting all of his professional life to conflict theory and the promulgation of Freud's ideas (C. Brenner, 2003). Interestingly, Brenner's challenge to the very theory he had espoused for decades went undiscussed in both his recently published memoir (C. Brenner, 2009a) and his interview with Robert Michaels (2009b). In his obituary, however, Jacobs emphasizes the maverick quality that Brenner possessed despite having been seen as the quintessential standard bearer of classical psychoanalysis (Jacobs, 2009). As a younger man, his earlier challenge to the prevailing views on psychosis because they did not fit the data of clinical experience earned him this reputation with his elders. Interestingly, he was roughly the age Freud had been when he put forth his theory of *Thanatos*. It is too soon to know whether Brenner's proposed revision will be forgotten or even dismissed as an aberrant flight of fancy by his followers, just as many loyal Freudians today choose to refute his forays into the "death instinct" as being too theoretical or perhaps autobiographically motivated. While Freud did also express his own uncertainty about these radical ideas, the reader nevertheless gets the impression of his subtle enjoyment in being the provocative "*advocatus diaboli*" (Freud, 1920g, p. 59).

In over three decades of my own clinical work with traumatized individuals, I, too, have had clinical experiences that have not conformed to prevailing theory, and I have felt the need to revise and ultimately extend some ideas about the effects of overwhelming life experience on the psyche (Akhtar & Brenner, 1979; I. Brenner, 2001, 2004, 2009a; Kestenberg & Brenner, 1996). The mutual influences of both external reality and internal psychic reality remain at the centre of the question as the latest developments in neurobiology, genetics, cognitive psychology, and trauma studies deepen our understanding of the mind–brain–body–environment question. It is in this very exciting climate where new discoveries made outside the consulting room may threaten to eclipse insights gleaned from the psychoanalytic situation unless the latter are revisited and integrated into a multidisciplinary approach to depth psychology. It is in this context that I would like to underscore the clinical importance of the repetition compulsion, which was so carefully explicated by Freud in *Beyond the Pleasure Principle*. While the extensive debate over its metapsychology and neurophysiology continues, the fact of its existence and relevance to treatment is not in question. Indeed, an appreciation of its presence, especially where trauma is concerned, has helped this author make sense of those conditions currently known as dissociative disorders, especially "multiple personality". This realm has traditionally been seen as, at best, either "not psychoanalysis" or, at worst, an iatrogenic creation of overzealous therapists (I. Brenner, 2001).

The dream and "waking dream" sequence

An unusual manifestation of the repetition compulsion may be observed in the mental life of those severely traumatized in childhood. It may only be observed where one is working analytically, because the extent of the patients' forgetting makes it impossible for them to see it on their own and because other forms of treatment would not allow the opportunity to examine the repeating relationship between dreams and altered states of consciousness. A typical scenario is as follows: The patient may report a disturbing dream or a recurring dream in which he/she is *watching another person—usually a child—get hurt in some specific way*. The dream often awakens the patient, who is left shaken up and confused about the manifest content. The child who is being victimized by others may be vaguely recognized by the dreamer or seem to be a total stranger. Moreover, the degree of upset is quite variable, ranging from mild concern, such as might be seen with the recall of a screen memory, to outright panic. Associations to the dream may, if the patient is able, be to the day residue, which, according to well-known classical principles, then enable the tentative conclusion to be drawn that some identifiable precipitant stimulated the creation of a dream that incorporates childhood determinants.

So far all is well and good. At this point, the analyst feels on the same solid ground that generations of dream interpreters have tread before, rediscovering Freud's formula that eventually, in a "good-enough" conducted analysis, the earlier material will emerge, which will enable a construction of childhood fantasy/ memory. However, in the situation under consideration, there is an additional component, and a most vexing one, that many clinicians might prefer to ignore or downplay, or they may simply fail to appreciate its profound significance. For if they do take it seriously, then a whole host of uncomfortable questions may follow which could even challenge some of our basic assumptions about psychic structure and the centrality of repression as the primary defence mechanism (I. Brenner, 2009a).

This second component of the sequence usually occurs within days of the dream. It could be as soon as the next analytic session or possibly up to a week later. At this time, the patient either presents in a different state of consciousness or undergoes an alteration in ego functioning or self-state during the session. It may be sudden and dramatic or seem subtle and imperceptible, especially if the patient is lying on the couch and the analyst is not aware of this phenomenon. It is referred to as "switching", in the jargon of those who typically treat dissociative disorders. Anxiety in the transference or a very dysphorically affect-laden topic may precede this shift (I. Brenner, 2004). At such times the patient may talk in a different way—that is, use different words or use words in a different way, with a different inflection, syntax, or cadence. The voice itself may sound different—perhaps as if it were coming from a younger person or from a person of the opposite gender. In addition, there may be fluttering of the eyelids as seen in an autohypnotic state or a dramatic change of facial expression in which the facial musculature is used differently. Body language may be different also as hand gestures and movements seem out of character. There may even be a sense of unfamiliarity or disorientation with the surroundings as the patient might come across as having just materialized in the analyst's office for the first time.

During this shift in the patient's demeanour, he or she may then relate a memory of being subjected to a horrendous situation that sounds very similar or even identical to the ordeal in the dream. This expression would appear to be an elaboration of the "night residue" (Leveton, 1961), where, according to the Morris Hypothesis (Akhtar, 2009a), the manifest dream gets lived out in the waking state. In contrast, however, the recounting of the memory is in the first person, as opposed to it being observed as happening to someone else in the dream. It may have the quality of an over-powering narrative or a psychological reliving of the trauma (Laub & Auerhahn, 1993), as the immediacy of the experience and the associated affect may have an abreactive quality to it. In addition, should the analyst happen to inquire about the aforementioned dream at this time or in any way try to make a connection or invite any connections between the two phenomena while the patient is in this mental state, he would typically hear that the patient has no knowledge, memory, or perhaps even any connection whatsoever with the process of dreaming. It is almost as though *someone else* had had the dream and was responsible for that realm of mental functioning which is of no concern to the patient at this time. One might even say that the patient's lack of curiosity has a qual-ity of indifference to it, not unlike "*la belle indifférence*" ascribed to hysteria.

What might be ascribed to unusually deep repression for this apparent "disconnect" becomes even more mystifying if at some point in the not-too-distant future the dream gets revisited. If the patient is queried about the subsequent abreaction in the aberrant state of mind, he/she denies any knowledge or recollection of having such a childhood memory, let alone having revealed it in a session. This denial appears sincere and genuine. At this point the analyst may experience his own momentary doubt over the accuracy of his memory and may either inquire further from the patient or simply let it pass as yet another inexplicable moment in the space–time continuum of analysis. I would contend, however, that such a clinical event is in the realm of dissociation and is of the greatest importance as it belies a type of forgetting or defensive not knowing that goes beyond repression and perhaps even precedes it developmentally (I. Brenner, 1994, 2009a, 2009b). It should also be noted that this sequence may also occur in reverse, such that the firsthand account in an altered state of consciousness may precede the reporting of the dream.

In a clinical example that represents some aspects of this situ-ation in reverse, Reiser describes a woman in analysis who, as a pre-teen many years earlier, had a "hysterical dissociative" episode following the accidental burning of her younger brother (Reiser, 1994). She was sent to the pharmacy to procure a medicine for the

badly scalded boy but went into an amnestic altered state for several
hours, became lost, and was found in a park in a daze hours later.
She was haunted by this mental lapse ever since and was obsessed
with trying to remember the name of the burn preparation she
never picked up. During a time when this material entered the
treatment, she had a dream of *consulting a travel agent about wanting to go to Germany but was not able to remember the name of the town
she wanted to visit. In addition, someone oddly complimented her on her
"tan"*. Through the analyst's empathic listening to her associations,
the patient was then able to recall that the elusive name of the
burn medicine was "*tannic* acid"—which Dr Reiser had already suspected by then. Significantly, *the travel agent* (analyst) in the dream
*was not able to help her plan the full itinerary for her travels throughout
Germany* (German was Freud's native language), which appears to
be a symbolic allusion to her frustration in analysis over not being
able to recall what was going on in her mind during this fugue
state many years earlier. A link between her dissociative episode
and the dream, catalysed by analysis, then became evident to this
perceptively attuned analyst, who helped the patient to remember
and integrate her traumatically induced flight into an altered state
of consciousness many years earlier. It appears that the psychological ingredients in this vignette are included in a more complex sequence where reciprocal amnesia (Janet, 1907) and a disturbance
in identity are present.

Case report: Cindy/Candy

In one such case, a patient in analysis was experiencing considerable anxiety over the prospect of a major surgical procedure for a
very painful condition (I. Brenner, 2001).

> The patient, Cindy, was asked by the surgeon, while she was giv-
> ing her consent to the operation, whether she would also give
> her permission for photographs to be taken. It was an academic
> teaching hospital, and, because of the exploratory nature of
> the operation, it was unclear what would be revealed inside
> her body as being the cause of this condition. Eager for relief,
> she naturally focused on the risks of the surgery and was rather

blasé about the request to be photographed. However, when she mentioned it during the session, she seemed to hesitate a bit and could not identify whether anything was, in fact, bothering her about it. The next hour, she reported a puzzling dream from the night before, which left her with a vague uneasiness. In that dream, *she was watching a young girl being taken to a barn by grownups to see the animals, but once she got there it was very strange, and there were many bizarre lights.* She awoke feeling disturbed by the images but could not elaborate. Then, several days later, during a session, the patient spontaneously underwent a mental transformation, "switched", and began to speak in a younger, more affect-laden, coquettish voice.

Having had some familiarity at this point in the treatment with these shifts, I recognized that at such times she insisted that she was not that "boring" other person, Cindy, who went to work every day, paid the bills, and was so very serious all the time. In great contrast, she loved to go out at night and dance and have a good time partying. She even insisted that I recognize her as a separate person and call her Candy. In fact, Candy loved to recount how she had recently "tricked" Cindy into planning a very expensive vacation to a resort. Cindy made all the arrangements, did all the packing, got on the plane, but then had no memory of the vacation until she got back on the plane to return home. From Candy's perspective, she "took over" and had the time of her life. From Cindy's perspective, however, she essentially went into a fugue.

However, it was not all fun and games for Candy: she had a crucial psychological job to perform. Candy was the one who protected Cindy from bad memories, and this time in the session she wanted to tell me about another time Cindy was tricked. It happened a long time ago, when "they" were young, when she went into a barn with her sneaky uncle and a friend of his that she did not know. They asked her if she wanted to see the farm animals and would even be able to pet them. Cindy was very excited about this idea and went with them, but when she got there it was not like it was supposed to be. Cindy got terrified and "hid" somewhere inside the mind; Candy then took over control of the body. There were many bright lights inside the barn, and the man wanted her to take her clothes off while he took pictures of her as she was touching the animals' private parts. The animals were also made to do painful things to her bottom. Although she was scared too and did not like it at all, she knew that Cindy would not be able to deal with it all, and so she, Candy, was the one who usually "came out" when these bad things were happening. In that state of mind, the patient, as Candy, had no knowledge of Cindy's dream. Then, when Cindy "returned" to the session, she had no memory of the time that Candy was out, describing this ordeal.

During this time Cindy's anxiety over the impending operation increased as her pain escalated. As "Candy", she could not comprehend the medical necessity of the procedure and was afraid that the "bad people" were tricking them again. Cindy experienced another such repetitive sequence of dream followed by a waking dream, as it were. As her fears of disfigurement came to the fore, Cindy reported a disturbing dream in which she was watching a teenage girl being held down on a table. The girl was naked and was being restrained by a woman who was a stranger while a man, whom she also did not know, savagely cut the girl's body. The girl screamed in pain while the people laughed and were totally indifferent to her suffering.

Several days later, Candy again reappeared in a session. This time she appeared quite paranoid, explaining that the "bad people" had intended to cut her completely open if she were to tell anyone what was going on. Since she had "heard" about the operation, she feared that "they" were the ones behind it and were going to really punish her this time. It seemed that talking to me was the reason she feared they were going to get her again. She then described a time when she was held down on a kitchen table by the mean girlfriend of her uncle while he inserted a knife into her vagina and cut her. Terrified, overwhelmed, and doubled over in pain as she relived this scenario, she was sure that he would make good on his promise to complete the job. There appeared to be a collapse of time in this "Candy" state of mind such that she could not appreciate the passage of time and feared that these perpetrators from childhood many years ago were still around to harm her. Furthermore, as with the previously mentioned sequence, Candy had no knowledge of Cindy's uncannily similar dream, wherein Cindy had amnesia for that part of the session when Candy took over.

It is known that such patients appear to be in a "waking dream" (Mark, 2009; Marmer, 1980, 1991) during their dissociative episodes. In my own observations of this dream-like state (I. Brenner, 1995, 2001), I have come to appreciate the importance of the so-called "functional phenomenon" (Silberer, 1909) as a mechanism to understand some of the symbolism seen in the accompanying dream imagery. Although alluded to by Freud (1900a), expounded upon by Rapaport (1949), and later rediscovered by Silber (1970, 1979), this aspect of dreams has been largely overshadowed by the classical theory of wish-fulfilment. This under-appreciated phenomenon refers to the ego's capacity to create imagery to symbolize its own various states of consciousness in metaphorical and very often anthropomorphic terms. In other words, this auto-symbolic function may result in the creation of people to represent its own different levels of alertness or awareness. A somewhat elusive quality of the human mind, Kohut (1977) apparently recognized its significance, applying it to his concept of self-state dreams in narcissistic patients. Here, the dream represents the attempts of the psyche to ward off threats of loss of cohesion. Even earlier, Fairbairn recognized the link between the endopsychic structures of the mind—that is, ego and internal objects—and the personae in dreams (Fairbairn, 1944). For a number of reasons, however, the functional phenomenon, Fairbairn's "state of affairs" dreams and the self-state dream have received limited attention in the literature (Slap & Trunnell, 1987), and any possible connection with the repetition compulsion has been obscure.

Auto-symbolism—a self report

Silberer (1909) described his own mind's creations in his efforts to stay awake in order to think and do his work. These creations included images of other people. For example, his conflict over maintaining his concentration was once represented as an unfriendly secretary in a library who ignored him and would not help him with his request for help, whereas, another time, a helpful assistant did await his orders. In my own experience, a recent dream in the early morning just before awakening further illustrates this phenomenon, which often occurs in hypnogogic/hypnopompic states: I had been up unusually late the night before trying to complete a project to meet a publishing deadline and was concerned about waking up on time the following morning. After my alarm went off, I drifted back to sleep for a few moments and dreamt that *I was crossing an international border back to the United States. The border guard asked me whether I had anything to declare. I said, "No". He then asked if I had been exposed to any diseases, such as the swine flu, that might be contagious and spread to others if I were let back in. Again, I said, "No". He seemed satisfied and was about to let me pass through. Just as I was proceeding, he suddenly sprayed a liquid into my eyes, which, he said, was a new procedure because of the pandemic. It surprised and annoyed me as I was not aware of this new protocol. I was also concerned that the disinfectant might burn my eyes, but I hardly felt it. I was relieved. I was more focused on having been let back in and was ready to proceed because I had somewhere to go and was on a tight schedule. Then, just as I was passing through the checkpoint,* I woke up and my eyes were stinging.

I was immediately aware of my dream, which amused me, as it seemed to symbolize my plight over having fallen back into a light sleep and knowing I had to get up. The conflict over my states of consciousness was apparently personified by the border guard, who took his time doing his job (of "guarding" my sleep and letting me rest for a few more moments) but eventually letting me pass through to the US territory, my homeland, and waking up back in my home. Then, the sudden action of the guard spraying me with the disinfectant, which I expected to burn my eyes, seemed to represent the experience of my suddenly waking up with sore eyes due to lack of sleep, which I wished would not happen this time.

In the larger reality at this time, the global anxiety over a swine flu/H1N1 pandemic and the precautions that were being implemented seemed to be part of the day residue in forming my mind's choice of scenarios. A determinant from childhood also came to mind during my self-analysis of the dream. An apocryphal story related to my ancestors' immigration to the United States was of a great-uncle who, as a boy, had endured the hardship of transatlantic passage in the bowels of an overcrowded ship, only to be refused entry at Ellis Island because his eyes were red. The immigration authorities were worried that his bloodshot eyes were indicative of a very infectious disease, and he had to return to Eastern Europe with his father while his mother and siblings were admitted. The uncertainty of being permitted to pass through the borders to safety became a cautionary tale in my growing up. It therefore appeared that the classical elements of dream formation, such as wish-fulfilment, day residue, and childhood factors, were also operative in this type of dream, which symbolized my passing through different states of consciousness—that is, from sleep to wakefulness.

Despite such "personification of drowsiness" (Rapaport, 1949), Rapaport reports that in normative circumstances "distinguishing between I and not I is presumed . . . [Whereas] in other states of consciousness parts of the self may not be as presumed. Multiple personalities . . . are commonly known examples" (p. 200). Under certain circumstances, therefore, this universal phenomenon may contribute to or reinforce a sense of multiple selves. It is therefore a very important clinical opportunity for the analyst to be able to point out to the patient the common origin of the content of both the dream and the altered state. Becoming aware of this manifestation of the compulsion to repeat may be a decisive moment for the patient to begin to accept formerly disowned aspects of the mind. When confronted with the possibility of a common origin to both the remembered dream and the dissociated self-state, the patient may experience this intervention as a well-timed interpretation.

Dreaming of defensive altered states

The representation in post-traumatic dreams of the defensive altered states employed by the patient in response to the traumatic experience itself is that obscure aspect of the repetition compulsion under examination here. It was illustrated by a patient in analysis, Karen, who was desperately warding off the belief that she had been sexually abused by her aunt, a most trusted relative who had taken care of Karen when she was young. Karen emphatically insisted that she had no memories of molestation and therefore could not verify it in her mind. Nevertheless, her exceedingly refractory symptoms of memory loss, fluctuating levels of consciousness, psychogenic pain, genital hallucinations, self-mutilation, eating disorder symptoms, alcohol abuse, precocious sexuality, and recurrent dreams of penetration by trusted women in authority had raised the question of abuse in a number of previous treating clinicians. In addition, she described hallucinatory experiences of "others" in her mind who could take over for periods of time, after which point she would then "come to" in the middle of an activity.

While she was in the throes of a crisis in treatment where she induced the kind of helplessness in me that she regularly lived with herself, she reported a dream where *her aunt suddenly jumped out from behind a curtain and stated that a prominent medical specialist had finally diagnosed her condition as a hormonal disturbance. The patient then replied that no one really thought that this was the case any more. The aunt then exclaimed that she knew what was causing her problem. The patient, who then became self-conscious because others were around, asked if they could talk about it more discreetly elsewhere. The aunt, however, persisted and declared that it was because the patient wanted to surpass everyone else but was really unimportant in her family and was neglected. At that point, the patient then started to cry and refuted the aunt, saying that her explanation could not cause her to feel pain so severe that it was like her bones were ripping through the skin and coming out of her body. Then the aunt became quite angry and approached the patient in a menacing and mechanical way, like a character in a horror movie. The patient could not move and then found herself sitting in a chair across the room. The aunt continued to approach her and said that the patient did not think that she could do something like this, at which point the aunt sat atop her with her legs wrapped around her. The aunt's breasts then came closer to the patient's face and felt like dangerous, disgusting weapons as Karen became overwhelmed with panic. These words formed in her mind: "It's true! It's true! I can't do this! How am I going to get through this?!?!"*

Suddenly, it became very misty, everything became blurry and everything in her body and mind began to feel fine. Then it was as though she were in a blackout. Karen reported that she remembered nothing more until she awoke in tremendous physical pain; she felt too paralysed with pain to move yet in too much pain to stay in bed. Her perpetual sense of being in a no-win situation was exemplified by the extent of her pain.

Significantly, one of the "selves" that the patient experienced as inhabiting her mind was known to her as the shadow, one who personified living in darkness. This "part" of her reportedly had memories of bad events and protected the patient by destroying her memory and inducing body pain in order to keep her from thinking and remembering too much. Thus it appeared as though the patient's dream represented her defensive altered state of consciousness in response to the overstimulating advances by her aunt. The dream imagery of mist, blurriness, and relief of both physical and mental pain suggested an autohypnotic flight from traumatic experience or experiences that may have been condensed into this one scenario.

Discussion

In severe dissociative psychopathology, where patients may shift between different levels of consciousness while awake, this mechanism also appears to be operative. In such cases, they may also employ a "pseudo-externalized displacement" in the service of negation. In so doing, they develop a quasidelusional insight enabling them to say, "*I* didn't think, say, do, feel or dream that—someone else did!" Thus, anthropomorphization of autohypnotic, dreamlike, hypnogogic, and hypnopompic states, a reflection of the functional phenomenon, seems to be a contributing factor to this psychological state. Under the influence of the repetition compulsion, a reciprocal amnesia between these dissociated states and post-traumatic dreams may further reinforce this process of disowning what is in the mind, even as the themes keep repeating themselves. As a result, this complex form of negation cannot be reversed by a mere lifting of repression through simple interpretation. While the timing of any interpretative effort is always crucial, it is especially important in helping the patient recognize and own these mental contents. Recognition of these complex operations in response to severe early trauma is necessary in the understanding of this defence/symptom compromise formation, which may be catalysed by analysis of the transference (I. Brenner, 2001, 2004, 2009b). When successfully handled, such patients, who initially have no conscious memory of trauma at a young age, may, over time, come to be able to own what in their "heart of hearts" they had known but did not *really* know was there all along (I. Brenner, 1997). As one patient on the verge of a breakthrough very succinctly and insightfully observed, "I cannot think about what I remember!"

My experience with hundreds of patients with severe dissociative pathology has shown that there is clinical value in viewing their recurrent dreams and their altered ego states from this perspective. In such cases, the striking similarities between the manifest content of traumatic dreams and the first-hand accounts of the personifications themselves suggest a common mental origin to both (Barrett, 1995; I. Brenner, 2001), as described above. These findings seem to suggest that the psychic fates of these altered states of consciousness, which originally occurred in response to severe early trauma, may be represented and repeated in the post-traumatic dream and then re-incorporated into repeated altered states.

A bridge from "hypnoid states" to psychic energy and beyond the pleasure principle

One of the major theoretical contributions in *Beyond the Pleasure Principle* is based upon Freud's elaboration of Breuer's hypothesis of bound and unbound energy, where the former is quiescent and the latter is free and mobile (Freud, 1895d). As such, the conscious would contain energy with the potential to be discharged freely due to the nature of mental activity and excitatory processes occurring there. For protection against overstimulation, however, a specialized function of the psyche develops, resulting in a psychological callous, as it were, in which "its outermost surface ceases to have the structure proper to living matter, becomes to some degree inorganic and then functions as a special envelope or membrane resistant to stimuli" (Freud, 1920g, p. 27). Therefore, "By its death, the outer layer has saved all the deeper ones from a similar fate—unless, that is to say—stimuli reach it which are so strong that they break through the protective shield" (Freud, 1920g, p. 27). Freud then goes on to say that it would be "traumatic [if] any excitations from the outside . . . are powerful enough to break through the protective shield [and therefore] provoke a disturbance on a large scale in the functioning of the organism's energy and to set in motion *every possible defensive measure*" (Freud, 1920g, p. 29; italics added). In this case, a defensive altered state of consciousness would be an example of such a desperate defensive measure. As a result, the pleasure principle is no longer in operation, and the major task of the psyche is to master, bind, and dispose of the excessive energy. This model of disposal is analogous to the function of metabolism in the liver whereby one method of disposal of toxic substances that enter the digestive system is to attach certain molecules to the intruding materials to make them water-soluble and easily excreted as a waste product. This process of chemical binding, known as conjugation, then enables the poison to be safely excreted in waste material in the faeces. In Freud's words, "The binding of an instinctual impulse would be a preliminary function designed to prepare the excitation for its final elimination in the pleasure of discharge" (Freud, 1920g, p. 62).

It then follows that the painful invasion due to the breach of the protective shell results in a deployment of high amounts of energy, "an "anticathexis" on a grand scale [for the purpose] of converting it into quiescent cathexis, that is, of binding it psychically" (Freud, 1920g, p. 30). Here, Freud's "principle of the insusceptibility to excitation of uncathected systems" (Freud, 1917d) suggests that the amount of quiescent cathexis is directly proportional to the psychic capacity for binding. As a result, the "importance of the element of fright . . . [due to] lack of any preparedness for anxiety [result in] those systems . . . not in a good position for binding the inflowing amounts of excitation" (Freud, 1920g, p. 31). Therefore, the "preparedness for anxiety and the hypercathexis of the receptive system constitutes the last line of defence . . ." (Freud, 1920g, p. 31). So, in order to "master the stimulus retrospectively by developing the anxiety whose omission was the cause of the traumatic neurosis . . . [traumatic dreams occur] in obedience to the compulsion to repeat" (Freud, 1920g, p. 32). So, "If there is a "beyond the pleasure principle", it is only consistent that there was also a time before the purpose of dreams was fulfilment of wishes . . . [i.e.] the binding of traumatic impressions . . . [which] obey the compulsion to repeat" (Freud, 1920g, p. 33).

Strachey noted that, surprisingly and repeatedly, Freud makes an "unexpected attribution to Breuer of the distinction between bound and unbound psychic energy and between the primary and secondary processes" (Freud, 1895d, p. xxvii). Originally, Freud did not elaborate on these ideas, but he was clearly influenced (Holt,

1962). Interestingly, Breuer's discourse on hypnoid states, which Freud never totally endorsed (I. Brenner, 2009), follows shortly after his comments on energy. His observation on these altered states of consciousness, which have all been forgotten by psycho-analysts, has particular relevance to the discussion here and serves as a starting point of an alternate pathway to understanding. Breuer conjectured that "If the split-off mind is in a constant state of exci-tation, as it was with Janet's hemi-anaesthetic patients, . . . so little cerebral functioning is left over for waking thought that the weak-ness of mind which Janet describes and regards as innate is fully accounted for" (in Freud, 1895d, p. 238). Moreover, he wonders whether, while in a state of autohypnosis, during "such a state of absorption and while the flow of ideas is inhibited, a group of affec-tively coloured ideas is active, it creates a high level of intracerebral excitation which is not used by mental work and is at the disposal of abnormal functioning such as conversion" (1895d, p. 218). While Breuer's ideas remain in the more physiological realm than in the psychological, the similarity to Freud's later ideas is quite evident. Regarding the debate over whether the hypnoid state precedes the traumatic excitation or is, in fact, caused by it, Freud concluded that "The affected self created a hypnoid state . . ." (p. 128), where-as Breuer suggested that "Autohypnosis has, so to speak, created the space or region of unconscious psychical activity into which the ideas which are fended off are driven" (p. 236). Therefore, the sharp distinction between hypnoid hysteria and defence hysteria, which Freud preferred, may have not been so clear-cut but more in the service of his effort to claim originality of his ideas. Regard-less, Breuer describes how "pathogenic autohypnosis would seem to come about in some people—by affect being introduced into a habitual reverie . . . [and] once this has happened the hypnosis-like state is repeated again and again when the same circumstances arise" (pp. 218–219). Breuer then suggests that the "recollection of the affective ideas, which is constantly being renewed, keeps on re-establishing the state of mind, 'hypnoid fright' . . . [which is] . . . the incubation stage of 'traumatic hysteria'" (p. 220). Breuer's way of explaining the compulsion to repeat is also based on energic considerations such that "fright inhibits the flow of ideas at the same time at which an affective idea (of danger) is very active . . .

[and] offers a complete parallel to a reverie charged with affect" (pp. 219–220).

Through Breuer's clinical observation and reasoning, therefore, he appears to conclude that the hypnoid state, an altered state of consciousness identical to an autohypnotic state, is what we would now consider a compromise formation that can be pathological or defensive and allow some gratification of an impulse that he described as a repetitive affectively charged idea. Furthermore, it is an ego-weakening mental state unable to bind the excessive stimu- lation entering the psyche and, in his oft-quoted words, "the split- ting of psychical activity which is so striking in the well-known cases in the form of 'double consciousness' is present to a rudimentary degree in every major hysteria and that the liability and tendency to such a dissociation is the basic phenomenon of this neurosis" (in Freud, 1895d, p. 227).

Perhaps in an effort of the overwhelmed ego to bind the pu- tative psychic energy that Breuer and then Freud described, the massively traumatized child has recurrent dreams at night of his defensive altered states during the day and may become confused by the mutual influences of one on the other. The result may be the formation of dissociated quasi-identities that attempt to keep mental contents separate and bind the psychic energy.

The sense of separateness in such patients' minds appears to be related to, but also extend beyond, the lack of integration of libidi- nally and aggressively derived self- and object representations. It is the quintessential expression of the lack of self-constancy, which is enhanced by the subjective experience of separate selves with their own cohesion. These personifications appear to be created with the help of a number of so-called "organizing influences", such as perverse sexuality, intergenerational transmission of trauma with identification with the aggressor, the divisive effects of aggression itself, near-death experiences, and the employment of these dream- like and "hysterical" mechanisms (I. Brenner, 2001).

There was reciprocal amnesia between Cindy's personifications with their monoideic fugues (Janet, 1907) and her dreams, which seemed to symbolize the anthropomorphization of her disturbance of consciousness (Silberer, 1909) during the original trauma. In other words, when Cindy switched into different alters, she had no memory of her dreams, whereas as Cindy she had no memory of what her alters knew yet she remembered her dreams. Through pseudo-externalized displacement, she attributed her impulses, affects, fantasies, and memories to her cadre of "inside people". This way, she could disown what was intolerable and thereby experience her intrapsychic conflicts as interpersonal conflicts. Her narcissistic investment in her separate selves (Kluft, 1987) posed a most powerful resistance, which, if confronted too soon, could have had suicidal implications.

The onset of Cindy's medical symptoms, which developed at a time of great intensity in the transference, resulted in further dissociative symptoms and absences and a regressive impasse. Her recurrent dreams at this time bore an undeniable resemblance to the first-hand accounts of the childhood sexual trauma reported by her as another self. With the help of treatment, the patient's eventual awareness of the internal consistency of those accounts enabled her to "feel it in her bones" and allowed her to become convinced that it was truly she herself who had been victimized. Similarly, the other patient, Karen, had a feeling in her bones too. She dreamt of bones literally ripping through her flesh, which was so painful that she, too, had to finally consider that something unthinkable must have happened to her in order to have created so much pain.

Concluding comment

In order for the realization and acceptance of ownership of the mind to occur, it seems crucial to help such a patient to realize how it may have operated during such intolerable experiences. By doing so, Cindy could begin to consider that the creation of her alters might indeed have been, in part, due to the spilling over of what usually remains in the realm of post-traumatic dreams. In the dreams, the symbolic representation of defensive altered states at the time of the original trauma may take the form of a child being violated while the patient enters such an autohypnotic state and "leaves" her body or experiences a "blackout". There seems to be a reciprocal influence on dreams, self-perception, and identity, as this cycle may apparently repeat itself for years. This phenomenon may then manifest itself through "switching" to other dissociated selves.

Containment and interpretive work on how her mind functions under these conditions may enable a movement towards a healing of the rifts in the psyche. Thus, the interrelationship between trauma, recurrent dreams, and defensive altered state present an unusual manifestation of the compulsion to repeat.

Freud's difficulty in explaining unconscious guilt via the topographic theory required him to revise his thinking and devise the structural theory (Freud, 1923b). Then, the problem of repetitive traumatic dreams required him to go "beyond the pleasure principle" (Freud, 1920g) and postulate the death instinct. Similarly, I would suggest that phenomena such as the relationship between dreams and amnestic self-states warrant a reconsideration of the role of dissociation in mental functioning. It is therefore ironic and, as Fleiss suggests, puzzling (Fleiss, 1953) that Freud omits the death instinct in the "Revision of Dreams" lecture of his *New Introductory Lectures* (Freud, 1933a, pp. 28–30). While he does discuss the role of the death instinct in the compulsion to repeat later on in his lecture on "Anxiety and Instinctual Life" (Freud, 1933a, pp. 107–108), he merely states that the function of the dream as the guardian of sleep has failed and that essentially a psychic overload has occurred. It is the fate of this overload that is the subject of exploration here. Regardless of the ultimate validity of the death instinct *per se*, the power of the repetition compulsion as fact of mental life enables the analyst to help certain patients to come to terms with most disturbing, traumatic experiences.

4

The dream in
Beyond the Pleasure Principle and beyond

Joshua Levy

This chapter compares Freud's traumatic dream theory in *Beyond the Pleasure Principle* (1920g) to his theory presented in *The Interpretation of Dreams* (1900a). Freud regarded these two dream theories as "independent". In an attempt to find the basis for their coexistence, four dream hypotheses are re-examined (the manifest and latent content, the day residue, the dream's motivations, and the dream-work) and their place in each of Freud's dream theories. Clinical material illustrates the relationship of the two theories.

Freud's two dream theories

In *Beyond the Pleasure Principle* Freud focused on the clinical manifestations of his patients' fixation on their traumatic situation, observed in repeated dreams and compulsive acting out, resulting in repeated failures. A second theory, radically "independent" of his original theory, was developed. Whereas in his first theory Freud stated that "a dream is a disguised fulfilment of a (suppressed or repressed) wish" (Freud, 1900a, p. 160), in his second dream theory he said:

Now dreams occurring in traumatic neuroses have the characteristic of repeatedly bringing the patient back into the situation
of his accident, a situation from which he wakes up in another
fright. [Freud, 1920g, p. 13]

Freud continued to elaborate:

> . . . dreams are here helping to carry out another task, which
> must be accomplished before the dominance of the pleasure
> principle can even begin. These dreams are endeavouring to
> master the stimulus retrospectively, by developing the anxiety
> whose omission was the cause of the traumatic neuroses. They
> thus afford us a view of the mental apparatus which, though
> it does not contradict the pleasure principle, is nevertheless
> independent of it and seems to be more primitive than the
> purpose of gaining pleasure and avoiding unpleasure. [Freud,
> 1920g, p. 32]

Freud's two dream theories are significantly different in structure
and function. In 1900 Freud argued that the manifest dream arises
in the context of a day residue, which serves the defensive purpose of warding off the latent dream content represented in the
manifest dream as disguised fulfilment of the dreamer's suppressed
and repressed wishes. This disguise results from the dream-work
(condensation, displacement, and means of representation) that
is "the essence of dreaming" (1900a, p. 506 [fn. added 1925]).
In 1920, however, Freud argued that the manifest dream displays
traumatic events as they occurred. By re-living the painful experience, the dreamer discharges the pent-up tension and belatedly
masters the trauma. In this second theory there is no reference to
the day residue, the latent content, or the role of dream-work. Instead, the disrupted psychic balance brought about by the trauma
is bound by the repeated dream. The dream is thereby motivated
not by the hope of pleasure, but by "a compulsion to repeat—something that seems more primitive, more elementary, more instinctual than the pleasure principle which it overrides" (Freud, 1920g,
pp. 20–23).

There is a vast difference in the clinical evidence that Freud provided for his two dream theories: while in 1900 his well-reasoned
clinical evidence allows for scrutiny of the development and conceptual clarity of Freud's original dream theory, the lack of clinical

evidence for his 1920 theory, in contrast, precludes assessment of the grounds for this second theory.

There have been a number of studies that assessed Freud's 1920 dream theory. For example, Loewenstein (1949), as a classical analyst, presented a post-traumatic dream within the analytic process and concluded that it was *not* an exact replica of the traumatic events. He stated that it had the dual function; as both mastering the threatened reality and as a wish-fulfilment. Three selected authors studied these issues from different angles and reached similar conclusions, which serve as building blocks towards my attempt to find the base for the coexistence of Freud's two dream theories.

Adams-Silvan and Silvan's (1990) contribution is one of the very few examples of the psychotherapeutic handling of post-traumatic nightmare. They were able to analyse it as a "true dream" with latent content. Brenneis (1994, 1997, 2002) scrutinized in great depth the available literature on the recovery of traumatic events through dreams. Briefly, he concluded that traumatic memories were remembered during treatment; in his view, the authors did not examine the effects of the unconscious communications between the patients and their therapists in the process of the recovery of traumatic memories via the patients' dreams. He presented his own psychotherapeutic work with a traumatized patient and revealed the power of subtle suggestion, based on his own countertransference, which significantly influenced the therapeutic process. It is of interest to recall Freud's assertion in the context of "reconstruction". Freud (1937d, p. 262) stated: "I can assert without boasting that such an abuse of 'suggestion' has never occurred in my practice." How can he be so certain? Freud's assertion contradicts the aim of this study to find the basis for the coexistence of Freud's two dream theories. The aim here is to examine the mutual effects of unconscious communication during the analytic process and to try to understand through the dream-work its influence in constructing the patients' dreams.

Lansky and his collaborators (Lansky, 1995) studied the dreams of Vietnam War veterans and found that there was a significant difference between the nightmare's scenario and the traumatic events. The dreams were not replicas of the traumas, and the manifest content served as a screen function, defending against the fulfilment of unconscious wishes. These post-traumatic nightmares were set off by daily experiences that evoked affective distress of shame, humiliation, threats to the self-cohesion, and narcissistic rage that were reminiscent of the original trauma. Their findings were used to challenge Freud's second dream theory. However, they omitted Freud's continuing struggles with the two dream theories. In his *New Introductory Lectures on Psychoanalysis* (Freud, 1933a, pp. 28–29), he returned to re-examining his two theories of dreams. Here he considers the role of wish-fulfilment in dreams in which a person who has . . . "experienced a severe psychic trauma . . . [is] . . . taken back in their dreams into the traumatic situation" (p. 28). Freud concluded that in these dreams the dream-work failed to fulfil its function because the wishes were connected with overwhelming fear and pain.

Again, Freud's conclusion was not backed up by clinical data, and his two dream theories remained un-integrated. It was not until 1933 that Freud could acknowledge a place for the dream-work within his second dream theory—but only to say that the dream-work did not work. How could this have come to pass? Were Freud's conclusions based on short analytic contacts or consultations that precluded the kind of analytic investigation that would have allowed him to compare his two dream theories in greater depth and to begin their integration? Again, the focus of this chapter is to investigate a basis for this integration.

Self psychology and Freud's two dream theories

Among current perspectives on dreams in psychoanalysis, self psychology is most similar to Freud's in his *Beyond the Pleasure Principle*. Other psychoanalytic perspectives either ignored Freud's second dream theory or implicitly rejected it. Kohut (1971) and his collaborators conceptualized the structure and function of the dream of the narcissistic personality disorder as being based on the vulnerability of the patient due to an underlying traumatic situation. They understood these dreams according to manifest content. Kohut (1971 p. 5) presented the following dream: "The patient is on a swing, swinging forward and backward, higher and higher—yet there is never a serious danger of either the patient's flying off, or of the swing uncontrollably entering a full circle." He considered this "self-state dream" to be typical of patients with "narcissistic person-ality disorder." Kohut extracted the patient's underlying traumatic situation from the dream's manifest content and asserted that its function was not primarily the fulfilment of disguised wishes as an end-product of unconscious processes (Freud's first dream theory). Its primary function was to regulate, maintain, develop, restore, and even creatively re-organize the internal reality of the dreamer (Kohut, 1977, pp. 18–19). For Kohut and for Freud (Freud, 1920g, pp. 13, 32), the dream's primary function was the restoration of the self by the mastery and the binding of the underlying overwhelm-ing tension. Kohut stated that the distinction between the manifest dream and the latent dream was untenable. Therefore there was no need to decode the dream with the aid of the patient's free associa-tions, as is commonly practiced within Freud's first dream theory. In fact, Kohut cautioned us that insisting on free associations may cause re-traumatization for the narcissistic personality disorder. In a critical note: neither Freud nor Kohut presented their theoretical assumptions and clinical conclusions with the support of clinical data to allow validity assessment.

In agreement with Kohut, Ornstein (1987) presented dreams with specific interactions between him and his analysand. From this data, the dreams, their day residues (weekend breaks) as well as the transference can be understood. He stated that his patient's "self state dreams portrayed the dreamer's inner experience of his/her acute or chronic self-disturbance, and with the aid of verbalizable dream imagery [the patient attempts] to bind the non-verbal ten-sions of the traumatic states." Thus, his aim was to demonstrate both an internal loss of balance of the self that is threatened with fragmentation and an effort to restore the integrity of the self. Ornstein's clinical data (1987, pp. 93–94) allow how the self psy-chology perspective understands the analysand's dreams by relying on Freud's second dream theory.

Agreeing with Freud (1920g) and Kohut, Ornstein asserted that he did not rely on free associations in his working with his patient's dreams because the distinction between the manifest and the la-tent dream contents was untenable: the patient's main concerns were already revealed in the manifest dreams. His patient's narcis-sistic vulnerabilities arising from a lack of early mirroring and the thwarted needs to idealize a parental figure were extracted from the manifest dream alone. Free associations would not have led to a deeper understanding of the dreams because the associations provided imagery that stayed at the same level as the manifest content. Ornstein emphasized that the structure and function of the self-state dream was different from the classical dream and therefore he rejected the hypothesis of the manifest dream as a disguise of latent dream content. The operations of the dream work in understanding dreams, in Freud's first theory, were not mentioned. The dream-work was inferred from the manifest content: the images were assessed for what they revealed, metaphorically and thematically, not for what they concealed. Unless the analyst appears directly in the dream or the dreamer immediately associates to the analyst, Ornstein does not assume that the dream relates to the transference. The dream figures are not necessarily disguised stand-ins for the analyst. Ornstein listened closely to the subtle nuances underlying his patient's traumatic state which was embedded in the dream's manifest content. He used the dream to interpret his patient's subjective experience and his self-object needs and contrasted his approach with one that aims at uncovering repressed, unconscious wishes. Ornstein claimed that this approach enabled the patient to accept and integrate disavowed feelings. Ornstein's self-psychological approach to understanding dreams is similar to Freud's second dream theory.

Is it possible to find space in the analyst's mind for the coexistence of Freud's two dream theories? Or are the two theories mutually exclusive?

This brings us to the role of the dream-work. As noted before, Ornstein did not find it necessary to rely on the operations of condensation and displacement because he assumed that the patient's psychic structure, his fragile self related to the traumatic situation, was directly represented in the manifest dream. Certainly, this approach created a soothing climate that encouraged the development of the self-object transferences that Ornstein attended to during the interpretations of his patient's dreams. However, did his approach divert him from hearing other themes in the transference? One of the dream elements, "rock", had been precipitated by the patient's recalling seeing the analyst's "stony face" only once. The "stony face" can be understood as a condensation, an integral part of Freud's first dream theory, and an exploration of the patient's unconscious perceptions of the analyst. Perhaps, then, the "stony face" was a subtle perception that neither the analyst nor his patient was aware of. Did Ornstein's approach foreclose examining the potential aggressive themes that would have disturbed both analyst and patient? Would deciphering the operations of the dream work according to Freud's first dream theory have risked destabilizing the patient's fragile psychological organization? Or can the hurts and the traumatic situation that may be disguised behind the patient's manifest dream figures ("rock") be heard as condensations and displacements that would include the patient's unconscious communications about the analyst's emphatic observational stance? Ornstein seems to have paid insufficient attention to how his theoretical perspective relied exclusively on Freud's second dream theory and affected his working with his patient's dreams. It seems that there are inevitable limitations resulting from exclusive adherence to a single viewpoint in understanding and interpreting our patients' dreams. An integration of Freud's two dream theories requires the analyst to listen to the patients' free associations to their dreams, to be in tune with potential multiple day residues that might have triggered the dreams, and to try to process the clinical material relying on the operations of the dream-work. These are the tasks of the following two sections.

The day residues in Freud's two theories of dreams

Freud referred to the events of the day as the day residues that stir up psychic problems and stimulate the night's dreams. This most innovative dream hypothesis endorsed by divergent analytic perspectives leads analysts to ask, with respect to all dreams: "Why now?"

Day residues may initially be regarded as incidental and insignificant matters, but Freud's associations to his reported dreams in *The Interpretation of Dreams* (1900a) allow understanding of his underlying conflicts and psychic reality. In teaching dream analysis to beginning and advanced candidates (Levy, 1996, 2009), special attention is given to identifying the conscious and unconscious sources of multiple day residues presented in patient's associations. Freud's first dream theory, with its extensive preambles, allows us to highlight the complexity of the day residues. Freud's second theory, in contrast, omits all day residue data and does not illustrate his utilization of these complex data in his analysis of traumatic dreams. Lansky (1995, 1997), however, clearly demonstrated that post-traumatic nightmares are set off by daily experiences that evoke affects reminiscent of the original trauma.

Three of Freud's well-known dreams—the "Irma dream", "R is my uncle", and the "botanical monograph"—are used here to illustrate the relevance of day residues to traumatic and non-traumatic dreams.

Lansky (2004) argued that Freud's daily experiences related to loss of professional status stirred up hidden shame that activated ego-ideal conflicts. Freud's competitive ambitions more visibly revealed screened the profound shame. For instance in "R is my uncle" his professorial appointment would not be confirmed because he was Jewish. In the "botanical monograph" Freud's cocaine contributions were passed over, aroused feelings of shame and humiliation, and, in Lansky's perspective, emphasized Freud's sense of failure and disgrace.

Lansky's selection of the day residues were supported by the available data. However, my perspective is quite different. These dreams were intimately related to Freud's traumatic situation. His meagre income threatened his capacity to feed his growing family and was activated by concerns for survival. Faced with an underlying anxiety of annihilation stirred by painful reality that re-awakened conflicts from levels of his development, the dangerous dream thoughts were transformed by the dream-work. His failure in the Irma dream aroused destructive aggression and death wishes towards his frustrating patient; towards his senior colleague, Dr M (Breuer), who had referred the patient to him; and towards Otto, the paediatrician of his six children. Freud's destructive aggression may be considered the traumatic situation underlying the dream. In his efforts to master the traumatic state—Freud's second dream theory—he resorted to psychological survival tactics to enhance his self-esteem, blamed Irma, depreciated Dr M, and portrayed Otto as a destructive and irresponsible physician who had injected Irma with a dirty syringe, which resulted in her severe physical illness.

In the "R is my uncle" dream shame experiences were aroused when Freud associated his esteemed friend with his uncle, who was a "scoundrel" and a "simpleton". Freud perceived his friend to be an obstacle to his becoming a professor and wished to get him out of the way. Again, a death wish stirred up a desperate psychic reality, and the dream's function was needed to master it.

In the "botanical monograph" dream the day residue was his seeing a botanical monograph during the day. His first associations connected "botany" and "flower" with his "wife" and a self-reproach for "so rarely remembering to bring her flowers." He then recalled an anecdote in which a woman recognizes that her husband's failure to bring the customary bouquet on her birthday indicates that "she no longer had the same place in his thoughts as she had formerly." The lady in this anecdote, formerly his patient, had spoken to his wife two days previously and had asked about him. Freud's associations and the "anecdote" would make any analyst suspect that his relationship with his wife was causing him great distress.

Another day residue that precipitated the "botanical monograph" was meeting and "congratulating a friend and his wife on their *blooming* looks". Did Freud compare the woman's *blooming* looks to that of his wife? These multiple day residues lead us to question whether the dream touched, in a disguised way, on Freud's deteriorating marital relations. Schur (1972, p. 159) linked Freud's forgetting an intimate friend's birthday to the death of their relationship. Did the triggers of Freud's dream of the botanical monograph touch off his death wishes towards his wife? Schur (1972, pp. 153–198) notes that throughout *The Interpretation of Dreams* (1900a) the links between Freud's dreams and death were quite prevalent.

Freud's three dreams and his associations provide data that suggest that behind the meaningless images lay multiple layers—including a traumatic situation. The triggers touched off "unconscious purposes" that threatened Freud's survival. The deeper implications of the daily events were transformed and disguised by the dream-work, resulting in condensed and displaced images that could be tolerated by his consciousness. Direct dream interpretation, unconnected to the implications of the multiple triggers, risks bypassing the possible traumatic situation behind the manifest dream content, leaving Freud's two dream theories unrelated.

In clinical analysis, the day residues may be derived from one or from a combination of sources—the transference, the analyst's interventions of the previous day, or from the intricacies of the analytic situation (Lewin, 1955). Analysts need to consider their countertransference as a powerful day residue, portrayed indirectly and symbolically in their patients' dreams. Countertransference impact on the patient may be helpful or may, when associated with the patient's traumatic situation, be assaultive. To maintain the vital analytic relationship, the patient may defensively distort the implications of such assaults. The patient's unconscious messages of compliance embedded in the patient's dreams and associations need to be understood as disguised, indirect, confused mental productions triggered by the analyst's interventions. It is essential to look for the dream-work in Freud's two dream theories. To ignore the effects of the analyst's contributions to the day residue may lead to misunderstanding between patient and analyst, resulting in what Ferenczi called a "confusion of tongues" (Ferenczi, 1933, p. 349).

The place of the dream-work in Freud's two dream theories

By re-evaluating his 1900 dream hypotheses in 1920, as applied to the traumatic dream, Freud opened the debate as to the value of the manifest dream content. In 1900 the manifest dream content, a distortion, concealed the latent content; in 1920 the manifest dream revealed the trauma *per se*. However, Freud never examined his modifications within the analytic process. While early psychoanalytic contributors underscored Freud's modifications (e.g. Nunberg, 1932; Waelder, 1930), subsequently there emerged a still present controversy. The central issues in the debate are related to finding the place of the dream-work in understanding the traumatic dream.

Freud's oft-quoted condensed footnote added in 1925 to his 1900 dream theory provides some understanding. In an effort to preserve the core of his discoveries in *The Interpretation of Dreams*, Freud realized later that the dream-work, considered to be the essence of the dream, was still misunderstood by many analysts. The function of the dream-work in facilitating an in-depth understanding of dreams during analytic treatment still remains ignored, dismissed outright, or poorly utilized. Levy's 1996 studies of interactions between analytic candidates or analysts and their patients repeatedly confirm that the intricacies of condensation, displacement, and the means of representation were not being integrated into the actual clinical work with dreams. Rather, the analysts often regarded the entire dream as portraying their patients' characteristic way of solving their problems. Freud would have been disappointed by this state of affairs. Highlights of Freud's footnote raise some questions.

1.   Freud initially expressed satisfaction that the distinction made in 1900 between the manifest dream content and its latent meanings had been accepted by analysts. Little did he suspect how problematic this distinction would become. Is this radical distinction between polar opposites in part responsible for Freud's finding that even analysts of his generation misunderstood what he considered "the essence of the dream"—namely, the dream-work?

2.   In the second part of his footnote Freud expressed concern that analyst were overlooking and confusing his other crucial distinction between the latent dream thoughts and the dream-work. This resulted in ignoring another significant discovery, that: " . . . at bottom, dreams are nothing other than a particular form of thinking made possible by the conditions of this state of sleep. It is the dream-work which creates that form, and it alone is the essence of dreaming—the explanation of its peculiar nature" (1900a, p. 313). Based on this conceptualization of the real nature of the dream, if, as suggested by Freud, the manifest content of a traumatic dream is the trauma *per se*, then is such a dream not a "true dream"? How could a "true dream" lack the operations of the dream-work—"the essence of dreaming" in its construction?

3.   In the third part of the footnote, Freud acknowledged that at least a part of dreams have a "prospective purpose" and can be concerned with problem-solving. However, he did not pursue this to inquire as to whether the dream-work has any role in solving the dreamer's conscious concerns.

Freud was expressing three different moods in this footnote while assessing the most fundamental issues related to the understanding of dreams. Starting with an optimistic mood, he shifted to disappointment that analysts were confused about the unique position of dream-work in his dream theory and ends with feeling indifferent to the problem-solving function of the dream. Indeed, Freud raised fundamental questions relevant to understanding dreams but did not assess them within the analytic process. Analysts were left with dichotomies: manifest content versus latent content, the dream-work versus latent dream content, the dream-work versus no dream-work and problem-solving unrelated to other possible dream functions. How than can traumatic dreams be understood as "genuine dreams"—similar to but also different from wish-fulfilment dreams? This requires defining the appropriate place and time for inquiring into the operations of the dream-work while analysing patients' traumatic dreams.

A critical study of Erikson's (1954) seminal article provides a comprehensive framework for understanding the structure and function of dreams, including the traumatic dream. Three of Erikson's conclusions assist in finding a place for the dream-work in understanding traumatic dreams. The focus is on the dream-work and its relations to (1) the multiple functions of dreams; (2) the relations between the manifest and the latent dream; and (3) the defences.

1. Relying on a thorough analysis of Freud's own associations, images, and experiences, Erikson demonstrated the complex meanings, the multiple layers, and the variegated functions of dreams. He argued that Freud's classical statement and foundation of his first dream theory—"a dream is a disguised fulfilment of a wish"—was one of the functions of the dream because Freud's own dream interpretations reflected the complexity and richness of human motives. Indeed, Freud (1917d, p. 223) had already stated that dreams had multiple *functions*: "one must view the dream among other things [as] a projection, an externalization of an internal situation." Within the dream's multiple functions, the original function of the traumatic dream is found. As stated in 1920, the repeated attempt to master the traumatic situation coexists with the other functions of the dream—namely, disguised "wish-fulfilment", "externalization", and so on. All of these functions propel the dream-work in the construction of all dreams, including traumatic dreams.

2. While Freud regarded the manifest dream content and the latent dream content as polar opposites, Erikson demonstrated that they coexist on a continuum that allows for a gradual transition from the manifest to the latent and vice versa. From associations to the dream elements Erikson extracted themes related to the dreamer's conflicts below the surface. These themes were then connected with the dream's latent content, the dreamer's unconscious wishes and conflicts, and the hypothetical transference. If this relationship between the manifest dream content and the dream's latent content is tested within current analytic practice, Freud's sharp separation between them was untenable. It is then possible to inquire how the dream-work in the construction of traumatic dreams fulfils both defensive and synthetic functions.

3. Analysis of the dreamer's perceptions, feelings, fantasies, and relations to the human figures in the dream assists in assessing the specific place of the dream-work in the construction and function of the dream. The dreamer's free associations may indicate how the dreamer experiences the dream figures on both conscious and unconscious levels. Is the dreamer feeling close to and identified with a certain figures (me) or distant from, even repugnant towards certain figures (not me), including the analyst. Can the analyst then work with the dynamic oscillations between the "me" dream figures and the "not me" dream figures? Fusion with, and projections onto, dream figures which might be due to the subtle operations of the dream-work in its effort to disguise the dreamer's identification with a consciously repugnant figure need to be noted. Unguarded moments when the dreamer blends with a dream figure and quickly re-establishes the conscious boundaries, shifting to the familiar perceptions and away from the emerging threatening latent dream content, can be significant in analyzing dreams.

In 1923 Freud was already aware of what he called "the multiplicity of egos" (p. 120), but he made no reference to this concept when he discussed the traumatic dream. He stated that: "the dreamer's ego can appear more than once in the same dream—in person and concealed behind other figures". Based on this hypothesis and his previous similar one in the chapter on the dream-work (Freud, 1900a, pp. 322–323), other analysts (Fairbairn, 1952; Segal, 1991; Winnicott, 1971) subsequently detailed and illuminated this hypothesis.

Erikson's seminal scrutiny of Freud's Irma dream teaches that traumatic and non-traumatic dreams have multiple functions; that their manifest and dream content may coexist on a continuum; that the dreamer may be represented directly or by one or more obscure or rejected figures, and that there is a potential for alternating and/or shifting between fusing with, and differentiating from, dream figures. Thus, the traumatic dream can be understood as being constructed through the dream work, like any other dream. To delve into the issues raised by Freud's two dream theories and to illustrate analytic work with traumatic dreams, extensive clinical material will now be presented.

Working with Freud's two dream theories within the analytic process

> . . . we have come across people all of whose human relationships have the same outcome: such as . . . the lover each of whose love affairs with a woman passes through the same phases and reaches the same conclusion . . . there really does exist in the mind a compulsion to repeat which over-rides the pleasure principle. [Freud, 1920g, p. 22]

Case report: John

John sought psychoanalysis at age 32. His history revealed two failed marriages and repetitive failure in relationships with women. Attractive to women and an intelligent and resourceful professional, he became irritable, anxious, and explosive, as if being attacked when a woman became "romantic". This behaviour ended the relationship and precipitated overwhelming regret, self-blame, aloneness, and "going to pieces". Previous therapies had led to symptomatic relief and then a sudden termination.

Early in his therapy John's depressive symptoms decreased and confidence in his work situation increased, but his anxieties related to women were only superficially mentioned. The analyst had felt guarded, fatigued, at times blocked and discouraged. Their interactions seemed mechanical and repetitive, and the analyst wondered whether John would leave.

An analytic session

John came in agitated and angry and said in a clipped, staccato rhythm that during the weekend he had "figured it all out". His fear of closeness, attributed to his father's aloofness and depression, was compounded by his mother's "logical, realistic, authoritarianism". In desperation he said that he now had to overcome his own difficulties. He abruptly got off the couch and opened the door, about to leave. The analyst asked him to stay, saying he was interested in what had happened to him over the weekend. John hesitated, hung onto the doorknob, then acquiesced and sat down.

Visibly frightened, his body shaking, John reported a vivid nightmare that had awakened him in a panic and had haunted him during the day. "It was a strange dream", he said, "but dreams are odd, why should it frighten me?" He then said: *"It was about Diane. She was having an affair with George." I told her: "It's your life, but if I ever see him with you, I'll punch him in the face."*

Encouraged to free-associate, John said that Diane was a former girlfriend, and that he had started treatment after their break-up. Sunday afternoon they had a pleasant visit.

Pt: "I guess I still care for her. . . . I had told you about the possibility of Diane and George having an affair. . . . I'm jealous. . . . It is so odd; George is my best friend, . . . so if they are having an affair, I really don't want to see them again. . . ."

[The dream seemed to him a replica of daily painful feelings, but he wondered]

Pt: "Why I am still frightened over this dream? Why am I still panicky right now?"

[A look of despair and fright accompanied the silence that followed.]

A: "This is the first dream that you dreamt, remembered, and told me since you started analysis."

Pt: "No, that's not true. I told you another dream."

A: "Yes you told me another dream, which you dreamt a couple of years ago."

Pt: "Yes . . . [very sadly] . . . you do remember what I told you . . . perhaps I'm beginning to trust you, I know I want to be more open with you, but I'm very scared . . . [pause] . . . I dream like crazy . . . I never told you a dream before, because I thought if I started with dreams I'd be here for ever . . . Last time I left with a feeling that I was getting close to you."

A: "You are beginning to feel close to me and to trust me. Trusting me scares you, and you tried to avoid the fear by leaving the session today."

Pt: "I'm still very scared . . . . [silent and looks away . . . and then in surprise and excitement] . . . You know what this scary feeling is all about? The dream reminded me of a feeling I had after the break-up with Joan. I was going in-sane; I had fits of rage, and entered psychotherapy. I felt better but soon became disappointed in my therapist and left town."

John cried about having being deceived, betrayed, and deserted by Diane and by Joan. Although he had been considerate to each, after a single outburst of anger from him they had left. With tears and anger he remembered that Diane had promised to love him—and now she wanted nothing to do with him. Or did she? He was still doubtful.

The analyst offered that John was afraid that the analyst would also suddenly withdraw and leave him isolated, when he needed him most, when he was beginning to feel close to him. Had John's fear of being deserted precipitated his angry outburst and his attempt to leave? The analyst suggested that while John was beginning to rely on him, he also felt obliged to suppress any negative feelings—for if he did not, then the analyst might withdraw, as his mother often had, and he would be left alone, desperate and in panic as he had been.

John was five minutes late for the session two days later. Although mostly in good spirits in the two hours before the session, he felt anger towards his previous therapists. Still standing, he launched an explosive attack on them.

Pt: "They deceived me. . . . They did not care for me. . . . They told me what to do without listening to me. . . . You all play games, you all play the trust number. . . . Why should you be different from other therapists?"

A: "You were feeling close and trusting me, in the last session. These feelings aroused great fear in you that I am going to suck you into trusting me, stir up hope that I would take care of you, but then suddenly, like your other therapists, I'll leave you disappointed and all alone. By your angry attacks on me today, you are trying to test me and provoke me, push me away from you and break up the closeness between us."

Pt [sobbing]: "I am glad that I felt free to get up and was about to leave the last session. If you did not call me back, I would have left the therapy . . . thank you."

Reflections

In response to John's impulsive move to leave, by asking him to stay and expressing interest, the analyst is trying to prevent a repetition of the suddenly ending therapy. Did John regard this expressed concern as an intention to maintain the analytic relationship? Had John experienced this intervention as an expression of the analyst's need to hold on to him and to restrict his independence? Or had the manner of intervention conveyed to John something of the analyst's wish to be rid of him in that John's traumatic situation was evoking aspects of the analyst's own conflicts? Was the patient in tune with the analyst's defences and attempting to rescue him by terminating the treatment? Most importantly, are these considerations about the analytic relationship relevant to understanding the dream?

Themes of betrayal and rage were part of the manifest dream content, but rather than responding directly, the analyst considered what aspects of the analytic relationship might have been a stimulus. Saying, "This is the first dream . . ." might seem to highlight a fact about therapeutic process. However, John's response—"you do remember what I told you . . ."—and his subsequent affects and associations provide some evidence of empathic comprehension of the patient's psychic reality, a necessary condition for subsequent productive dream conversation. Could John's association—"I dream like crazy. I never told you a dream before, because I thought if I started with a dream, I'd be here forever . . ."—be thought to validate the intervention?

Instead of pursuing a collaborative understanding of the dream as disguised unconscious processes, the analyst attended to the underlying traumatic experiences associated with John's repeatedly ending intimate relationships. As with many patients, the interpersonal aspects of the dream that are embedded in the analytic relationship need to be attended to before mutual exploration of the intrapsychic structure of the dream can be worked through productively.

The analyst understood that for John, closeness and intimate contacts stirred up overwhelming anxieties associated with his inability to trust and anticipation of betrayal—all unconsciously derived from his experiences of his depressive mother repeatedly withdrawing, leaving him to cope with an inner state of panic, disorganization, and explosive rage. The analyst wondered whether this dynamic had been enacted in the session and hidden in the dream, and what, in the analytic relationship, had been perceived as a betrayal. Reflecting on his own feelings during this session with John, the analyst offered that: "He stirred in me fears of going to pieces and being all by myself."

Dreams related during analysis have many purposes. These dreams occur within a dynamic of external and internal factors. John was terribly anxious about his dreams because they were experienced as a breakthrough of threatening forces that evoke the overwhelming pain of a traumatic situation. In exploring the sequences of his shame and remorse over his poor judgement and related depressions, John was challenging the analyst to find in his dream a creative potential and utilize it to benefit treatment. Too hasty an interpretation would probably have interfered with achieving this benefit. Instead, the analyst tried to be in touch with John's affective experiences by considering within the safety of the treatment situation what was frightening, shameful, and rageful. While the underlying dynamic common to John's psychic conflicts and dream was developing in the session, the analyst communicated, behaviourally and verbally, that he would not abandon the patient if he lost control, thereby establishing sufficient containment within the analytic relationship. Later it would be possible to return to further analysis of the dream.

The analyst also tried to be aware of his countertransference, wondering: "What is the patient trying to tell me, both in his behaviour and in his dream, about unrealized aspects of myself? Had the patient's perception of our interactions been a stimulus for the dream? Do I share an underlying depressive–obsessional structure that impedes progress?"

Interpreting the dream material as transference or as self-representation at this stage—before the analyst recognizes his potential contribution to the patient's dynamics—would have been premature.

John's conscious and unconscious responses to the analyst's interventions were quite mixed. He became more calm and relaxed, yet was also very angry and suspicious. He asked the analyst to stop psychological explorations and to tell him how to resolve his predicament with women. John's experience of being understood established a space for him to think about the consequences of his behaviour—but it also interfered with his tendency to act out, which aroused intense feelings of deprivation. The analyst was convinced that maintaining the analytic frame—minimizing reassurance, suggestions, exhortation, and casual conversations—would further ensure the safety of the analytic situation and facilitate genuine dream conversation.

Eventually the patient returned to the dream because it had personal significance that he did not understand. He urged the analyst to tell him what it meant but did not insist and began collaborating and associating to the dream. He came to understand that Diane, an image in the manifest content, evoked memories of women. Diane was a condensation, illuminating similar emotional experiences with multiple women, from various levels of his life, including his childhood with his mother. The anger, highly significant in the manifest dream, was understood now as disguising his despair over previous betrayals. His anger was not only modified, but was also displaced from Diane to George. John's memories, affects, and associations about Diane and George led to his anxious feelings and fantasies about the analyst. In the later stages of the treatment both the dream's latent meanings and its contributions to the working through of the transference–countertransference were interrelated.

These examples of condensation and displacement were the essence of dreaming in Freud's first dream theory. When the timing and dosage of dream interpretations are right, the patient becomes emotionally involved and interested in applying his new understandings during the dream conversations. As analyst and patient work together to understand the complexities of dreams, there is fostered in the patient an identification with the way in which the analyst understands the dream-work. While this happened in the case under discussion here—and a long-term analytic treatment followed—it is not invariably the case.

Two dreams from three years later

During the subsequent three years John repeatedly expressed intense feelings of rage when he anticipated being exploited and abandoned by his analyst. The working through of his impulses to suddenly terminate would follow. The analyst was often discouraged and at times felt that helping John master his present traumatic experiences and all they evoked from his past seemed beyond their capacity. However, as analysis continued, John's work stabilized, and an intimate relation with a woman endured for the last year.

John also had a teen-aged daughter, and his wish for closeness evoked anxieties that he was unsuitable to be a father. He feared losing control over his incestuous impulses. He needed to prepare a room for her but was overwrought that she would want to stay overnight.

Pt: "I left here yesterday morning. . . . I felt this huge weight lift off my shoulders. I suddenly realized that the problem I have in my life about my daughter. . . . I can't go back and change history. . . . There are things I can do, finish

painting the room. . . . I can tell her that she is welcome. It
is very scary. . . ."

"I had a dream about you last night. *I was sitting and talking
to you face to face. I was telling you, I was a perfectly average guy,
not a dangerous person.*"

"In the second dream, *Bill, my friend, drove up next to me. He
has a nice white Prelude and I have my old Datsun and he eyed my
car as if mine were nicer.*"

"My project was published yesterday. . . . A friend told me
I'm much too hard on myself. . . . Bill was always envious
of me . . . that my father would get me anything . . . yet Bill
had way more clothes than me. . . . I felt positive about the
dreams as if Bill was admiring my common sense . . . the
dream about us is a dream about equality. I don't like to be
average . . . but the interpretation was that you aren't a danger to your daughter . . . needn't fear your masculinity. . . .
I screwed up my computer course and could kick myself
now . . . changing perspective in that dream of you. Sometimes I feel a window rising and I can see more clearly; other
times it is closed, and I feel distant from you. . . . I spoke to
Nancy (his partner) about coming here. She says she doesn't
know who will be coming home at night."

A.: "What comes to mind is that you aren't sure how I take your
positive feelings. Your mother interpreted your enthusiasms
as being out of control . . . like the man molesting a child.

[Here the analyst is referring to an early memory of an older guy
touching a boy at a sandpit. Of this incident, that patient had
said: "Something went terribly wrong there, and I feel to this day
that I should be punished for not doing something about it."]

Pt: "For the school patrol they chose the kids whose instincts
were pushed down the furthest."

A: "You see your impulses as dangerous, leading to all sorts of
misery for others and you see that psychoanalysis should
hold you down and control you."

. . . . . .

Pt: "Terrible impulses . . . and terrible things may happen to me or may happen to you. . . . I caused my parents to fight with my sister. . . . I feel I hurt others . . . or perhaps I killed my mother. . . . My great fear in life was to be embarrassed. . . . I disobeyed my mother, refused to accompany her to the neighbours. She threw herself on the couch and cried that I was turning out like my father . . . it was a terrible embarrassment. . . ."

Reflections

John's associations suggested that he was ready to continue working through traumatic conflicts related to the sadistic and incestuous maternal introject, a recent focus of the analysis. The analyst was interpreting John's projection of being seen as controlling and of destroying positive achievement and spontaneity. Given that the fear of losing control over his sexual and aggressive drives was an integral part of John's traumatic situation, John's wishful interpretation of his dream of speaking with his analyst as " . . . you aren't a danger" was insufficiently explored.

After the session the analyst recognized the emerging signs of the father transference that could have been integrated with the maternal one. Previously the analyst had been experienced as promoting John's autonomy, perhaps reawakening infantile longings for close contact with a caring parent. His enthusiasm and triumph that his project had been published could be seen as a wish that the analyst reinforce his positive self-regard. Within this context, John had said: "Sometimes I feel a window rising, and I see more clearly."

The analyst recalled that John retained vivid memories from childhood of his father playing with him and buying him toys. The parents' relationship deteriorated when John was about 4 years old—his father frequently leaving and abandoning his son who was without protection from mother's onslaughts on his autonomy and spontaneity.

These aspects of John's history suggest the operations of the dream-work. Contradictions and uncertainty about who was envious of whom can be seen. Was his friend Bill envious of John because his father would get him "anything"? Yet Bill had a "nice white Prelude", and John had his "old Datsun." Was a reversal operating as a protection against re-experiencing painful relations with his father? Was the patient experiencing in the transference anxieties about feeling close to the father/analyst? Did he fear the repetition of abandonment that would destroy the longed-for intimacy between them? Had this prompted the wish-fulfilling fantasy of Bill being envious of John?

The analyst wondered why he had realized the significance of the father transference only after the session. The transference meanings of the patient's enthusiasm and buoyancy had escaped him as he interpreted the mother transference. Had the analyst understood the dream's day residue in the previous session and paid attention to how the dream-work represented the patient's positive feelings towards the analyst, he might have found a way of communicating this to the patient. The analyst's reflections highlight the complexity of the working through of the multiple components of the patient's traumatic situation and the countertransference influence. The analysis of a dream is always incomplete, but Freud offered a guide: "One must be content if the attempt at an interpretation brings a single pathologic wishful impulse to light" (p. 93).

Discussion

Freud presented his theory of the manifest content of traumatic dreams without clinical evidence and without reference to the pivotal concepts of his earlier dream theory—the latent content, the dream-work, and unconscious wish-fulfilment. Consequently there were no grounds for assessing the validity of his second dream theory and no conceptual basis for integrating his original dream theory. Psychoanalysis was then left with two separate, seemingly unrelated dream theories.

One of Freud's major conclusions about traumatic dreams remains relevant: "These dreams are endeavouring to master the stimulus retrospectively, by developing the anxiety whose omission was the cause of the traumatic neurosis" (Freud, 1900a, p. 32). Here Freud focused on this restorative function of traumatic dreams without making reference to the day residues which in his first dream theory he understood as a trigger of dreams. However, his conclusion provides the basis for the integration of his two dream theories, as illustrated in the clinical example outlined above.

In clinical practice it is crucial to work with the manifest dream content of traumatic dreams to alleviate re-awakened painful affects that Freud's second dream theory emphasizes. However, while focusing on the manifest dream content strengthens the patient's fragile self, this focus may bypass deeper issues concealed by dream-work.

Further, the analyst's contribution to the structure and function of the traumatic dream must be considered. Patients may enact transference perceptions of the analyst's countertransference, which, understandably, analysts may minimize in interpreting traumatic dreams. Recognition of the analyst's representation in traumatic dreams enriches the working through of the dream's latent meanings.

In 1900 Freud offered: " . . . that the interpretation of dreams is like a window through which we can get a glimpse of that apparatus" (p. 219)—meaning the patient's mental apparatus. He went on to explain that dreams often have more than one meaning, and in a footnote that he added in 1914 he stated: "dreams are arranged in superimposed layers . . ." (p. 219 fn.). Relevant to the present study, Freud's "window" is like a prism that reflects the various aspects of the multiple components that may be revealed during the uncovering of the dreamer's psychic reality—aspects that are encoded symbolically and metaphorically in the dream. This "window" provides a glimpse—from different levels of awareness and from different periods of the patient's life—into traumatic experiences and related representations of conflicts, unconscious wishes, and internal object relations. A glimpse is also gained of the dream-work in its disguising and revealing of the dreamer's traumatic experiences, conflicts, wishes, and object relationships. Stimulated by the dream's multiple day residues, by childhood memories, by fantasies, and by somatic stimuli, the dream, as expressed via the dream-work, may have a unique relation to what is currently active in the dreamer's imagination. While the window metaphor provides a perspective on the intrapsychic world of the dreamer, it also provides a perspective on the psychic structure and dynamics of the analyst. Dreams may be shed on the analyst's interventions as they are unconsciously perceived by the dreamer—whether these interventions have been experienced as helpful or as traumatic.

You may recall that John related a dream in which he spoke of a "window": "Sometimes I feel a window rising and I can see more clearly; other times it is closed and I feel distant from you . . . I spoke to my partner about coming here. She says she doesn't know who will be coming home at night."

This resonated with the analyst's experience that John's close-ness and trust in the analytic situation vacillated and only occasion-ally offered a window into the disguised aspects of his intrapsychic life. However, this window would close quickly, leaving mainly John's disorganized affects. These dynamic cycles became the fo-cus of analytic enquiry. In listening to the affects that accompanied John's interactions, the analyst heard that he experienced him as expressing care and patient acceptance—as waiting for his storm to subside or for his withdrawal to abate.

John came to recognize how frequently he felt blocked by a "wrong look" or a "wrong tone" from his boss or a colleague. He would become obsessively convinced that he was going to lose his job, and thoughts and dreams of vengeful murder would be pre-cipitated. A central theme of the analysis was developing an un-derstanding of the relationship of this oft-repeated cycle to John's original traumatic situation. Also, experiences of success would lead John to overwhelming and disorganizing expansive fantasies of moving from partner to partner—evidencing an unconscious self-destructive urge that was disturbing to the analyst.

The feelings of dread generated by either side of John's trau-matic experiences made the analyst realize that he had to be pre-pared to "not know who would be coming to the session" and had to anticipate the paradoxical effects of his interventions. In time the analyst's staying with and analysing John's feelings, fanta-sies, sensations, and images reduced his impulsivity and feelings of doom. Analytic data after three years of analysis—and the partial dream analysis reported above—suggest John's increased capacity to develop positive relationships between his cycles of psychic dis-turbances and to work through the components of his traumatic situation.

Conclusion

This exploration—that Freud's two dream theories could coexist in the analyst's mind during analytic treatment—needs to be continued by a systematic comparison between our current diverse dream theories and Freud's. Hopefully, this expanded exploration can lay the ground for a comprehensive dream theory that meets the needs of our patients during analytic treatment. It will incorporate Freud's dream theories and go beyond them.

5

Does the death-instinct-based theory of aggression hold up?

Henri Parens

Many who speak of Freud assert him to have been dogmatic; they fail to credit him for his caution and occasional declaration of awareness that what he asserts is not set with certainty in his own mind but that, rather, clinical findings at times stirred in him speculations he found difficult to dismiss. He did so twice in his highly controversial "Some Psychical Consequences of the Anatomical Distinction between the Sexes" (1925j),[1] and he had also done so five years earlier in *Beyond the Pleasure Principle* (1920g) in declaring: "What follows is speculation, often far-fetched speculation, which the reader will consider or dismiss according to his individual predilection" (p. 25). This follows upon his dismissing the highly plausible likelihood that *the compulsion to repeat* follows from an effort *to make passive into active,* which, in turn, might be reflective of an *instinct to master* (p. 16). Why, he wondered, would the child repeat, repeatedly in fact, an event that causes him pain or anxiety? What makes him seek such pain or a situation he experiences as dangerous? Driven by factors we can only speculate about—as Max Schur has done with regard to Freud's nearly life-long preoccupation with death (1972)—Freud developed a strikingly circuitous argument in 1920 to assert that the compulsion to repeat is reflective of an inner need to return to one's inorganic state. It is essential to underscore that Freud's theory of aggression made the destruction of others secondary to a primary need to destroy oneself, thrust by the death instinct to seek return to one's original inorganic state.

As I wrote in my 1979 review of Freud's evolving instinctual drive theory, "while Freud had only tentatively put forward the death instinct in 1920, by 1930, despite the resistance met with 'even in analytic circles', he noted that the death instinct had 'gained such a hold on me that I can no longer think in any other way' ([Freud, 1930], p. 119)" (Parens, 1979, p. 55). It is established history that in the United States pre-eminent psychoanalytic theorists challenged the death-instinct basis of aggression, asserting that psychoanalysis would not be able to ascertain, let alone prove, that we humans are driven by a death instinct.

As a psychoanalyst who holds to much of what Freud wrote, let me first say how I came to doubt the validity of his death-instinct-based theory of aggression.

How I came to doubt the death-instinct basis of aggression

In 1973, I reported on what I felt was a striking adventitious finding, namely, a "Brief running commentary on a problematical observation . . . frequently made in normal, well-cared-for infants 3–5 months of age" (Parens, 1973, p. 35).

Jane was 15 weeks old when, after a 25-minute nap, she woke up and we recorded on film (Parens, Pollock, & Prall, 1974) "excerpts from one continuous 30-minute period of activity" (Parens, 1973, p. 35), which, I felt, posed a serious challenge to the death-instinct-based theory of aggression.

> Within minutes of waking Jane begins to look at objects—her mother and observers. She smiles broadly, already . . . focusing on her mother. She then looks around at articles on the floor, looking at several quite intently as she briefly fixes on these in passing. She now turns her attention to a set of plastic rings on a string, which she very busily explores. She begins by pulling them apart, mouthing them. The sensorimotor effort is visible on her face; one soon also hears vocal concomitants of that effort. She moves the rings back and forth while she looks at

them, a serious look on her face, and a good deal of pressure can be inferred from the way she seems to be "working". She waves her arms as she attempts to reach the rings which she inadvertently just pushed out of reach. Her mother (cooperating with us) then advances the rings so that she can reach them again, and Jane does so promptly, her attention continuing to be focused on those rings. The affect which bespeaks the effort she makes to bring the rings to her mouth, the effort with which she pushes and pulls them, suggests that this pressure is in the service of assimilating the rings. The activity is of course interrupted by physiological needs, as well as socialization. She looks around and smiles at her mother. She then returns to the rings. Notable is the intent, work-like affect, the constancy of the effort she invests in exploring the rings, the inner-drivenness of that activity. Much energy seems to be invested in the exploratory mouthing, pulling, and pushing of the rings. While she explores these rings, there is no thumb-sucking activity. Repeatedly she mouths the rings, sometimes with simultaneous pulling movements of her arms and lifting of her torso; her legs are activated as well, and indeed her entire body is involved in her effort. Her facial expression and entire body posture indicate the tension of, and the large effort invested in that protracted activity. After 18 minutes of nearly continuous effort, she pauses, lying down on the mat. One sees she is tiring. She pauses for about 15 seconds, looks up at her mother, smiles softly and returns to the rings, at once very busy. Soon she pauses again, and one begins to see signs of unpleasure on her face. She cries as if annoyed and stops her exploratory activity, rings in hand; and now, for the first time in a 20-minute period, she puts her thumb in her mouth and lies quietly. [After a brief pause] she returns to the rings. . . . From here on she alternates between exploration of the rings and thumb-sucking . . . giving the impression that she is recovering from tiredness and unexplained frustration . . . she cries momentarily, and looks up at her mother. . . . She spits up a bit. Her mother picks her up to comfort her. Jane has now been awake for about 25 minutes and has been continually busy. [Parens, 1973, pp. 35–36]

This . . . type of pressured, driven, "exploratory" activity was observed in 8 or our (then) 9 infants from the ages of 8 to 16 weeks on, during periods of wakefulness and physiologic and psychic comfort. . . . In Jane, the strong pressure and duration of this exploratory activity from the time she was nine weeks old was impressive. . . . The persistence of this . . . exploratory activity is compelling; Jane, like our other children, did not elect to look; she seemed driven from within to look, and at the risk of thinking teleologically, I would add, to gratify the push from within to assimilate, to control, to master her visual experience. [Parens, 1973, p. 37]

This behaviour challenged the model of aggression I used up to that time to try to understand the vicissitudes of aggression in my patients and in life activity. Why did this behaviour challenge this model?

The model I had come to accept derived directly for Freud's death-instinct-based theory of aggression. In 1949, Hartmann, Kris, and Loewenstein argued in favour of this model but rejected its death-instinct basis—that is, they rejected the basis on which Freud developed his model of aggression, namely the hypothesis that the aggressive drive is the psychic representative of a death instinct, but they retained the superstructure the death-instinct hypothesis had generated. As Freud himself noted in 1930, a number among his colleagues rejected the death-instinct hypothesis. I did not see the problems inherent in Hartmann, Kris, and Loewenstein's model of aggression until we observed a number of times and filmed the type of behaviour I reported, as quoted above.

As I first argued in 1973 and further elaborated in *The Development of Aggression in Early Childhood* (1979), Hartmann, Kris, and Loewenstein's 1949 model assumed an inherent, inborn disposition to destructiveness. As a clinician, a child psychoanalyst accepting Hartmann and colleagues' theorizing on aggression, I interpreted Jane's behaviour as the by-product of aggression that was neutralized. Clinically, Jane's behaviour looked as if it was driven by neutralized aggression.[2] Neutralized, this aggression was in the service of the ego and was assumed then to drive much nondestructive energy. But the neutralization of aggression I assumed would require the functioning of an ego sufficiently mature to erect such a defence. According to Hartmann (1939), the structuring of the ego into an organ of adaptation—in contrast to its being one of reactivity—does not occur until about 6 months of age. But Jane was only 15 weeks old: and we saw such pressured exploratory activity in babies even younger than 15 weeks. Could this have been driven by what Hartmann had identified as "neutral ego energy" (1939)?

Could we assume that neutral ego energy would drive neutralized aggressive energy? I could not equate "neutralized aggressive energy" with *ab ovo* "neutral ego energy", both of which were much used by Hartmann in his theorizing. It brought to mind Freud's (1914c) dismay at finding himself having to differentiate between self-directed libido and self-preservative instincts. He wondered whether are they not the same. I have even postulated that this dilemma contributed to his replacing his first drive theory with the second (Parens, 1979).

In turn, the type of data I just reported created for me a sequence of dilemmas. First, while others might construe Jane's behaviour to not be aggression, I have, and I continue to do so. But, then, given my above-stated argument, I could only see it as an *inherently non-destructive aggression*. To research this question, and given my determination to be guided by the data of observation—convinced as I have long been that as Charcot is said to have said: "theory does not prevent facts from being what they are"—I welcomed Ernst Kris's (1950) and Heinz Hartmann's (1950) urging psychoanalysts to take up "depth-psychological" direct observational research. Given serious disagreements about theoretical assumptions regarding early development that organized into baseline positions on development and what these assumptions gave rise to, Kris and Hartmann emphatically recommended that we test our early developmental assumptions by direct observation of live human infants and young children. In 1958, Anna Freud echoed their position, stating that behaviour gives evidence of unconscious determinants of that behaviour, of what is manifest, of what is visible and readily, plausibly inferable. Jane's behaviour, more or less clearly observable in all children, and what I construed from it, challenged the death-instinct-based theory of aggression.

In 1973, I proposed that rather than one inherent (inborn) type of aggression—that is, that derived from the tendency to destroy, first oneself and, secondarily, others—there are two inborn currents of aggression: (1) one "inherently nondestructive" and (2) one "inherently destructive" (1973, p. 55). I even wondered whether "a spectral metaphor rather than one of two currents [might] better reflect the innate character of the aggressive drive, with nondestructive aggression at one pole and destructiveness at the other" (p. 55).

But what I came to—which was published in 1973—left me with a serious dilemma and with the following question: With all due respect for Hartmann, Kris, and Loewenstein, who held to the superstructure of Freud's death-instinct-derived theory of aggression, if a death instinct does not drive that basic form of aggression that gives rise to hostility and hate, then what does? Is it, as I said in 1973, that destructiveness is inborn, inherent? Observed behaviour seemed to me to give clear evidence of a nondestructive current of aggression. Could *direct observation* further inform the question of *inherent destructiveness*? That took months of twice-weekly 2-hour observations to address.

In time, observing the babies and their mothers opened to view a pattern of behaviour that pointed to a possible answer verbalized by the mothers: whenever an infant would fuss, cry, or start kicking up a storm, a mother would say, "Oh, oh, something's wrong", and the mother, in those remarkable ways mothers have for doing so—often good, sometimes bad—would try to ascertain "*what* was wrong with the baby". Noting this phenomenon again and again, I came to assume that most commonly "something was wrong": pain of one kind or another seemed to cause the infant to cry, and if mother did not intervene soon enough, the infant would commonly show signs of being angry. Magically, mother's soothing or doing whatever she felt was needed seemed to stop the crying and anger, often just on the first try! I then began to test this clinically: what seemed to have caused anger in my patients? What I learned from watching the babies with their mothers seemed to be cogently applicable towards my understanding of my patients. In fact, applying the findings of observation clarified the sources of anger in my patients: it was not difficult to reconstruct anamnestically and in the transference that they had experienced some intense psychic pain, in a myriad possible ways—abuse, maltreatment, neglect, shaming, insults, intense frustrations of all kinds, some lesser, some greater. This led me to hypothesize that *psychic pain*—not just physical pain, *except when intentionally caused to hurt*—triggers anger and hostility, not some inborn disposition.

Not yet understanding well enough how psychic pain triggers hostility and hate, the death-instinct basis of aggression no longer worked for me. The aggressive behaviours I observed so far in the infants were quite different along one critical parameter: one was hostile, the other was not. Yes, it could have been seen as neutralized hostile aggression, except that, as I noted before, the ego in our young subjects was too immature to neutralize it! I had to start afresh: I "discarded" the death-instinct hypothesis; I had to keep on looking. Eventually 18 months of twice-a-week, 2-hour observation sessions of babies and their mothers yielded aggressive behaviours that defied cataloguing into the two types of aggression I had found.

The outcome for this investigator
of continuing direct longitudinal observation

Discarding a theory is fine if cogent and convincing findings dictate its failure to account under test. This is so for the sciences, mathematics, philosophy, history. The problem I found, though, was: What do you replace that attractive but now discarded theory with? Starting *ab ovo*, assuming no theory of aggression, what do the data of observation suggest? The manifestations of aggression in early childhood are multiform! My adventitious finding was bringing with it another dilemma. How does one catalogue the awesome, varied manifestations of aggressive behaviour? In time, after much cogitation, deliberation, testing, and dreaming,[3] I organized these into *four categories of aggressive behaviours*:

1. *unpleasure-related destructiveness (rage reaction of infancy);*
2. *non-affective destructiveness (feeding activity);*
3. *nondestructive aggression (pressured sensorimotor activity);*
4. *pleasure-related destructiveness (teasing and taunting activity).*

These, in turn, led me to conceptualize the following three trends in aggression:

1. *hostile destructiveness (Categories a and d);*
2. *non-affective destructiveness (Category b);*
3. *nondestructive aggression (Category c).*

By 2000, according to my records (a Powerpoint document), I had entitled this model, "The Multi-Trends Theory of Aggression "

(Parens, 2008). Of these, the trend that accounts for hostility and hate is

Hostile Destructiveness (HD: the trend that ranges from anger to hostility, rage, hate, etc.)

> *It is not inborn, and it is not biologically generated.*
>
> *What is inborn is the mechanism for its generation.*
>
> *But the mechanism must be activated to generate HD.*
>
> *It is activated by an experience of excessive unpleasure/psychic pain (EU).*
>
> *Excessive psychic pain is required for the generation of HD.*
>
> *Psychic pain gives to aggression the affective quality characteristic of anger, hostility, hate, etc.*
>
> *Most critical is that HD can be moderated or heightened by experience.*

While I laboured to research and conceptualize *the multi-trends theory of aggression,* I launched on a review of the vast psychoanalytic and psychoanalysis-relevant literature on aggression. I found that quite a few analysts over time were also challenging the explanatory value and validity of the death-instinct-based theory of aggression.

Brief review of selected psychoanalysis-relevant models of aggression

I found in my review that the death-instinct-based theory of aggression had been and was being challenged by a number of psychoanalytically relevant models, including several psychoanalytic and two major psychological ones—namely, Dollard's "frustration–aggression" model and Tomkins' affect theory model. I catalogued these models as follows.

Death-instinct-based models

I should note that Freud's death-instinct model is still widely used today by clinicians who base their work on that of Melanie Klein. Winnicott (1947) was influenced by Klein even though, in the

1950s, he did speak of aggression as a "vital force" of growth (see Parens, 2008, pp. 71–74). It is at times forgotten that Freud believed the death-instinct-based aggression to be inherently "*self*-destructive", not simply "destructive" (Freud, 1920g). To protect the self against it, aggression, Freud proposed, has to be inhibited, externalized, or neutralized (Freud, 1923b).

As I noted earlier, the model proposed by Hartmann, Kris, and Loewenstein (1949) is a variant of Freud's 1920 theory of aggression. Hartmann and colleagues' model was long continued by Brenner (1982). As already noted, the great problem with this model is that by removing the death-instinct basis, it proposed a drive with no psychogenetic underpinnings. Unlike the academic psychology concept, where "aggression" is *descriptive of behaviour that is hostile and destructive,* in the Hartmann–Kris–Loewenstein model the inference is that aggression is an instinctual drive that is inherently destructive.

Experience-dependent models

In 1979 I reported that, from 1949 on, a number of psychoanalysts progressively saw a need for a major modification in the theory of aggression. As Freud said, within his own circle, analysts, including Hartmann (1939), Bibring (1941), Fenichel (1945), and Waelder (1956), protested that psychoanalysis could not by its clinical method prove—or disprove—the existence of a death instinct. Later analysts, however, further questioned Freud's death-instinct-based theory. Over four decades they reported not only that their clinical work compelled them to assume that aggression consists of an amply clinically demonstrable destructive trend, but that they found evidence that there must also be an *inherently nondestructive trend.* Up to the mid-1970s, these included B. Rank (1949), Winnicott (1950), Waelder (1956), Lantos (1958), Greenacre (1960, 1971), Storr (1968, 1972), Spitz (1969), Solnit (1970, 1972), Rangell (1972), and a number of others, each of whom doubted that all human aggression arises from an inherently destructive drive.

I should note here that the classical academic psychology model that separates "assertiveness" from "aggression" (hostility) based these concepts on manifest behaviours and did not ascribe it to an instinctual drive. Also, in psychology the concept of "aggression" is not assumed to derive from a death instinct. It is reasonable to say that the behaviours these concepts represent are relevant to the multi-trends model, allowing that one not insist on aggression being an instinctual drive—a point I emphasized in 2008. Setting aside the question of psychoanalytic theorizing (i.e., depth-psychological-based theorizing) as compared to classical psychological theorizing (i.e., empirically based theorizing), this academic psychology model—which distinguishes and separates *assertiveness* from *aggression*—seems to be the basis for the model proposed by Stechler and Halton (1983). Stechler and Halton, who have long been in dialogue with psychoanalytic aggression theorists, developed their systems theory model following on findings arising from their own longitudinal direct child observation research. Particularly in the context of Stechler and Halton's model, the academic psychology concepts of assertiveness and aggression seem to address the same psychodynamics as those of the two trends considered by many analysts to be inherently nondestructive and destructive trends in aggression.

Dollard's *frustration–aggression theory* (Dollard, Doob, Miller, Mowner, & Sears, 1939) may well have been the first to challenge the death-instinct-based theory of aggression. Much researched and criticized, it is very pertinent to the multi-trends theory of aggression I have developed. Here I want to say two things: (1) that although intensification of frustration, which is, of course, experienced as psychically unpleasurable, will be expected to generate and activate hostile destructiveness, it is not the only experience that will do so, as I shall note in a moment. And (2) the theorizing did not sufficiently account for the fact that defence against its outward expression often leads to no *manifest* evidence of hostile destructiveness following on excessive frustration. Due to this, documenting evidence of the frustration–aggression hypothesis appeared at times unconvincing. Considering our findings and the operation of defence mechanisms, I think that this is a convincing hypothesis; but it is insufficient to explain the generation and activation of all human hostile destructiveness ("aggression" in Dollard's sense). As I wrote earlier (1984, 1989, 2008, p. xxv), the frustration–aggression hypothesis can easily be subsumed into the multi-trends theory of aggression.

Deriving from their clinical work, Rochlin (1973) and Kohut (1977) each developed a model of aggression based on the central assumption that *narcissistic injury* activates hostile destructiveness in humans. There are differences in their explanations, theorizing, and in their models. These differences notwithstanding, Rochlin and Kohut both postulated that the vicissitudes of narcissism are centrally determining in the generation of what I have called hostile destructiveness—that is, it is the "self" that experiences "excessive unpleasure", which activates the bio-psychological mechanism that generates "hostile destructive" feelings within the self.

As I detailed in 1989, Rochlin views aggression as a defence activated by any threat to one's narcissism. He said: "To restore our self-esteem, assert our value . . . the defensive functions of aggression are invoked. The aggression generated by the need for restitution may be enormous, but it is not, fortunately, always destructive; it may well be turned into creativity" (Rochlin, 1973, p. 1). Rochlin did not speak of any form of *inherent* nondestructive aggression; he saw hostile destructiveness being turned into creativity as the product of a defensive operation.

By contrast, Kohut's evolving views on aggression led him to propose (Kohut, 1977)—along lines notably in agreement with the model I proposed (1973, 1979)[4]—that aggression may be inherently nondestructive and "that man's destructiveness as a psychological phenomenon is *secondary;* that it arises originally as the result of the failure of the self-object environment to meet the child's need for optimal . . . empathic responses" (Kohut, 1977, p. 116; italics added). Thus, in Kohut's model, what I call *"nondestructive aggression"* is the earliest and most basic form of aggression and human destructiveness is generated secondarily in reaction to narcissistically painful experience. As I discussed in 1989 (Parens, 1989, p. 104), Gunther, who elaborated on Kohut's theory of aggression, developed an attractive explanation for how assertiveness converts into rage by virtue of a *"primitivization* of the [aggression] response" (Gunther, 1980, pp. 188–189). I had come to a somewhat similar assumption: namely, that nondestructive aggression and/or nonaffective destructiveness is converted into hostile destructiveness by means of the influence on aggression of the affective state created by excessive unpleasure experiences, a process I described in 1979 (p. 111). All in all, like the Dollard frustration–aggression hypothesis, the Rochlin/Kohut narcissistic injury–aggression/destructiveness hypothesis can be readily subsumed into the multi-trends theory, given that I have held that the "excessive unpleasure generates hostile destructiveness" hypothesis of the multi-trends theory is "the lowest common denominator" of both intense frustration and narcissistic injury.

Kernberg (1982, 1991) has proposed that early-life affective self-object experiences are the "building blocks" for what becomes organized into an aggressive drive. He also has proposed that the *experience of rage* is the specific affective component that serves as building block for the aggressive drive. There is a cardinal feature in this hypothesis with which my research and clinical findings are in accord, which is that experience is the obligatory determiner of the hostile destructive trend in aggression. Psychoanalysts agree that the cumulative experiences of rage reactive to excessively unpleasurable handling by one's libidinal objects influence the quality of hostile destructiveness in humans by generating a large load of hate in them that determines the quality of their current and future object relations as well as of their intrapsychic conflicts and coping mechanisms. Kernberg has held that severely troubled humans—including those with borderline character disorders—may have a biogenetically facilitated tendency to experience rage and envy (Kernberg, 1975). Newer knowledge on the effects of severe early trauma on the child's brain patterning and biologic make-up support Kernberg's 1975 hypothesis; but I have differed with Kernberg in that I ascribe greater pathogenicity to the effects of trauma in these individuals than to their genetic endowment and diatheses (Parens, 1994). In addition, considering Kernberg's model, I should point out that, like others, he considers aggression to be only what I call "hostile destructiveness". I have three problems viewing aggression this way:

1.   Does human aggression have any bearing on aggression in animal life? "Hostile destructiveness" as a paradigm for aggression cannot account for the nature of *prey aggression,* which is pervasive in nature to a far greater extent than is the rage of *Homo sapiens.* As a number of aggression theorists have asserted, prey aggression—which is in the service of self preservation, not self-destructiveness—is produced by the biological (physiological),

inherently self-preservative instinct activated by bodily needs. This destructiveness is not driven by hostility or, strictly speaking, by any affect.

2. Longitudinal infant observation of a normal population (Parens, 1979) as well as much clinical work with children (Lantos, 1958; Rank, 1949; Solnit, 1970, 1972; and others) have revealed much evidence from the early months of life onward of aggressive behaviours that show no evidence of arising from rage experiencing.

3. But more to the point is this (and I find it with Tomkins' affect theory as well): although rage is no doubt a powerful affective expression of aggression, rage *of itself is not a generator of hostile destructive aggression,* whereas the experience of psychic pain—that is, *the experience of "excessive unpleasure"*—is. If Kernberg holds, as I too, the affect-self-object to be the building block of the aggressive drive, is it not an *experiential dyadic event* that causes the affect rage? It is not rage that generates rage, it is the object-self interaction that does. Note also that the death-instinct-based aggression theory asserts that the death instinct is what thrusts the manifestation of aggression in humans, and not the manifestation itself: that is, anger, hostility, or hate. These manifestations of aggression are caused by the death instinct. But my research and clinical findings suggest that excessive unpleasure and psychic pain can generate or activate these various intensities of hostile destructiveness. We do not need the death instinct to explain the bio-psychological cause of "hostile destructiveness". As I proposed in 1979,

> No doubt the expression of unpleasure has a somatic root: irritability of the protoplasm. By virtue of the irritability of the protoplasm . . . the noxious accumulation of tension in the cell [organism/self] is experienced psychically as "unpleasure". This sensory reactivity of live matter serves to protect against the destruction of the cell [self] and acts primarily to rid the cell [self] of noxious tension. . . . The somato-psychic force in this ridding activity is "aggression". This activity is effected by primary autonomous *pleasure-ego* functions under the aegis of primary narcissism. Insured by this vital somato-psychic protective mechanism, the aggressive-ridding

impulse is brought about *reactively* to rid the self of the noxious agent which instigates the excessively-felt unpleasure (irritability). [Parens, 1979, p. 110]

In this 1979 work I elaborate how this "ridding aggressive activity", affectively suffused by "unpleasure", becomes hostility; but, given the unpleasure-intensity-determined range of variability of hostility that this trend contains—that is, from anger, to hostility, hate, and rage—I labelled this trend, generically, "hostile destructiveness".

Systems theory models

Another attractive model of aggression, proposed by Lichtenberg (1989), is based on the assumption of inborn reactivity systems that serve adaptation. Lichtenberg's 1989 model is compatible with ethological conceptualization, a domain of thought handsomely populated—for example, by Lorenz, Hinde, and Tinbergen. We could say that Stechler and Halton's 1983 model is also such a model, given its systems theory basis, but it is conceptualized along the lines of academic psychology.

Affect-theory-based models of aggression

Sylvan S. Tomkins (1962, 1991), a foremost personality theorist, left us an elegant, complex model of the nature and place of affects in his long-term project on a theory of personality. As is common in correlating models, differences in Tomkins' theoretical frame, concepts, and term definitions makes for difficulty in efforts at correlation of Freud's death-instinct model and the experience-based models I have here briefly noted, including the multi-trends model I developed. For example, we would no doubt all agree that, as Tomkins proposes, affects are *innate responses* to varying experiencing. But Tomkins argues that, contrary to Freud's view, affects are not "subordinated to the drives", nor are they by-products of the drives (1962, p. 6). Here, our theory correlation problem lies in the fact that Tomkins's definition of the drives is quite different from Freud's. In 1962, as he affirmed in 1991, Tomkins asserted that, while both drives and affects are motivational systems, "the primary motivational system is the affective system, and [that] the *biological drives* have motivational impact only when amplified by the affective system" (1962, p. 6, italics added; for further details see Parens, 2008, pp. xxx–xxxiv.) Needless to say, Tomkins put aside Freud's death-instinct-based theory.

Summing up this section, note that I have not included a number of aggression models from varied disciplines—for example, from *psychiatry*, those of Patterson, Littman, and Bricker (1967) and of Hamburg and Trudeau (1981); from *psychology*, those of Bandura and Walters (1959, 1963), De Wit and Hartup (1974), and Feshbach (1970); nor those from *genetics* (Ginsberg, 1982), *physiology* (Moyer, 1968), *neurophysiology* (Reis, 1973, 1974), *ethology* (Goodall, 1979; Lorenz, 1963b; Tinbergen, 1969), or *sociology* (McCord, McCord, & Zola, 1959). But in my reviews of these I found no endorsement of the psychoanalytic death-instinct-based theory of aggression.

I must add one major vote in favour of a model of aggression that assumes aggression to be constituted of both destructive and nondestructive trends, from among especially well-qualified non-analysts. Konrad Lorenz paid tribute to Anthony Storr when he wrote in his Foreword to Storr's book that he, Lorenz, wished he himself had thought of the conceptualization of aggression proposed by Storr in his works of 1968 and 1972. What makes this important is that Lorenz had proposed that animal fighting—that is, nonspecified destructiveness—can be spontaneous, the implications of which include, therefore, that it is inborn. According to Tinbergen (1969), Robert Hinde challenged this assumption, asserting that fighting in the animal world is determined by the situation, not by an inner need to fight. This was reviewed by Tinbergen, who, in fact, felt that Lorenz and Hinde were less in disagreement than their words suggested: he showed that both Lorenz and Hinde assumed that both internal, that is, "spontaneous", and external, that is, situational, factors operate to trigger animal fighting (Tinbergen, 1969, pp. 29–33). And, of course, Storr's hypotheses, which Lorenz praised, do assume the operation of both internal and external factors in the eliciting of destructive aggression. It is important to note, however, that while Storr recognized that unpleasure experience plays a part in the appearance of what I call "hostile destructiveness", he did not attribute *the generation* of hostile destructiveness specifically to experiences of excessive unpleasure. But because of his clear delineation of two major trends in aggression, Storr's model was, up to 1979, the farthest advanced towards a conceptualization of the multi-trends theory of aggression—a fact that I became aware of only after I had developed the latter theory.

Is the death-instinct-based aggression theory wrong?

I have not *proven* the death-instinct-based theory of aggression wrong. What I have found is that, following the disciplined approach reasoned and recommended by Kris (1950), Hartmann (1950), and Anna Freud (1958), which corresponds with my commitment to replicable data-based hypothesis generation and the direct, longitudinal, twice-weekly observation of children from the first weeks of life on, do not support the theory that aggression is driven by a psychic representative of a death instinct in humans. But these findings compelled my proposing a theory of aggression that could be documented and replicated by others, directly and by inference—that is, clinically. Directly observable is that the normal average-expectable neonate does not give the impression of being "a cauldron of seething excitations". The normal-enough newborn, following his/her initial show of distress and screaming on emergence from the birth canal—a process that puts great strain not only on the mother but also on the foetus, whose entire body is squeezed and strained under great pressure in order to come out—soon quiets and acclimates to her/his new environment without great fuss or flailing. To be sure, infants born with varied physiological disregulations, be they the product of foetal developmental and/or intrauterine chemical irregularities or of premature termination of pregnancy, may evidence respiratory or gastrointestinal central nervous system dysfunctions or other distress symptoms that do give the impression of being evidence of greater or lesser discharges of aggression. While some might ascribe these manifestations of infantile aggression to arising from a death-instinct-driven force, how do we explain that this does not manifest in most infants with good APGARs?[5] Rather, the jeopardized infants' dysphoric behaviours can be explained by the hypothesis that excessive psychic pain activates within them the mechanism that generates the earliest manifestations of "hostile destructiveness", in the generic sense I proposed (Parens, 1973, 1979). Though I have not proved the death-instinct theory wrong, I do show that it is unnecessary for a sound and valid understanding of human aggression. Unlike what can be said for the death-instinct-based theory of aggression, I assert that the "multi-trends theory of aggression" (Parens, 2008) is directly observable and readily inferable in our clinical work.

Allow what the reader may think to be an outrageous question. Do automobiles, wood and brick houses, marble statues in Venice, Rome, Athens, and other parts of the world rich in ancient art deteriorate because of a death instinct in them too? The passage of time brings with it friction, over-use, accidents, and nigh-invisible to the eye air pollutants that destroy all structures, whatever their composition, organic and inorganic. Do we need to postulate a tendency in any structure to return to its inorganic state by virtue of a self-destructive tendency? In inanimate structures, does not the assumption that forces external to the structure operate to bring about its destruction? And with regard to animate structure, might not such external forces, as well as such internal processes as infectious processes, mechanistic and biochemical disorders, and the proliferation of abnormal cells, achieve the destruction of the organism, animal or plant, without needing to invoke an inborn self-destructive obligatory compulsion?

Does the death-instinct model of aggression hold up?

Does it hold up, 90 years after its publication? Since I am asking this question, I should myself face the same question, since I started to report on the multi-trends theory of aggression nearly 40 years ago: Has it held up over these nearly four decades? Two questions follow:

1. Can we document direct or even strongly inferable evidence of aggression driven by a death instinct? Can we document direct or even strong evidence for the multi-trends model?
2. Since both are "working models", what is the heuristic value of each?

Can we document evidence of the death instinct?

Can we document evidence, directly or strongly inferably, of such an inherent force at play in our patients, whether children or adults? When, in the transference, we are the object of our patient's hostility, is it our tendency to ascribe it to their untamed death-instinct-derived aggression? Are we not likely to look for an underlying past *experience* externalized into the transference that gave rise to this hostility? My clinical experience, and for long now my bias, is to look for a (or more) past experiential source responsible and determining of the patient's currently transferentially experienced hostility.

Does the psychoanalytically advanced assumption that infants come into the world driven to attack the object hold up? I have not seen such evidence. A word of caution: as I noted before, infants with pain-inducing diatheses (eczema or asthma, for instance) or somatic immaturities (low thresholds of irritability, gastric atresias, or even just plain colic) may become angry, cry, and even scream. Pain = excessive unpleasure; not a death-instinct derivative.

Some have invoked phenomena as "cell death" and the rare but dramatic medical disorder, progeria, as proof of a self-destructive tendency in living organisms. Accepted explanations for these phenomena do not support the notion of a self-destructive compulsion to return to an inorganic state. "Cell death" has been explained[6] to be a normal neonatal phenomenon believed to serve to reduce overcrowding of neurons to optimize space for the formation of specific neural pathways. Progeria is an insufficiently understood acceleration of aging; attempts to document the play of a death instinct in this disorder have proven as challenging as it is to ascertain it in the psychoanalytic situation.

Do we need the concept of *instinctual drive* to understand aggression? The concept of *instinctual drive* does not install aggression as a phenomenon of great concern to us all, nor should it. What matters, rather, is that we recognize that not all aggression is destructive and that hostility and hate do not arise from an inborn disposition but from experience. This makes it clear that *hostile destructiveness* is amenable to prevention measures and that ultimately war is not inevitable—as Freud told Einstein.

Notes

1. In the third paragraph of "Some Psychical Consequences of the Anatomical Distinction between the Sexes", 69-year-old Freud writes: "The time before me is limited. The whole of it is no longer spent in working, so that my opportunities for making fresh observations are not so numerous. If I see something new, I am uncertain whether I can wait for it to be confirmed. . . . On this occasion, therefore, I feel justified in publishing something which stands in urgent need of confirmation before its value . . . can be decided" (1925j, p. 249). Then, in the penultimate paragraph of the same paper, Freud says again: "I am inclined to set some value on [these] considerations. . . . I am aware, however, that this opinion can only be maintained if my findings . . . turn out to have general validity and to be typical. If not, they would remain no more than a contribution to our knowledge of the different paths along which sexual life develops" (p. 258).

2. Interested in the *neutralization of aggression* in intelligent children who were failing in school, Alex Weech and I studied the effects of our psychotherapy with a small sample of such children (Parens & Weech, 1966). Our hypothesis was that if we could help them neutralize some of their excessive hostility and hate by redirecting those psychic energies to adaptive functioning, they might do better in school. In the 1950–1960s, the idea that neutralized aggressive energy was put into the service of sublimation was felt to be attractive and to give us some guidelines to help capable children struggling in school. So, Weech and I developed some degree of clinical skill in looking for evidence of *neutralized aggression.*

3. In fact, the solution came to me in a dream.

4. For this information, which extended my review of Kohut's work on aggression, I am indebted to M. & E. Shane (1982).

5. Paediatric observational assessment of the newborn's degree of functional normalcy or disturbance. A good APGAR generally suggests good structural development and systems functioning of the newborn.

6. The author apologizes for no longer being able to access the references from which he gathered his information regarding both "cell death" and progeria. Needless to say, if the reader can in fact find documentation to the contrary of the author's claim, the author would be indebted to the reader for sharing this information with him.

6

The concept of the death drive:
a clinical perspective

Otto Kernberg

I believe that it is quite evident that the two major controversies that have been raised by Freud's monumental discoveries are his theory of libido or the sexual drive and his theory of the death drive, representing, respectively, the struggle between life as centred in erotic impulses and aggression. Freud considered the two drives as the fundamental motivational principles determining unconscious conflict and symptom formation (Freud, 1920g). In a broader sense, they were what drives human beings towards the search for gratification and happiness, on the one hand, and to severely destructive and self-destructive aggression, on the other. Freud's stress on the infantile origins of sexual orientation, infantile sexuality, and particularly its sadomasochistic components, have raised shock, opposition, and efforts at denial in the general culture (Freud, 1905d). The death drive runs deeply against more optimistic views of human nature, based on the assumption that if severe frustrations or trauma were absent in early development, then aggression would not be a major human problem.

These perennial cultural reactions towards Freud's theories are mirrored within the psychoanalytic community proper. Recent tendencies, particularly in American psychoanalysis, reflected by the relational approach, tend to de-emphasize both infantile sexuality and aggression, in contrast to their centrality in the psychoanalytic focus in European and Latin American psychoanalytic contributions (Kernberg, 2001). Additionally, Freud's concept of the death drive has been questioned within American ego psychology, and the debate about whether aggression is primary or a secondary response to trauma and frustration permeates the psychological field far beyond psychoanalysis proper.

In this chapter I wish to focus exclusively on the controversies surrounding Freud's theory of the death drive. The importance of this controversy relates directly to the social and cultural problems of the twentieth century and the beginning of this new century. The fundamentalist regimes of the last century were unprecedented in their primitive and brutal aggression, both systematic and daily. The tens of millions killed in the name of German National Socialism and Marxist communism are beginning to be replicated under new banners in this century. But no society, no country is free from the history of senseless, wholesale massacre of imagined or real enemies. The relative ubiquity of these phenomena throughout the history of civilization cannot be ignored. The question of the existence of the death drive as part of the core of human psychology is, unfortunately, a practical and not merely a theoretical problem (Kernberg, 2003a, 2003b).

To begin, regarding Freud's theory of motivation: the study of the unconscious conflicts that patients with neurotic syndromes and character pathology experience led Freud to successive formulations regarding the ultimate drives, culminating in the dual drive theory of libido and the death drive. The practical implication of these proposed two major motivational systems is that, as mentioned before, at the bottom, all unconscious conflicts involve conflicts between love and aggression at some level of development. This, I believe, makes eminent sense clinically, as does Freud's careful warning that the only thing we know about these two drives is their expression in mental representations and affects.

Here begins the problem: Freud had postponed linking psychological functions and structures with underlying neurobiological developments because of the primitive nature of the neurobiology of his time. He expressed the hope, however, that eventually more specific relationships between psychological functions and neurobiological developments might become clearer. From today's developments in neurobiological science and advances in our knowledge about instinctive behaviour and its organization in mammals, particularly primates, it emerges that the primary motivational systems consist of affects of a positive and negative kind. Affects are primary motivational systems in the sense that their activation, under certain circumstances, by mechanisms of the limbic brain initiates strong motivation to movement towards other objects or away from them. The entire series of libidinal affects—joyous encounter, euphoria, sensual gratification, and erotic arousal—are all directed towards early libidinal objects, while the negative affects of rage, anger, disgust, anxiety, and, later, envy and hatred motivate us to withdraw from dangerous objects or attempt to control or to eliminate them (Panksepp, 1998). All affects are embedded in mental representations: that is, a cognitive organization of the context in which affects emerge, an emerging definition of the desired objects as well as of the feared and hated ones, and wishful fantasies towards erotic objects as well as about the elimination of threatening objects. The very fantasies that reflect unconscious conflicts between love and hatred are always representations embedded in respective positive or negative affects.

In the study of patients with severe psychopathology, the borderline conditions, at the Institute of Personality Disorders at the Weill Cornell Medical College, we have been able to confirm that borderline patients who suffer from inordinate aggressive impulses and lack of impulse control—in other words, a strong predominance of negative affects and impulsivity—regularly show hyperactivity of the amygdala, a limbic structure related to the activation of negative affect. They also show a primary inhibition of the dorsolateral prefrontal cortex, which is related to cognitive framing of affects and the establishment of priorities of focus, attention, and action following such affective activation (Silbersweig et al., 2007). These and other related findings have been confirmed also in various other centres, so that we are at the beginning of establishing a more direct relationship between neurobiological function and affect activation. But what does all of this say to the theory of drives?

The psychoanalytic community is struggling nowadays with the problem of whether drives should continue to be considered as the primary motivational systems or whether they should be replaced by the consideration of affects as primary motivational system (Kernberg, 2004a). The absence of any biological evidence for the original, primary nature of drives, the abundant evidence for the primary motivational function of affects, and the fact that affects always imply representations at the same time raise the question of whether affective representations are the building blocks of more complex human motivational developments, thus replacing the concept of drives. Against such a radical assumption lies the fact that, clinically, the replacement of drive theory by affect theory does not do justice to the stable organization of unconscious conflicts. The multiplicity of affects and the shifting affective relationship to objects and their representations does not lend itself to meaningful conceptualization of the organization of those conflicts. On the other hand, a pure drive theory that does not consider the specific vicissitudes of affects tends to acquire over-generalized and rigidly dogmatic aspects that also run counter to clinical experience: to explain unconscious conflict as simple struggles between libido and aggressive drives does not do justice to the complexity of clinical experience.

I proposed, years ago—and am no longer alone in this view—that affects constitute the primary motivational system and that they are integrated into supraordinate positive and negative drives: namely, libido and aggression. The drives, in turn, manifest themselves as activation of their constituent affects with varying intensity, along the line of libidinal and aggressive investments. In short, I believe that affects are the primary motivators. They organize into hierarchically supra-ordinate motivations, or the Freudian drives, and the drives, in turn, become activated in the form of their component affectively valenced representations manifest as unconscious fantasies (Kernberg, 1992).

Within the context of these formulations I shall propose, in the present chapter, that the concept of the death drive as a designation for the dominant unconscious motivation towards self-destructiveness is warranted in severe cases of psychopathology. I shall question, however, whether severe self-destructive aggression is a primary tendency and propose that the unconscious function of self-destructiveness is not simply to destroy the self, but to destroy significant others as well.

It will be noted that, earlier in this chapter, I talked about aggression and then about aggressive drive rather than the death drive *per se*. That our patients suffer from conflicts involving love and aggression and from their ambivalence towards those they love and need and who gratify and frustrate them, who can never satisfy all desires and sometimes dramatically withhold the gratification of basic psychological needs, seems reasonable enough. We are talking here about aggression secondary to frustration, which conforms with the type of aggression delineated by Freud as arising from the conflict between the pleasure principle and the reality principle. And the basis of such aggression, mingling with our deepest needs for closeness and love, may naturally be related to the biological disposition to aggression, as inborn as that to love and eroticism, and which we encounter as a common property of all mammals. I am referring to the aggressive dispositions that are a normal mechanism in the defence of the new-born mammal and its early development that requires parental protection: the aggression at the service of territoriality that protects the sources of nutrition, and the aggressive disposition involved in the competition of males for the possession of females. These biologically anchored instincts have corresponding instinctive dispositions in human beings as well and explain the mechanism of aggression secondary to danger or frustration. But Freud discovered clinical phenomena in which aggression could not be accounted for by mere frustration of the pleasure principle and became an overriding, self-destructive motivation that proved to offer enormous resistances to its modification in psychoanalytic treatment. The clinical experience accumulated, throughout time, on the basis of psychoanalytic practice has added new evidence in support of the prevalence of severely self-destructive psychopathological constellations, indirectly supporting the theory of a death drive.

The phenomena that led Freud to the establishment and, later, to the reinforcement of the hypothesis of the death drive as opposed to a simple aggressive drive include (Freud, 1920g, 1921c, 1923b, 1924c, 1930a):

1. the phenomenon of repetition compulsion;
2. sadism and masochism;

3. negative therapeutic reaction;
4. suicide in severe depression (and in non-depressive charactero-
    logical structures);
5. destructive and self-destructive developments in group processes
    and their social implications.

Let us examine these phenomena.

First, regarding repetition compulsion, the main clinical constellation referred to by Freud in his original proposal: as the
name implies, the patient engages in an endless repetition of the
same—usually destructive—behaviour that resists the interpretation of assumed, and very often well-documented, unconscious
conflicts involved. Originally described as a "resistance of the id",
a somewhat mysterious force from the dynamic unconscious, clinical experience has demonstrated that repetition compulsion may
have multiple functions that have different prognostic implications.
Sometimes it is simply the repetitive working through of a conflict
that demands patience and gradual elaboration; at other times, it
represents the unconscious repetition of a traumatic relationship
with a frustrating or traumatizing object, with the hidden hope that
"this time" the other will gratify the needs and wishes of the patient,
thus being transformed, at last, into the much needed good object.
Many unconscious fixations to traumatic situations have this origin,
although they may sometimes reflect more primitive neurobiological processes. These primitive processes deal with the incessant
rekindling of a very early behavioural chain deeply engrained in
the limbic structures and their neural connections with the prefrontal and preorbital cortex. In many cases of post-traumatic stress
disorder we find that repetition compulsion is an effort to come to
terms with an originally overwhelming situation. If such a repetition compulsion is tolerated and facilitated in the context of a safe
and protective environment, gradual resolution may obtain.

In other cases, however, particularly when post-traumatic stress
syndrome is no longer an active syndrome but operates as an etiological factor behind severe characterological distortions, the repetition compulsion may reflect an effort to overcome the traumatic
situation by an unconscious identification with the source of the
trauma. Here the patient identifies with the perpetrator of the
trauma while projecting on somebody else the function of victim.

It is as if the world had become exclusively a relationship between perpetrators and victims, and the patient repeats, unconsciously, the traumatic situation in an effort to reverse the roles and place somebody else in the role of victim (Kernberg, 1992, 2004b). The unconscious triumph that such a reversal may provide the patient then maintains repetition compulsion endlessly. There are still more malignant cases of repetition compulsion, such as the unconscious effort to destroy a potentially helpful relationship out of an unconscious sense of triumph over the person who tries to help, who is envied for not having suffered what the patient, in his mind, has suffered. It is an unconscious triumph that coincides, of course, at the same time, with the defeat of the patient himself.

André Green, a leading contributor to the exploration of severe psychopathologies, has described the unconscious identification with a "dead mother"—that is, a severely depressed mother who had chronically frustrated the needs for love and dependency of her infant and child. At the same time, such a mother, desperately needed, cannot be abandoned. The patient, in unconscious identification with a fantasied "dead mother", denies the existence of all live relationships in reality as if he himself were dead to the world (Green, 1993a, 1993b).

In patients with severe narcissistic pathology, repetition compulsion may have the function of an active destruction of the passage of time, as an expression of denial of aging and death, combined with the triumphant destruction of the work of the envied therapist. That denial, on the surface, reassures the patient and protects him from the anxiety over his self-destructive avoidance of his life tasks, including the analytic work. It is a manifestation of what Kleinian authors describe as a destructive narcissistic organization (Rosenfeld, 1971). Repetition compulsion, in short, provides clinical support to the theory of a relentless self-destructive motivation, one of the sources of the concept of the death drive (Segal, 1993).

Severe manifestations of sexual sadism and masochism are a second type of a fundamental drive to self-destruct. Cases of sexual perversion—that is, a significant restriction of sexual behaviour to a specific interaction that becomes an indispensable condition for sexual excitement and orgasm—may be linked to a dangerously sadistic or masochistic behaviour, reflected in severe self-injurious or self-mutilating behaviour as a precondition for sexual enjoyment.

In the most severe cases, inordinate cruelty towards others and inordinate cruelty towards the self are often combined. Patients with borderline psychopathology often show severe self-mutilation, cutting, burning, and, in the most severe cases, self-mutilation leading to the loss of limbs as a relentless drive that, at times, causes all therapeutic efforts to fail. The frequent syndrome of anorexia nervosa, particularly in its most severe manifestations, may also correspond to such relentless, irreducible self-destructiveness. The unconscious conflicts of anorectic patients cover a broad spectrum of dynamics: from oedipal rivalry and rebellious protest against mother and unconscious guilt over a girl's developing sexuality to primitive hatred of the patient's own body identified with an extremely sadistic maternal image and the enactment of a self-destructive unconscious omnipotence (Kernberg, 2004d).

One clinical syndrome that is particularly difficult to handle is that of perversity (not sexual perversion). Perversity involves the recruitment of love at the service of aggression: the effort to seduce another person towards love or helpfulness as a trap that will end with the destruction, symbolic or real, in a social and sometimes even in a physical sense, of the person so seduced (Kernberg, 1992). In normal love relations small doses of aggression intensify erotic pleasure. However, under pathological conditions perversity may destroy erotic pleasure and, even more, its object. The mildest cases of all these sadomasochistic developments are found in those patients who, because of unconscious guilt, usually related to profoundly forbidden oedipal urges or unconscious aggression to an early object of their dependency needs, destroy what they received. These developments are easier to understand and to treat; here self-destructiveness has the function of the "price" that must be paid in order to permit a gratifying relationship to develop and does not have the primary function of the destruction of a potentially good relationship.

This brings us to the third type of manifestation of severe self-directed aggression: namely, the negative therapeutic reaction. Freud described one type of negative therapeutic reaction in his clinical observation of patients who appeared to get worse under conditions when they experienced a helpful intervention by the analyst, as an expression of unconscious guilt over being helped (Freud, 1923b). Negative therapeutic reaction out of unconscious guilt is, in effect, the mildest form of this reaction. A much more frequent and more severe, although eminently treatable, form is the negative therapeutic reaction out of unconscious envy of the therapist, which is particularly characteristic of narcissistic patients. It is an expression of a humiliating envy on the part of the narcissistic patient of the therapist's capacity to help him, of the analyst's creativity in his efforts to help the patient.

There is an even more severe form of negative therapeutic reaction, and one that has the unmistakable signs of a highly motivated self-destructiveness: namely, an unconscious identification with an extremely sadistic object, so that it is as if the patient felt that the only real relationship he may have is with someone who destroys him. This dynamic constellation is prevalent in the case of patients presenting severe self-mutilating behaviour. One patient successively cut off segments of fingers of her hands and severed major nerves in one arm: she presented the syndrome of malignant narcissism, and her psychoanalytic psychotherapy was carried out, in part, during extended hospitalizations. She was not psychotic at any point. In the transference, the identification with an extreme aggressive and incestuous paternal image was a dominant element. It is difficult to understand this development from a position of ordinary common sense, but there are patients who relentlessly provoke the analyst until the analyst succumbs to an uncontainable negative countertransference reaction. The analyst, manoeuvred into a countertransference enactment, manifests some negative behaviour to which the patient triumphantly responds with further escalation of his provocative self-destructive behaviour. Very often these treatments end precipitously, leaving the therapist with a sense of impotence, frustration, and guilt feelings. These patients represent severe borderline conditions and what I have described as the syndrome of malignant narcissism—that is, severe narcissistic features, paranoid tendencies, ego-syntonic aggression against self and others, and antisocial behaviour. These patients may utilize the treatment as a perversely gratifying form of self-destruction because they draw others into their deadly self-attacks. One of our patients presenting this syndrome repeatedly consumed rat poison, which interferes with blood clotting, to the extent of provoking severe internal hemorrhages, while she smilingly denied to her therapist and to the staff that she had done so. Even hospitalized, and with the prothrombin time extending by the day, and despite careful searches by the nursing staff, we were not able to control the self-mutilating behaviour and the pleasurable nature with which this patient expressed it, to the extent that, finally, she was transferred to another institution for custodial care.

A fourth type of severe self-destructive impulse is reflected in suicidal urges and behaviour. Freud considered suicidal tendencies in melancholia as another expression of the death drive. He described the essential mechanism of this development as the introjection of an ambivalently loved and lost object that would then draw the aggression towards that object into the ego, which is now identified with the lost object. Although Freud (1917e) had originally explained suicide in melancholia as a result of turning hatred of the lost object inward, after the formulation of his dual drive theory (Freud, 1920) he revised his view in *The Ego and the Id* (Freud, 1923b), stating about melancholia: "What is now holding sway in the super-ego is, as it were, a pure culture of the death instinct, and in fact it often enough succeeds in driving the ego into death, if the latter does not fend off its tyrant in time by the change round into mania" (p. 53).

The work of Melanie Klein showed that such ambivalence is a normal aspect of all love relations (Klein, 1940, 1957). She described the task of the depressive position in overcoming the split between positive, idealized internalized relations with the object and aggressively invested and projected relations with the object of a persecutory type. She described, in short, the normal integration between split-off idealized and paranoid relationships as part of normal development, the depressive position, in contrast to the earlier, splitting-dominated paranoid-schizoid position. This integration, Melanie Klein convincingly proposed, constitutes a normal early developmental phase, repeated in all later mourning processes, so that in all losses there is not only the loss of an external object and the working through of that loss by its internalization, but a reactivation of the depressive position with the working through of ambivalences towards all earlier object losses. In short, normal ambivalence is an unavoidable aspect of all mourning reactions.

It is only under conditions of severe aggressive—particularly unconsciously aggressive—impulses towards the lost object where

the pathology of the depressive position evolves in the form of relentless self-attacks now derived from the internalization of aggressive aspects of the object into the superego and an attack of the self from the superego, and the simultaneous identification of the object with the ego or the self. This combination leads to potentially severely dangerous and very often actualized suicidal tendencies. But we do find such self-destructive suicidal behaviour also in patients who are not depressed—precisely, in severe narcissistic personalities. Here a sense of defeat, failure, humiliation, in essence, the loss of their grandiosity, may bring about not only feelings of extremely devastating shameful defeat and inferiority, but a compensatory sense of triumph over reality by taking their own life, thus demonstrating to themselves and to the world that they are not afraid of pain and death. On the contrary: death emerges as an even elegant abandonment of a depreciated, worthless world (Kernberg, 2007).

We have seen that severe self-destructive psychopathology warrants the clinical assumption of powerful, sometimes uncontrollable self-destructive impulses reflected in the phenomena of repetition compulsion, sadism and masochism, negative therapeutic reaction, and suicide, both in severe depression as well as in other forms of psychopathology. But, in addition, Freud also described severe self-destructiveness as a social phenomenon in the behaviour of large social group processes, in human masses as ideologically united conglomerates, in mutual identification with a grandiose and aggressive leader (Freud, 1921c). In this process, the group projects their individual superego functions onto the group leader, with the consequence of group-sanctioned expression of primitive, ordinarily suppressed impulses, particularly of an aggressive type. A mass movement may coalesce around a drive to search and destroy enemy formations, the sense of power derived from their liberated, now focused aggression, their sense of protected dependency by their allegiance to the leader, and the regression to the most primitive dissociation of object relations into idealized and persecutory ones. This development represented for Freud the activation of severe destructiveness at a social level. The projection of the superego onto the leader, the mutual identification of all participants with that person, as well as the sanctioned expression of aggression are the fundamental explanation for the aggressive behaviour of mass movements and large social structures, applying even to international conflicts. But the aggression activated in regressive group processes may also be channelled onto the group itself, guided by a grandiose, self-destructive leader, ending in a religiously or ideologically rationalized mass suicide.

Freud's theory of mass psychology, dramatically demonstrated in a thousand forms in the mass psychology of the fundamentalist movements of the last century, has been complemented by Bion's (1961) work with small groups of 10–15 individuals and that of Pierre Turquet (1975) and Didier Anzieu (1981) with large groups of 100–150 individuals. I do not have space here to describe in detail all these findings but would summarize them by stating that, when small or large groups are unstructured—that is, without a clear task and its corresponding structure relating that group constructively to its environment—and when, in contrast, the only task of such groups is meeting to study their own reactions for, say, an hour and a half during a sequence of several days or a few weeks, they present striking and similar phenomena. They show the immediate activation of intense anxiety and an effort to escape that anxiety by some soothing *ad hoc* philosophy expounded by a friendly, mediocre, grandfatherly leader who calms the group's anxiety with clichés. When this effort fails, they show a tendency to the development of intense violence, a search for a paranoid leader, the division of the group itself—or its perception of the surrounding social environment—into an idealized and a persecutory one, with active aggression directed against what is perceived as the hostile segment of the world in order to protect the perfection and the security of the ideal group.

Vamik Volkan (2004), who has applied psychoanalytic theory to the study of inter-group and international conflicts, has expanded these observations by systematically studying the nature of the ideal world of fundamentalists groups, the reason for their need to search for and destroy enemies, their strivings to preserve rigid boundaries and the purity of their group, and the obvious connection between these categories and fundamentalist political, racial, and religious movements. In conclusion of this point, there is impressive clinical and sociological evidence for a universal potential for violence in human beings that can be triggered too easily under certain conditions of group regression and corresponding leadership and that may, from the perspective of survival of human societies, be considered as fundamentally self-destructive.

These are the leading clinical arguments in support of Freud's theory of the death drive. Freud also attempted to link it to a biological disposition to self-destruction, tracing a parallel of the psychological attraction of the "nirvana principle" with the physiological mechanisms of self-destruction in biology. In effect, the biological function of apoptosis, the controlled orders for self-destruction of certain cells, may be seen as one illustration of such a biological mechanism. While it may be tempting to explain psychological functions by analogical ones from biology, this runs the risk of reductionism by relating complex phenomena at widely different structural levels to each other. What we do have is the powerful clinical evidence for severe, relentless self-destructiveness in many cases of psychopathology. If anything, the experience over the last 30 years with severe types of character pathology and the borderline conditions has given even further evidence of the fundamental nature of deep self-destructive tendencies in human beings that clinically would support the concept of a death drive.

If we accept that severe self-destructiveness functions as a major motivational system, we may explore, from this perspective, the concept of the death drive. In my view, one solution to this theoretical challenge is a combination of several conclusions. First, if death drive is a designation for the dominant unconscious motivation towards self-destructiveness in severe cases of psychopathology, this concept is, undoubtedly, warranted. Second, severe self-destructive aggression is, however, not a primary tendency, as far as we can tell, but a particularly grave, organized motivational system that is not simply "secondary to trauma", although it may be influenced and stimulated by traumatic experience. Third, the unconscious functions of self-destructiveness are not simply to destroy the self but, very essentially, to destroy significant others as well, be it out of guilt, revenge, envy, or triumph.

Exploring jointly the clinical constellations that reflect most clearly the dominance of self-destructive impulses, they all reveal intrapsychic struggles between internalized sadistic representations of objects and masochistically submitting representations of self. Internalized sadistic object representations may represent both projected and reintrojected aggressive impulses and realistic traumatic experiences, while masochistic self-representation may represent a combination of the erotization of painful traumatic experiences and unconscious guilt-induced expiational suffering. In the case of the repetition compulsion, I have referred to the unconscious identification with the perpetrator and victim of a traumatic past, the unconscious identification with a "dead mother", and the triumph over a potentially helpful yet envied object by destruction of the self. In the cases of sadomasochistic pathology, the strong predominance of aggressive conflicts may turn the internalized relation with a sadistic object into overwhelming self-destructiveness. In the case of negative therapeutic reaction, the spectrum of self-directed aggression may vary from the superego-induced attacks on the self in better integrated patients to the primitive intrapsychic relation with a battering object of dependency. Freud's and Melanie Klein's clarification of the psychopathology of suicidal depression first pointed to the self-destructive consequence of a sadistic superego, so that what is sought in self-destructive motivation is not simply "nirvana", but active destruction of significant libidinal relations with significant others.

In short, aggression as a major motivational system is always present in the mind, based on the integration of primary negative affects, but I propose that it deserves the designation of death drive only when such aggression becomes dominant, when it recruits libidinal impulses such as in the syndrome of perversity, and when its main objective is, to use André Green's (1993a) terms, the achievement of "de-objectalization", the elimination of the representations of all significant others, and, in that context, the elimination of the self as well. The death drive, I propose, is not a primary drive, but represents a significant complication of aggression as a major motivational system, is central in the therapeutic work with severe psychopathology, and as such is eminently useful as a concept in the clinical realm.

What determines whether aggression will be predominantly structured into internalized object relations that direct it externally, or against the individual's own body or mind? Under what circumstances will self-directed aggression become the dominant unconscious motivational system? I believe we have only partial answers to these questions at this time. There is evidence for genetically determined and constitutionally given dominance of negative affect activation and for inadequate cognitive contextualization of affect, expressed in temperamental dispositions that influence the internalization of early object relations. Insecure attachment may significantly contribute to a disposition for predominantly negative affect activation. Traumatic experiences in infancy and childhood and severely disorganized family structures are clearly related to severe personality disorders with self-destructive tendencies (Paris, 2009). But some patients with severe self-destructive tendencies do not evince such a background. Clinically, however, in those latter cases, as well as in the most severe cases of major self-destructiveness, we typically find narcissistic personality disorders, both of the apparently milder, self-assured, grandiose kind and of the most regressed, aggression-infiltrated pathological grandiose self of the syndrome of malignant narcissism (Kernberg, 1992), the cases that Kleinian authors describe as destructive narcissism (Britton, 2003) or pathological organization (Steiner, 1993), and as negative narcissism (Green, 1983) and de-objectalization (Green, 1993a). In short, a combination of intensity of aggressive affect and the particular structuralization of internalized object relations of narcissistic personalities emerges as the leading aspect of the malignant transformation of aggression into a dominant motivation for self-destruction.

The self-destructiveness of melancholia, its superego-determined suicidal tendencies, constitutes a special case, again illustrating the influence of both genetically and environmentally determined hyperreactivity of depressive affect activation and the importance of a particular structuralization of internalized object relations—namely, the pathological superego of these patients (Panksepp, 1998).

This brings us, of course, to the question of the therapeutic implications of this conceptualization: Where do we stand? What has psychoanalysis achieved in this regard? Under the influence of contemporary object relations theory, psychoanalytic structural theory has evolved into the analysis of the building blocks of ego, superego, and id—namely, their constituent internalized relations with significant others that are integrated in the form of primitive, affectively determined representations of self and significant others or objects (Kernberg, 2004c). I have proposed that dyadic representations of self and others, under the dominance of a particular affective valence, are internalized as a parallel series of positive and negative internalized object relations. They consolidate according to their specific function into superego structures when they have a commanding or prohibitive quality, or into ego structures when they correspond to potentially conscious and preconscious identifications and the organization of character formations, and id structures when such internalized object relations correspond to primitive, aggressive or erotic fantasied desired and feared relation with objects that cannot be tolerated in consciousness.

The importance of this reformulation of the psychic structures in terms of the internalization of object relations resides in the fact that in the most primitive types of structures that we find in severe psychopathologies, it is such early split idealized and persecutory object relations that dominate the transferential field rather than the manifestations of mature ego and superego functions, and the treatment has to be centred on the analysis of each of these dyadic units as they emerge in the transference. Regarding our understanding of these psychopathologies, perhaps the greatest advance in recent years has been in the treatment of severe character pathologies, particularly narcissistic and the borderline conditions.

In typical cases of predominantly self-destructive efforts in the transference, behind what appears to be a disdainful rejection and ruthless tearing apart of the analyst's interpretative interventions, the problem is not a simple manifestation of the death drive, but its reflection in an internalized object relation between a sadistic, murderous object representation and a submissive, paralysed representation of self that enters into collusion with the aggressor. It is the collusive aspect of the self that, at first, becomes evident in the patient's manifest ignoring of the analyst's interventions and the lack of concern for himself. The unconscious pleasure in the defeat of the analyst, out of hate or envy, emerges more slowly in the transference situation. The analyst's tolerance of such regressive transferences is the key to their eventual resolution.

Our application of psychoanalytic principles to the descriptive and structural characteristics of these patients has permitted a clearer indication of differential treatments based on a psychoanalytic modality.

It is important to diagnose early syndromes in which severe self-destructive aggression may dominate. These include particularly the syndrome of the "dead mother", which I referred to, and the syndrome of malignant narcissism; cases with severe ego-syntonic aggression manifest in arrogance, perversity, and identification with a sadistic superego, as well as self-destructive behaviour that affects patients' survival in their social environment (Kernberg, 1992, 2004b, 2007). With these cases, it would seem essential to analyse the developments of such self-aggressive tendencies in the transference from the very beginning of the treatment, with particular attention paid to tendency to destroy what is provided by the analyst, and to whatever hope the patient may have for the survival of the therapist in spite of the patient's aggression. It may become important to structure the treatment, in the sense of ensuring the stability of its boundaries. We have learned how to prevent severe physical acting out of aggression that would threaten the treatment boundaries by careful initial contract setting, and to analyse any countertransferential deviation from technical neutrality—that is, from the normal attitude of concerned objectivity of the analyst as a result of intensively hostile transferences.

It may become particularly important to explore the pleasure in the patient's aggression against the self and others. In this regard, we might say that the death drive is not inconsistent with the pleasure principle, as evidenced by the triumphant pleasure these patients get in defeating all efforts to help them. I have suggested in earlier work (Kernberg, 1992) that it is important to transform psychopathic transferences in which the patient manifests dishonesty or dangerous withholding, and perverse transferences in which the patient tries to recruit the benign efforts of the therapist for malignant purposes. We have to transform these psychopathic transferences into paranoid ones—that is, to analyse why the patient has to behave in a deceptive way to avoid deep fear and suspicion of the analyst, on to whom such aggressive impulses are projected. Full development of paranoid transferences is the first step towards a gradual recognition of the projection, the acknowledgement of the origin of aggression in oneself, and the development of depressive transferences—that is, transferences in which, under the influence of the development of guilt feelings related to the recognition of his own aggression, the patient may be able to integrate and elaborate his aggressive tendencies.

In some cases one needs to be alert to an absence both of affects and of representations in what may appear to be "pure" affects, so that both affect storms, on the one hand, and an apparent total absence of affect on the other have to be explored systematically to unveil the underlying activated object relations. Some cases with extended therapeutic stalemates are in reality deadly repetitions of self-destructive efforts to escape conflicts and to deny the passage of time. There are times where, under the influence of extreme aggressive impulses and their projection, the reality testing of the patient decreases. The patient may develop micro-psychotic episodes in the sessions, and it may become important for the analyst to spell out the existence of incompatible realities in which patient and analyst live and how to understand them and resolve them.

In short, an object relations perspective on the predominance of severely self-destructive transferences has provided analytic tools to treat such patients and has, we might say, become a major front on the struggle to apply psychoanalytic principles to this area of most challenging and prognostically reserved cases. Whether the growing psychoanalytic understanding of aggressive and self-aggressive behaviour of large groups and its relation to regressive processes in the social realm will lead to a contribution to their prevention and management remains to be seen. In conclusion, Freud's dramatic concept of the death drive may not reflect an inborn disposition as such, but it is eminently relevant in clinical practice.

7

Addiction to near-death

Betty Joseph

There is a very malignant type of self-destructiveness, which we see in a small group of our patients and which is, I think, in the nature of an addiction—an addiction to near-death. It dominates these patients' lives; for long periods it dominates the way they bring material to the analysis and the type of relationship they establish with the analyst; it dominates their internal relationships, their so-called thinking, and the way they communicate with themselves. It is not a drive towards a Nirvana type of peace or relief from problems, and it has to be sharply differentiated from this.

The picture that these patients present is, I am sure, a familiar one: in their external lives these patients get more and more absorbed into hopelessness and involved in activities that seem destined to destroy them physically as well as mentally—for example, considerable over-working, almost no sleep, avoiding eating properly or secretly over-eating if the need is to lose weight, drinking more and more, and perhaps cutting off from relationships. In other patients this type of addiction is probably less striking in their actual living but equally important in their relationship with the analyst and the analysis. Indeed, in all these patients the place where the pull towards near-death is most obvious is in the transference. As I want to illustrate in this chapter, these patients bring material to analysis in a very particular way: for example, they may speak in a way that seems calculated to communicate or create despair and a sense of hopelessness in themselves and in the analyst, although apparently wanting understanding. It is not just that they make progress, forget it, lose it, or take no responsibility for it. They do show a strong though frequently silent negative therapeutic reaction, but this negative therapeutic reaction is only one part of a much broader and more insidious picture. The pull towards despair and death in such patients is not, as I have said, a longing for peace and freedom from effort; indeed, as I sorted out with one such patient, just to die, although attractive, would be no good. There is a felt need to know and to have the satisfaction of seeing oneself being destroyed.

So I am stressing here that a powerful masochism is at work, and these patients will try to create despair in the analyst and then get him to collude with the despair or become actively involved by being harsh, critical, or in some way or another verbally sadistic to the patient. If they succeed in getting themselves hurt or in creating despair, they triumph, since the analyst has lost his analytic balance or his capacity to understand and help and then both patient and analyst go down into failure. At the same time the analyst will sense that there is real misery and anxiety around, and this will have to be sorted out and differentiated from the masochistic use and exploitation of misery.

The other area that I am going to discuss as part of this whole constellation is that of the patient's internal relationships and a particular type of communication with himself—because I believe that in all such patients one will find a type of mental activity consisting of a going over and over again about happenings or anticipations of an accusatory or self-accusatory type in which the patient becomes completely absorbed.

I have described in this introduction the pull of the death instincts, the pull towards near-death, a kind of mental or physical brinkmanship in which the seeing of the self in this dilemma, unable to be helped, is an essential aspect. It is, however, important also to consider where the pull towards life and sanity is. I believe that this part of the patient is located in the analyst, which accounts, in part, for the patient's apparent extreme passivity and indifference. This I shall return to later.

It will be seen that much that I have outlined in this introduction has already been described in the analytic literature. For example, Freud (1924c) discusses the working of the death instinct in masochism and distinguishes the nature of the inner conflict in a negative therapeutic reaction from that seen in moral masochism. He adds at the end of the essay, "even the subject's destruction of himself cannot take place without libidinal satisfaction". In the patients that I am describing it seems to me that the near-destruction of the self takes place with considerable libidinal satisfaction, however much the concomitant pain. The main additional aspects, however, that I want to discuss are: the way in which these problems make themselves felt in the transference and in the patient's internal relationships and his thinking, and the deeply addictive nature of this type of masochistic constellation and the fascination and hold on them that it has. Later I want to add a note on some possible aspects of the infantile history of these patients. I shall start by getting into the middle of the problem by bringing a dream.

This dream comes from a patient who is typical of this group. He started analysis many years ago, and was then cold, rather cruel, loveless, highly competent, intelligent, articulate, and successful in his work—but basically very unhappy. During the treatment he had become much warmer, was struggling to build real relationships, and had become deeply but ambivalently emotionally involved with a gifted but probably disturbed young woman. This was a very important experience for him. He was also now deeply attached to the analysis, although he did not speak of it, did not acknowledge it, was often late, and seemed not to notice or be aware of almost anything about me as a human being. He often had sudden feelings of great hatred towards me.

I am going to bring a dream from a Wednesday. On the Monday he had consolidated the work we had been doing on a particular type of provocation and cruelty silently achieved. By the end of the session he had seemed relieved and in good contact. But on the Tuesday he phoned just at the time of the end of his session and said that he had only just woken up. He sounded very distressed but said that he had hardly slept in the night and would be here the following day. When he arrived on Wednesday, he spoke about the Monday, how surprised he was that following the better feeling in the session he had felt so terrible and tense physically, in his stomach, and in every way on the Monday night. He had felt much warmer towards K, the girlfriend, and really wanted to see her, but she was out for the evening. She said she would phone him when she got back, but she didn't, so he must have been lying awake getting into a bad state. He also knew that he very much wanted to get to analysis, and he expressed a strong positive feeling that he felt was emerging since the last session. He had found the work we had done during the Monday session very convincing and a real culmination of the work of the last period of analysis. He altogether sounded unusually appreciative and absolutely puzzled about the complete sense of breakdown, sleeplessness, and the missing of the Tuesday session.

When he was describing the pain and misery of the Monday night, he said that he was reminded of the feeling that he had expressed at the beginning of the Monday session: the feeling that perhaps he was too far into this awful state ever to be helped out by me or to get out himself. At the same time during and immediately after the session there had been feelings of insight and more hope.

He then told a dream:

He was in a long kind of cave, almost a cavern. It was dark and smoky, and it was as if he and other people had been taken captive by brigands. There was a feeling of confusion, as if they had been drinking. They, the captives, were lined up along a wall, and he was sitting next to a young man. This man was subsequently described as looking gentle, in the mid-twenties, with a small moustache. The man suddenly turned towards him, grabbed at him and at his genitals, as if he were homosexual, and was about to knife my patient, who was completely terrified. He knew that if he tried to resist the man would knife him, and there was tremendous pain.

After telling the dream, he went on to describe some of the happenings of the last two days. He particularly spoke first about K. He then spoke about a meeting he had been to, in which a business acquaintance had said that a colleague told him that he, the colleague, was so frightened of my patient, A, that he positively trembled when on the phone to him. My patient was amazed but linked this with something that I had shown him on the Monday, when I had commented on a very cold, cruel way in which he dealt with me when I queried a point about another dream. This association was connected with the idea of the man in the dream looking so gentle but acting in this violent way, and so he felt that the man must somehow be connected with himself, but what about the moustache? Then suddenly he had the notion of D. H. Lawrence—he had been reading a new biography of Lawrence and remembered that he was enormously attracted to him in his adolescence and felt identified with him. Lawrence was a bit homosexual and clearly a strange and violent man.

I worked out with him that it seemed therefore that this long, dark cavern stood for the place where he had felt he was too far in to be pulled out by himself or by me; as if it was his mind, but perhaps also part of his body. But the too-far-in seems to be linked with the notion that he was completely captured and captivated, possibly, by the brigands. But the brigands are manifestly associated with himself, the little man linked with Lawrence, who is experienced as part of himself. We can also see that the giving-in to this brigand is absolutely terrifying, it is a complete nightmare, and yet sexually exciting. The man grabs his genitals.

Here I need to interpose—I had been impressed for some time about the pull of despair and self-destructiveness in this man and one or two other patients with similar difficulties, and was driven to conclude that the actual despair, or the describing of it in the session, contained real masochistic excitement, concretely experienced. We can see it in the way these patients go over and over their unhappinesses, failures, things they feel they ought to feel guilty about. They talk as if they are attempting unconsciously to pull the analyst into concurring with the misery or with the descriptions or they unconsciously try to make the analyst give critical or disturbing interpretations. This becomes a very important pattern in the way that they speak. It is familiar to us and has been well described in the literature (Meltzer, 1973; Rosenfeld, 1971; Steiner, 1982) that such patients feel in thrall to a part of the self that dominates and imprisons them and will not let them escape, even though they see life beckoning outside, as expressed in my patient's dream, out-side the cavern. The point I want to add here is that the patient's experience of sexual gratification in being in such pain, in being dominated, is one of the major reasons for the grip that the drive towards death has on him. These patients are literally "enthralled" by it. In this patient A, for example, no ordinary pleasure, genital, sexual, or other, offered such delight as this type of terrible and exciting self-annihilation which annihilates also the object and is basic to his important relationships to a greater or less extent.

So, I think the dream is clearly a response, not just to the girl-friend K being out on the Monday night and A lying in bed getting more and more disturbed about it, of which he was conscious, but to the fact that he had felt better, knew he had, and could not al-low himself to get out of his misery and self-destruction—the long cavern—or allow me to help him out. He was forced back by a part of himself, essentially sadomasochistic, which operated also as a negative therapeutic reaction, and which used the distress about the girlfriend as fuel. I also stressed here, and shall return to, his triumph over me when our work and the hope of the last weeks is knocked down and he and I go under.

I am discussing here, therefore, that it is not only that he is dom-inated by an aggressive part of himself, which attempts to control and destroy my work, but that this part is actively sadistic towards another part of the self that is masochistically caught up in this process, and that this has become an addiction. This process has al-ways, I believe, an internal counterpart, and in patients really dedi-cated to self-destructiveness, this internal situation has a very strong hold over their thinking and their quiet moments, their capacity for mulling things over or the lack of it. The kind of thing that one sees is this. These patients pick up very readily something that has been going on in their minds or in an external relationship and start to use it over and over again in some circular type of mental activity, in which they get completely caught up, so that they go over and over with very little variation the same actual or anticipated issue. This mental activity, which I think is best described by the word "chuntering", is very important. The *Compact Oxford English Dictionary* describes chuntering as "mutter, murmur, grumble, find fault, complain". To give an example, A, in the period when I was trying to explore in him this dedication to masochism, described one day how he had been upset the previous evening because K had been going out with somebody else. He realized that on the previous evening he had, in his mind, been rehearsing what he might say to K about this. For example, he would talk about how he could not go on like this with her, while she was going around with another man; how he would have to give up the whole relationship; he could not go on like this, and so on. As he went on speaking about what he was planning to say to K, I got the feeling, not only from the ideas, but from his whole tone, that he was not just thinking what he might say to K but was caught up in some kind of active cruel dialogue with her. Slowly then he clarified the ideas that he had had, and how he had been going over things in his mind. On this occasion and indeed on others, he realized that he would be saying something cruel, for example, and that K in the fantasy would reply or cry or plead or cling, she would become provocative, he would get cruel back, and so on. In other words, what he then called "thinking about what he would say" is actually actively being caught up in his mind in a provocative sadomasochistic fantasy in which he both hurts and is hurt, verbally repeats and is humiliated, until the fantasy activity has such a grip on him that it almost has a life of its own and the content becomes secondary. In such cases, unless I could begin to be aware of the problem of their being caught up in these fantasies and start to draw my patients' attention to them, these fantasies would not come into the analysis, although in some way or other they are conscious. Patients who get so caught up in these activities, chuntering, tend to believe that they are thinking at such times, but of course they are living out experiences, which becomes the complete antithesis of thought.

Another patient, when we had finally managed to open up very clearly the enormous importance and sadistic grip that such going over and over in his mind had on him, told me that he felt that he probably spent two thirds of his free time absorbed in such activities; then in the period when he was trying to give them up, he felt that he had almost too much free time on his hands and had a vague feeling of let-down or disillusionment as he began to do without them, the sense of let-down coming from the relinquishing of the exciting pain of this internal dialogue.

My point about the circular mental activities being the antithesis of thought is, of course, important in the analytic situation. I am stressing that the internal dialogue, the chuntering, is lived out in the analytic dialogue as well as in these patients' lives. Such patients use a great deal of analytic time apparently bringing material to be analysed and understood, but actually unconsciously for other purposes. We are all familiar with the kind of patient who talks in such a way as—they hope unconsciously—to provoke the analyst to be disturbed, repetitive, reproachful, or actually critical. This can then be used by the silently watchful masochistic part of the patient to beat himself with, and an external "difficulty" can be established in the analysis and perpetuated internally, during the session, with the patient silent and apparently hurt; or outside in an internal dialogue. We can then see that it is not "understanding" that the patient wants, though the words are presented as if it were so. These self-destructive patients appear very often to be passive in their lives, as on one level did A, and a very important step is taken when they can see how active they are, by projective identification, for example through the kind of provocation that I am describing or in their thinking and fantasy. But there are other ways of expressing this type of self-destructiveness in the analysis. For example, some patients present "real" situations, but in such a way as silently and extremely convincingly to make the analyst feel quite hopeless and despairing. The patient appears to feel the same. I think we have here a type of projective identification in which despair is so effectively loaded into the analyst that he seems crushed by it and can see no way out. The analyst is then internalized in this form by the patient, who becomes caught up in this internal crushing and crushed situation, and paralysis and deep gratification ensue.

Two issues arise from all this: first, that this type of patient usually finds it very difficult to see and to acknowledge the awful pleasure that is achieved in this way; and, second, I believe it is technically extremely important to be clear as to whether the patient is telling us about and communicating to us real despair, depression, or fear and persecution, which he wants us to understand and to help him with, or whether he is communicating it in such a way as primarily to create a masochistic situation in which he can become caught up. If this distinction is not clearly made in the analysis from moment to moment, one cannot analyse adequately the underlying deep anxieties because of the whole masochistic overlay and the use that is being made of this. Further, I think that one needs to distinguish very clearly between the masochistic use of anxieties that I am discussing and dramatization. I am here describing something much more malignant and much more desperate to the personality than dramatization.

I want now to bring an example to illustrate further this connection between actual anxieties and the exploitation of anxieties for masochistic purposes, and that between genuinely persecuted feelings and the building up of a kind of pseudo-paranoia for masochistic purposes. I shall bring material from the patient A in a period when he was in great distress. It had been indicated to him that he would be likely to be promoted to a very senior position in the firm where he worked, but he got into a bad relationship with a principal man—himself probably a difficult and tormenting person. For a period of about two years things quietly deteriorated, until there was a major reorganization in which he was to be demoted. He was deeply disturbed and decided he would almost certainly have to leave rather than be put in an inferior position. It should, however, be remembered that in his position there would be no likelihood of his having difficulty in finding other high-grade and financially rewarding work.

> I bring a session from a Monday at this time. The patient came in most distressed, then remembered he had not brought his cheque, but would bring it the following day; then described the happenings of the weekend and his talk with his principal on Friday and how worried he felt about his job. K, his girlfriend, had been helpful and kind, but he felt sexually dead and as if she was wanting sex from him, which became rather horrifying. Then he queried, "was he trying to be cruel to her?"—already that question has something a bit suspect about it, as if I was supposed to agree that he was trying to be cruel to her and get caught up in some kind of reproaching of him, so that the

question became in itself masochistic rather than thoughtful.
He then brought a dream. In the dream,

> *he was in an old-fashioned shop, at a counter, but he was small, about
> the height of the counter. There was someone behind it, a shop assistant.
> She was by a ledger but was holding his hand. He was asking her, "was
> she a witch?" as if wanting a reply, persistently asking, almost as if he
> wanted to hear from her that she was a witch. He felt she was getting
> fed up with him and would withdraw her hand. There were rows of
> people somewhere in the dream and a vague feeling of being blamed for
> something he had done. In the shop a horse was being shod but with a
> piece of white plastic-looking material, about the shape and the size of
> the material one would put on the heel of a man's shoe.*

In his associations he spoke about his anxiety about his relationship with K at the moment and his sexuality. He was the height
of a child in the dream. He had tremendous feelings of panic
and anxiety at night. What would he do? Would he really run
out of money, and what would happen to his whole position?
We spoke about the realities of this a bit more.

He had seen a lot of horses being shod as a child and well remembered the smell of the iron going into the horse's hoof.
He spoke about his guilt about the situation that he felt he had
helped to create at work, and he realized that he must actually
have acted very arrogantly with his principal and that this had
probably really helped to bring the ceiling down on him.

I linked the ledger with the forgotten cheque and his anxiety
about finances. He is worried about his lack of sexual interest
at the moment, but he seems to want me to be nasty about
the cheque, and K about his lack of libido. In the dream he
wanted the woman to say that she was a witch, and this attitude
appears to be an old story, since he is the height of a child.
The guilt, I believe, is not just about his faulty handling of his
work situation, his arrogance and harsh attitude, which has really led to serious work problems, but this is used both in his
mind and actively in the transference in an attempt to draw me
into agreement with his despair, to criticize his arrogance in his
relationship with K and to shatter him and create utter despair
and a sense of uselessness in both of us. This is the masochistic

use of anxiety in his mind and in the session. We can then see something about the sexualized excitement, of a very cruel kind, that he gets in this attitude by looking at the associations to the shoeing of the horse. There is the picture of a burning iron being put into the horse's foot and the fascination and horror of this as a child, feeling that it is bound to hurt, though in fact one subsequently knows it doesn't. So I could then show him the indulgence in a tremendously masochistic attitude that was going on visibly in the dream, currently in the session, as misery, despair and pseudo-paranoia were being built up. There is almost a fragment of insight in this dream, as when he demands that the woman tell him if she is a witch, and vaguely he knows that he hopes that she will agree that she is. As we went over this, he began to see it again very clearly, and his whole attitude became more thoughtful and quiet, as opposed to desperate and hopeless. He slowly added that, of course, there is the problem that this kind of sexual excitement and horror seems so great that nothing else can be so important and exciting to him. Now, when he said this, at first there was clearly a sense of insight and truth about, but then there began to be a different feeling in the session, as if he really meant that there was nothing one could do about it. Even the insight began to contain a different message. So I showed him that there was not only insight, not only anxiety and despair about being so much caught up in this kind of masturbatory excitement, but now there was also a triumph and a kind of sadistic jab at me, as if he were digging a burning iron into my heart to make me feel that nothing we were achieving was really worth anything and nothing could be done. Once again he could see this, and so it was possible to link the desperate sexualized masochistic excitement with the triumphant doing down of his object, external and internal.

I have tried to show in this example how this masochistic excitement was covering up at that time deep anxieties stirred up by A's work situation, connected with feelings of rejection, being unwanted, failure, and guilt. But it is only possible to get through to them if the masochistic use, exploitation, is first dealt with. If one does not do this, then one gets a situation that is so common with these patients: that interpretations may appear to be listened to, but some part of the patient's personality will treat the analyst with contempt, with sneering, and with mockery, though the mockery and contempt will be silent.

But we are still left with a major problem as to why this type of masochistic self-destruction is so self-perpetuating—why it has such a grip on this type of patient. One reason that I have discussed in this chapter—the sheer unequalled sexual delight of the grim masochism—is undeniable, yet it is usually very difficult and it takes a long time for such patients to see that they are suffering from an addiction, that they are "hooked" to this kind of self-destruction. With A, by the time we reached the dream about the sexual assault in the cavern, we had worked through a lot of this, and he felt consciously that he was in the grip of an addiction from which he believed he would like to be free. But he felt that the part of him that would like to be freed was nothing like as powerful, nor were the possible results as attractive as was the pull of his addiction. And this he could not understand.

This problem needs considering from the angle of these patients' passivity that I mentioned at the beginning of the chapter when I described how the pull towards life and sanity seems to be split off and projected into the analyst. One can see this in the transference, in severe cases, going on sometimes over years, roughly like this. The patient comes, talks, dreams, and so on, but one gets the impression of very little real active interest in changing, improving, remembering, getting anywhere with the treatment. Slowly the picture builds up. The analyst seems to be the only person in the room who is actively concerned about change, about progress, about development—as if all the active parts of the patient have been projected into the analyst. If the analyst is not aware of this and therefore does not concentrate his interpretations around this process, then a collusion can arise in which the analyst carefully, maybe tactfully, pushes, tries to get the patient's interest or to alert him. The patient briefly responds, only quietly to withdraw again and leave the next move to the analyst, and a major piece of psychopathology is acted out in the transference. The patient is constantly pulling back towards a silent kind of deadly paralysis and near-complete passivity. When these lively parts of the patient remain so constantly split off, it means that his whole capacity for wanting and appreciating, missing, feeling disturbed at losing, and so on: the very stuff that makes for real whole-object relating is projected, and the patient remains with his addiction and without the psychological means of combating this. To me, therefore, the understanding of the nature of this apparent passivity is technically of primary importance with these patients. Moreover, it means that with such splitting-off of the life instincts and of loving, ambivalence and guilt is largely evaded. As these patients improve and begin to become more integrated and relationships become more real, they begin to feel acute pain, sometimes experienced as almost physical—undifferentiated but extremely intense.

I think it is often at these periods of analysis, when concern and pain near to guilt begin to be experienced, that one can see a quick regression to earlier masochistic methods of avoiding pain linked essentially with infantile and childhood behaviour. To give a very brief example

> A, following a good analytic experience, had a dream in which *his mother, dead or near dead, was lying on a slab or couch, and he, to his horror, was pulling off bits of sunburnt skin from one side of her face and eating them.*

I think that instead of becoming aware of, and guilty about, the spoiling of the good experience, he is showing here how he again becomes identified with his damaged object by eating it up, and it is also important to see the link between the painful exciting physical horror and his earlier nail-biting and skin-tearing, which is familiar to us.

Freud, of course, describes this process of identification in "Mourning and Melancholia" (1917e), and he also adds, "the self tormenting in melancholia . . . is without doubt enjoyable. . . ." (p. 251). Despite certain important similarities, the patients that I am describing are not "melancholic"—their guilt and self-reproach being so much evaded or swallowed up by their masochism.

My impression is that as infants, these patients, because of their pathology, have not just turned away from frustrations or jealousies or envies into a withdrawn state, nor have they been able to rage and yell at their objects. I think they have withdrawn into a secret world of violence, where part of the self has been turned against another part, parts of the body being identified with parts of the offending object, and that this violence has been highly sexualized, masturbatory in nature, and often physically expressed. One sees it, for example, in head-banging, digging nails into fists, pulling at one's own hair and twisting and splitting it until it hurts, and this is what we are still seeing in the verbal chuntering that goes on and on. As one gets into this area and these patients are able to recognize, usually at first with great difficulty and resentment, the excitement and pleasure they get from these apparent self-attacks, they can usually show us their own particular personal predilection. One of my young male patients of this group was still pulling at and splitting his hair when he was well into his analysis. Another, an older man, who spoke of the amount of time used up by his chuntering, used, in times of great disturbance, to lie on the floor drinking and putting on his radio as loud as possible, as if caught up in a wild orgy of rhythmical bodily experience. It seems to me that instead of moving forward and using real relationships, contact with people or with bodies, as infants, they apparently retreated into themselves and lived out their relationships in this sexualized way, in fantasy or fantasy expressed in violent bodily activity. This deeply masochistic state, then, has a hold on the patient that is much stronger than the pull towards human relationships. Sometimes this is to be seen as an aspect of an actual perversion, in others it is part of a character perversion.

It will be seen that in this chapter I have not attempted to discuss the defensive value of the addiction, but there is one aspect of this problem that I would like to mention before ending. It has something to do with torture and survival. None of the patients whom I have in mind as particularly belonging to this addictive group have really very seriously bad childhood histories, though psychologically in a sense they almost certainly have—as, for example, a lack of warm contact and real understanding, and sometimes a very violent parent. Yet in the transference one gets the feeling of being driven up to the edge of things, as I indicated, and both patient and analyst feel tortured. I get the impression from the difficulty these patients experience in waiting and being aware of gaps and aware of even the simplest type of guilt that such potentially depressive experiences have been felt by them in infancy as terrible pain that goes over into torment, and that they have tried to alleviate this by taking over the torment, the inflicting of mental pain, on to themselves and building it into a world of perverse excitement, and this necessarily militates against any real progress towards the depressive position.

It is very hard for our patients to find it possible to abandon such terrible delights for the uncertain pleasures of real relationships.

8

Manifestations of the death instinct in the consulting room

Michael Feldman

In his paper on "The "Uncanny", Freud wrote,

> ... It is possible to recognize the dominance in the uncon-
> scious mind of a "compulsion to repeat" proceeding from the
> instinctual impulses and probably inherent in the very nature
> of the instincts—a compulsion powerful enough to overrule the
> pleasure principle, leading to certain aspects of the mind *their
> daemonic character.* [Freud, 1919h, p. 238; emphasis added]

In *Beyond the Pleasure Principle* (1920g), Freud continued this exploration of the forces that drive and maintain certain striking
patterns of behaviour, where the more obvious aims of the relief of
tension or "unpleasure" and the achievement of "pleasure" do not
seem to apply. Freud, the astute clinician, struggled to account for
the fact that "The compulsion to repeat ... recalls from the past
experiences which include no possibility of pleasure, and which can
never, even long ago, have brought satisfaction even to instinctual
impulses which have since been repressed" (p. 20). He linked such
observations with dreams in traumatic neuroses and the impulse
that leads children to play certain repetitive games. He raised the

question of whether the child's repetition of the unpleasant experience of play carried "a yield of pleasure of another sort *but none the less a direct one*" (italics added) (p. 16).

In keeping with his interest in the theoretical model of instinctual drives, Freud attributed to the compulsion to repeat the characteristics of an instinct, linking it in particular, for the first time, with the death instinct. Throughout the paper he moved between his clinical observations and his speculations about fundamental biological forces present in all living creatures.

Freud seems to me to have been very aware of the limitations of our understanding of the nature of the *psychological* forces involved in these obscure and disturbing human impulses and behaviour that he had observed. Indeed, he writes about people feeling "an obscure fear—a dread of rousing something that, so they feel, is better left sleeping—what they are afraid of at bottom is the emergence of this compulsion with its hint of possession by some 'daemonic' power" (p. 35).

Some ten years after the publication of *Beyond the Pleasure Principle*, Freud summarized the theoretical position he had arrived at in the following way:

> Starting from speculations on the beginning of life and from biological parallels, I drew the conclusion that, besides the instinct to preserve living substance and to join it into ever larger units, there must exist another, contrary instinct seeking to dissolve those units and to bring them back to their primeval, inorganic state. That is to say, as well as Eros there was an instinct of death. The phenomena of life could be explained from the concurrent or mutually opposing action of these two instincts. It was not easy, however, to demonstrate the activities of this supposed death instinct. The manifestations of Eros were conspicuous and noisy enough. It might be assumed that the death instinct operated silently within the organism towards its dissolution, but that, of course, was no proof. A more fruitful idea was that a portion of the instinct is diverted towards the external world and comes to light as an instinct of aggressiveness and destructiveness. In this way the instinct itself could be pressed into the service of Eros, in that the organism was destroying some other thing, whether animate or inanimate, instead of destroying its own self. [Freud, 1930a, pp. 118–119]

In her discussion of the conflict between the life and death instincts, Segal points out that in the individual's response to needs
there can be two reactions: "One, to seek satisfaction for the needs:
that is life-promoting and leads to object seeking, love, and eventually object concern. The other is the drive to annihilate: the need
to annihilate the perceiving experiencing self, as well as anything
that is perceived" (Segal, 1997, p. 18).

Freud envisaged a primary drive that remains mute and hidden, silently driving the individual towards death. The gratification of this basic instinctual drive would be the annihilation of
the self. However, the clinical phenomena he encountered forced
him to postulate that this drive was always partly "fused" with the
life instinct, resulting in what Segal has described as a variety of
"compromises", with the accompanying libidinization and equali-
zation we observe clinically. She suggests that it is when these "fu-
sions" or "compromises" fail that the death instinct triumphs and
the instinctual wish is fulfilled in the actual destruction of the self
(Segal, 1997).

It is not difficult to appreciate the power of a theoretical model
of the human psyche permanently subject to a struggle between the
basic instincts of life and death. In keeping with this model, we can
almost always find evidence of a force within the patient, defending him against the full expression of the death instinct—namely,
physical and psychic annihilation. Nevertheless, I believe Freud
continued to struggle to evolve a satisfactory psychological model
of the death instinct. As a reflection of the difficulties inherent in
the concept, it has remained controversial, and the debate concerning its philosophical status and its clinical usefulness continues.

In this chapter I wish to use the clinical phenomena encountered in our patients to reconsider the nature and aims of the
drive, which he termed *Todestriebe*, that Freud found it necessary
to postulate; however, as he acknowledged in the quotation above,
"It was not easy . . . to demonstrate the activities of this supposed
death instinct" (1930a, p. 119). I believe our clinical research does
indeed point to the fundamental importance of a destructive drive.
However, it seems to me that the gratification of this psychological
drive does not lie in the annihilation of the perceiving and experiencing self, or indeed in literal death or annihilation. On the
contrary, what is often clinically more compelling is the extent to

which certain patients, rather than seeking to annihilate their perceiving selves, attack and distort their capacities for perception and judgement, incorporating their distorted perceptions into ways of structuring their experience that gratify deep destructive impulses. A precondition for the gratification of this drive is the survival of both the patient and his object, but severely reduced and undermined. The aim seems to be largely, but not entirely, to eliminate anything that gives rise to admiration, dependence, rivalry, and particularly envy, in ways I hope to describe.

Indeed when, in 1937, Freud returned to his theory of the death instinct to further his understanding of deep-seated resistances against analytic treatment, he wrote: "No stronger impression arises from the resistances during the work of analysis than of there being a force which is defending itself by every possible means against recovery and which is absolutely resolved to hold on to illness and suffering" (Freud, 1937c, p. 242).

Rosenfeld suggests that while a wish to die or to withdraw into a state of nothingness resembles Freud's description of the unfused death instinct: "On detailed clinical examination we find that the death instinct cannot be observed in its original form, since it always becomes manifest as a destructive process directed against objects and the self. These processes seem to operate in their most virulent form in severe narcissistic conditions" (Rosenfeld, 1971, p. 169).

I believe that these are manifestations of the same force that Freud referred to in his 1937 paper, where he described the patient's apparent determination not to die but to hold on to illness and suffering. These studies by Segal and Rosenfeld represent important further research into the disturbing, even frightening psychological phenomena that Freud had identified in his earlier work, which he was so concerned to account for in terms of universal biological forces.

What I want to discuss, therefore, is the value of the original concept of the death instinct, the aim of which is the total destruction of the self. Certainly, examples are quoted of extreme situations in which someone actually seems impelled towards death. It follows from the nature of these particular situations that they are difficult to study, and our knowledge of them is inevitably incomplete. The question I am raising is whether, on the basis of the clinical phenomena we have been able to investigate in depth, what we encounter clinically are not derivatives or compromises, "fused" or "bound" with life instinct, but the direct expression of a primary destructive drive directed towards the self and others. In my view, it is striking that when we examine its manifestations, we find that this drive does not actually seem to be directed to death, although threats of death or annihilation and a fascination with omnipotent destruction may contribute to its power and addictive hold on the individual and to its destructive impact on any analytic work. We are often aware of the conscious gratification the patient obtains from attacking and distorting the meaning and value both of the analyst's thinking and of his work, as well as his own capacities for thought and creativity, although the gratification is often unconscious. Klein developed a powerful explanatory model to account for these phenomena, which she regarded as usually driven by a deadly envious process, the aim of which is to spoil and devalue, rendering everything the same and therefore useless. In a certain sense, of course, these activities are murderous and suicidal, but I am suggesting their primary aim is not totally to destroy life, but to take the life out. I hope to discuss these points further in relation to the clinical illustrations that follow.

Segal (1997) describes a patient, Mrs A, who, shortly before a break, complained of her own passivity and brought material into the session that was fragmented and persecutory. When Segal related the patient's state of mind to the forthcoming break, the patient immediately expressed her violent hatred of last sessions and her wish to press a button and make the last session disappear. Segal connected this with earlier material where the patient had spoken of her fears of nuclear war and her concern with whose finger was on the button. Segal interpreted that the patient's response to the impending separation was a wish to annihilate everything. The patient acknowledged this, relaxed, and the atmosphere of the session changed. She said she wouldn't mind a nuclear war—indeed she might even wish for it, if she and her child would die immediately. She couldn't bear the thought of surviving in a post-nuclear-war world—"perpetual fall-out and all".

Although the patient articulates phantasies and wishes for total annihilation, I believe the analyst is confronted with a situation in which the patient is already caught up in the living out of her violent destructiveness. This was being expressed not by a single obliterating explosion, but by multiple, dispersed attacks on her own mind and body, as well as the analyst's work—in small packets of "fall-out". The patient feels driven to sustain such attacks, which do not totally destroy her capacities for perception and experience. These attacks are not just defensive in nature but seem to provide gratification of a powerful need that is predicated upon phantasies of the individual's psychic survival.

The patient claims that her nightmare is surviving, with her mind intact, in a world of endless devastation. The total obliteration of herself and her child would, by contrast, be a relief—completely curing her of the anxiety and pain of living and her awareness of separations. However, from Segal's description of the patient, it does seem at times that she is already living in a tormenting, fragmented world full of devastation and persecution. I suspect that this is not only an experience the patient suffers in a helpless and passive way and seeks to obliterate. On the contrary, I assume Mrs A derived a good deal of open or hidden gratification from the phantasy of the possession of such omnipotent destructive power, seeking also by this means to avoid the problems of dependency and loss and rendering the analyst and the meaning of her work useless. It is indeed often possible to recognize the active role the patient's finger plays in sustaining such a world, the awful gratification derived from inhabiting it, and drawing the analyst into it. However, in the session that Segal describes, it seems that the analyst's freedom and capacity to understand and interpret the impact of the forthcoming separation, and the destructiveness that it provoked, could modify the situation. It gave Mrs A relief and enabled her to speak about her wishes and fears, rather than enacting her destructive phantasies.

The compulsion and gratification involved was vividly exemplified in an example from another patient Segal describes, who dreamt he was in a deep, dark, wet cave, extremely gloomy and oppressed. In the dream he asked himself, "Why do I want to stay here?" Segal refers to the "sadistic pleasure of triumph over the defeated analyst but also the masochistic pleasure of the triumph over that part of oneself that wishes to live and to grow" (1997, p. 23).

In the third clinical example in this thought-provoking paper, Segal describes a patient's dream in which "There was an area in which everything and everybody was immobile and nearly dead. Around that area, at regular intervals, there were nuclear weapons facing outwards. If anybody approached the area the weapons would automatically trigger off. Amongst the near dead people in the area were his parents" (Segal, 1997, p. 23).

I think this describes the powerful tyrannical control the patient exerts, which presumably contributes to the terrible state of his objects. While there is certainly the threat of annihilation, it is important that his objects (including his analyst), remain just alive. Segal links this with Joseph's description of addiction to near-death (1982—chapter 7, this volume), where life is allowed to continue just so long as nothing is really alive and functioning. "The dream is meant to warn the analyst that approaching this area would disturb the deathly balance, would mobilise unbound destructiveness" (Segal, 1997, p. 23). The patient thus seeks to replace the analyst's world of thought, creativity, meaning, and change with one dominated by paralysis and terror.

Rosenfeld captures in a vivid fashion the gratification involved. In a dream, a narcissistic patient described *a small boy dying from some kind of poisoning, and further endangered by the hot midday sun that was beginning to shine on him. The patient did nothing to move or protect the boy.* "He only felt critical and superior to the doctor treating the child, since it was he who should have seen that the child was moved into the shade" (1971, p. 174). Rosenfeld interpreted the way in which the patient maintained his dependent libidinal self in a dying condition by preventing it from getting help and nourishment from his analyst:

> Even when he came close to realising the seriousness of his mental state, experienced as a dying condition, he did not lift a finger to help himself or to help the analyst to make a move towards saving him, because he was using the killing of his infantile dependent self to triumph over the analyst and to show him up as a failure. The dream illustrates clearly that the destructive narcissistic state is maintained in power by keeping the libidinal infantile self in a constant dead or dying condition. [Rosenfeld, 1971, p. 174]

Rosenfeld refers to "a constant dead or dying condition", but I think the distinction is important. In the clinical examples I have quoted, it is significant that the objects are not dead, but poisoned, weakened, immobilized, and, one suspects, forever dying.

There often seems to be present in the patient's mind the phantasy of some violent cataclysmic event. This may be located at some undefined point in the past, and/or something the patient and analyst feel threatened by in the present or the future. This event is associated with varying degrees of helplessness, terror, excitement, and triumph. It is striking that in two of the dreams quoted by Segal it is the patient who has the power (and the desire) to release the devastating attack. It is, of course, the recognition of the drive towards this annihilatory attack that leads us to invoke the concept of the death instinct. However, what we encounter clinically suggests that the gratifying devastating force for which nuclear war is chosen as a metaphor is often already present, but fragmented and dispersed into small destructive operations: what Segal's patient Mrs A described as "perpetual fall-out and all". These invade, not in order to annihilate or even to kill, but to attack meaning, clarity, movement, exploration, and any form of creative interchange, as an expression of hatred towards life and liveliness.

It is not always easy to follow precisely how this destructive force operates: it is often subtle and silent. However, in her 1977 paper Segal quotes an example that seems to me to illustrate the processes that express this destructiveness. The patient dreamed *he was breaking the links in a chain with great fury*. In the previous session the analyst had referred to "links" and had also spoken of "a train of thoughts". When she said this, the patient had had an angry thought that he had not verbalized.

"It's not a train, it's a chain." He was in a temper after the session. He said he didn't want to be chained by his thoughts. He wanted to tear the chain apart and be free of it. "He felt his own train of linked thoughts as a prison and a persecution, because it interfered with the belief in his omnipotence" (1977, p. 220).

In addition to the important point Segal makes, I think this exemplifies the way the patient was able omnipotently to intrude, and to transform the interpretation, telling himself: "It's not a train, it's a chain." He does not feel freed by the different perspective offered to him but enacts his gratifying destructive power by seizing the interpretation, silently changing a word, stripping the meaning, and remaining angry and aggrieved.

Joseph (1982—chapter 7, this volume) points out how certain patients bring material apparently to be analysed and understood but actually to be used unconsciously for other purposes. She suggests that these patients do not want "understanding", though the words are presented as if it were so. The patient may express his destructiveness and self-destructiveness through the use of projective identification, as a means of silently and powerfully leading the analyst to feel quite hopeless and despairing.

> I think we have here a type of projective identification in which despair is so effectively loaded into the analyst that he seems crushed by it and can see no way out. The analyst is then internalised in this form by the patient, who becomes caught up in this internal crushing and crushed situation, and paralysis and deep gratification ensue. [Joseph, 1982, p. 452—chapter 7, this volume]

She continues,

> . . . this type of patient usually finds it very difficult to see and to acknowledge the awful pleasure that is achieved in this way. . . . It is technically extremely important to be clear as to whether the patient is telling us about and communicating to us real despair, depression, or fear and persecution, which he wants us to understand and to help him with, or whether he is communicating it in such a way as primarily to create a masochistic situation in which he can become caught up. If this distinction is not clearly made in the analysis from moment to moment, one cannot analyse adequately the underlying deep anxieties because of the whole masochistic overlay and the use that is being made of this. [Joseph, 1982, pp. 452–453—chapter 7, this volume]

I believe the patient I wish to describe exemplifies many of these processes. He seemed often to be caught in a vicious interplay between actual frustration and disappointment and the gratification and sadistic pleasure he obtained from using experiences of suffering and despair to undermine and torment his objects, and himself.

Case example: Mr B

History

The patient, Mr B, is an intelligent, talented, and creative man. In his childhood his father was frequently absent for long periods, and he was left alone with his mother, whom he saw as lonely and full of bitter resentment. Mr B's father had died of cancer ten years earlier. He felt burdened by the responsibility of caring for his mother, who was unhappy and demanding.

In the course of his studies Mr B had come to rely a good deal on his tutor, a brilliant and charismatic man who had helped Mr B a great deal with his career and had functioned as a wise mentor. However, before Mr B had completed his thesis, Dr A had had to return rather abruptly to his native Italy for family reasons, and Mr B found this painful and difficult. The experience revived many of the reactions to his father's absences in the past. Several years later, Mr B came into this analysis depressed, virtually unable to work, and convinced that he was himself suffering from cancer, with symptoms similar to his father's. Within a short time these symptoms disappeared, and he became more vigorous and creative in his work.

He continued to find his mother's condition and her demands difficult, and he could become angry and exasperated with her complaints. On one occasion she provoked an angry outburst from him, which was followed shortly afterwards by his mother being taken to hospital with a stroke. This seemed to confirm Mr B's belief in the awful consequences that resulted from the expression of his rage, and he was tormented with feelings of persecution and guilt. He was greatly relieved when his mother survived this attack, and he was able to restore warmer contact between them before she died some two years later.

Clinical material

The first session I am going to describe took place after an extended weekend break. The patient arrived for the session on Wednesday morning and began musing in a flat, hopeless voice about whether he could afford the analysis much longer—the financial cost, and the time. If it were not for the analysis, he could have continued his work by accepting a well-paid post abroad.

Mr B continued, "On the way here I was thinking of three dreams that I had last night. As you know, I like bringing dreams, partly because it is something to talk about, and I like stories. But another reason I like remembering dreams is because I think some truth may escape from me—something I am trying to control or hide, even from myself. The dreams are a way of finding something out that would otherwise be hidden, or at least I would attempt to hide it, either consciously or unconsciously". Mr B spoke in a way that was detached, superior, and rather "knowing". He conveyed that he found the analysis burdensome and unhelpful. While apparently wishing to be cooperative, his dreams had already become "stories", or a means of demonstrating his analytic insight, and the basis for a psychoanalytic discourse.

He went on to say that his dreams were a strange threesome, and he debated the order in which they had appeared. "In one *I was with a set of animals. I was sitting on the same settee as them, and they all had black and white stripes, like racoons, but they weren't racoons. The others were like very large insects, like tarantulas.* In real life I can't stand spiders, I have a phobia of them. In the dream *they were next to me, and some of them were probably poisonous. I stroked some of the animals. I was in two minds whether they were safe or not."*

"I've been trying to think what the dream means—my own association is the numerous times you pointed out how I tend to paint things black and white. I suppose the last thing that happened in the Friday session was to do with that. My talking about what I was just starting, but something more complex, it was both true and not true. (He went on speaking in a complicated way that I found confusing and could not understand.)

"The next dream was about *my mother. She had been ill. My father had been absent for a while, and she was talking about his absences. She said, every time he goes away, I get weaker, and soon, when he next goes away, I will not be able to fight the disease, whatever it is, I will be too weak."*

"When I was young my father used to go away on long trips, and I used to miss him quite a lot. Of course my mother must have missed him most of all. It's funny; I have long conversations with her in my head on the way here. I was explaining something to her, something about my father, but I can't remember what. She was a strange mixture—very intelligent and very naive at the same time".

"The last dream was also about absence. *Dr A had returned to Italy because he had to look after his wife who was ill. He arranged for me to be supervised by someone else, a younger man. Then it became more as if I was having analysis, but I wasn't lying on the couch—we were facing each other, in a place that looked like a restaurant. There was a large area, with lots of people, and I couldn't properly hear what he was saying. After a while I thought, 'This is not going to work, it's impossible, I don't know why I am having treatment with this person'."*

After a silence Mr B said that during the preceding two days he had been waiting for a response to his proposal for a new project. The organization involved kept delaying, and he felt it was going on and on. He thought he might be able to get on with his other work. His old laptop was dying, but a friend managed to find a second-hand computer for him. Then his printer started playing up. The patient said, in a very gloomy voice, "Really, I don't know how long I can go on like this".

The patient initially spoke in a lifeless, negative way that felt undermining of any hope that either of us would get anywhere. He conveyed his resentment at the claims the analysis made on him, and how it prevented him from pursuing his career with a rewarding project abroad. He became more animated at the prospect of describing his dreams, because he liked telling "stories" and also because they gave him an opportunity to organize and explain.

I commented that he had referred to his father going away and in his dream Dr A goes away, leaving him with someone he felt

was unable to help him. However, he made no direct reference
to the fact that there had just been an unusually long break.
I thought that when he felt threatened by having to be aware
of waiting or of missing someone, he felt driven to take over
the functions of the one who understood and who managed,
and he then found himself explaining things to me, as he had
done with his naïve mother. When this didn't work well enough,
however, he became not only frustrated and depressed, as he
had conveyed to me, but something quite poisonous and hateful became evoked. What he had communicated in the dream
about his mother was the extent to which he was invaded by her
hopelessness and despair in a way that felt hateful and poisonous. I thought I was similarly placed in the position of having
helplessly to witness the hopeless and demoralizing situation
he found himself in. I thought his awareness that he was drawn
to stroking the dangerous creatures of his dream reflected the
seductive pull this interaction had for him.

The patient responded to my interpretation initially by saying,
politely, that he recognized that he had a very strong tendency,
when faced with disappointment, to cut off his nose to spite
his face. He then described how he had recently undertaken
some difficult work for a voluntary organization. He knew they
didn't have much money, but he expected a modest fee. When
he raised the matter, there was "a terrific to-do", and the head
of the organization said they couldn't pay him at all. Mr B
had been in a real rage. He felt he was being made to pay for
a misunderstanding within the organization. "I wanted to do
something really destructive to them, and to myself. I suppose
the difference this time, unlike similar situations in the past, is
that I realized what was going on in me. I thought, 'I am enjoy-
ing this feeling of resentment too much'."

I thought it was important that there were moments, such as
this one, in which the patient could acknowledge the work that
had gone on in the analysis and could tell me that he was able
to recognize the sadistic pleasure he indulged in.

I interpreted that when he felt left out, pushed aside, he became
involved in something that he could see was more complicated

than cutting off his nose. He had spoken of the way he would dwell on phantasies of revenge, retaliation, often quite sadistic and pleasurable, which he sometimes played out. When he felt not properly acknowledged or paid and was made to wait, he recognized how this led him to retreat into a familiar place, where there was a mixture of pain, pleasure, and cruelty. It disturbed him when he realized what a grip this process had on him and how much pleasure he derived from it.

This long weekend break, which evoked experiences of having been left in the past, also stirred up this pleasurable and deadly negativity, which was referred to in his dream and which I thought had been manifested in the way he began this session, ruminating in a way that created an atmosphere of guilt, resentment, and hopelessness.

While his detached, rather intellectual way of narrating and commenting on his dreams seemed to invite me to admire the story-like quality of his dreams and the links he made to the past and to the analysis, he did not convey the sense that anything useful would come out of our interchange. On the contrary, I suspect he anticipated I would respond with a feeling of helplessness and frustration and engage with him in a way that would probably fuel the resentful and bitter "chuntering" (Joseph, 1982—chapter 7, this volume) he was already engaged in when he arrived after the break.

I believe Mr B becomes identified with his mother as she is portrayed in his dream, reacting to absence and loss not by acknowledging it, thinking about it, or experiencing distress, pain, or anger, but by sinking into progressive reproachful weakness and illness. Much of the time I am consequently exposed to the disheartening impact of this. Mr B. seemed to find comfort only in turning to the poisonous black-and-white creatures of his mind that he stroked in a sensuous way, manifested in the session by cultivating and stroking his grievance and hopelessness, or, as he had at other times, by turning to cruel and violent sexual phantasies.

Although his initial response to my interpretation of this process sounded superficial and propitiating, he was able to acknowledge how his frustration and sense of being badly treated gave rise, briefly, to rage and then to phantasies of violent and destructive attacks on his objects and on himself. He recognized the pleasure involved in these destructive phantasies and the way he tended to go over and over them in his mind, and he felt troubled by it. At this point in the session it was evident that he was less caught up in the gratifying destructive rumination, and he could briefly acknowledge, and be disturbed by, his recognition of the process that so often gripped him. By emerging from the rumination, by being able to represent the process in words and in his dreams, he is, by contrast, able to express a more constructive and cooperative aspect of his personality that is interested in communicating with me in a way that makes it easier for him to be helped.

Many of these issues emerged more clearly in the next session. I was slightly delayed, so we started about two minutes late, which was unusual. Mr B subjected me to an intense, hostile scrutiny. After a silence of three or four minutes, he said, "I have a few desultory thoughts, but nothing I was thinking about was holding my attention. There is one thing that I didn't mention yesterday. I suppose it's a stage of grief, it is classical that one always blames the doctor or the hospital when someone dies. Then there comes a time when you reconsider it. Over the weekend I realized that once my mother had had the first attack, it was over for her really. She was so weakened, she could hardly survive. If she had survived the second attack, her quality of life would have been zero. I have been very, very angry with the hospital, because they refused to put her on kidney dialysis, or anything else, but I think they were probably right" (he sighed), "it was too late".

Although Mr B might seem to be describing his acceptance of the distressing reality, in the way he spoke he conveyed a terrible and gratifying hopelessness into which he immersed himself. This tended thus to evoke a response not so much of sympathy and concern, but of helplessness and hopelessness in the analyst.

Mr B continued, "But what came to my mind was an image of her when she used to get very, very worked up. It didn't happen

often, but I remember some occasions when there was some issue between her and my father, and she became really very upset
and would shout in a way I found very distressing. . . ."

The patient then told me about a meeting with his accountant
the previous day. Some of his current financial difficulties had
resulted from Mr B's failure to deal with a particular professional matter in time. In the course of the meeting Mr B said
he was shocked to discover that the accountant's assistant had
failed to pass on certain documents that would have made it
easier for Mr B to sort out the problem. The accountant, whom
he has known for many years, had not told Mr B about his assistant's incompetence. He had now sacked the assistant but was
evidently worried that the patient might sue him.

There were indications in the patient's behaviour, and in his
material, of his capacity for overt hostility and vigorous protest.
He referred to his intense anger and protest against the doctors'
resignation in the face of his mother's terminal illness. In the
course of this session he also recovered a version of his mother
able to express intense anger and complaints towards his father.
However, these more direct responses and vital ways of engaging
his objects seemed to become overwhelmed by a more deadly
process. There was no evidence at this time that the brief delay
at the start of the session had caused Mr B particular anxiety or
distress, but it fuelled instead his anger and resentment, which
could not be directly acknowledged or expressed, except in the
initial hostile look. As in his initial response to the long weekend in the previous session, he spoke instead in a desultory way,
resigned to the hopelessness of his mother's condition and his
own. This was not a direct, angry criticism or attack but a way
of creating an atmosphere that was imprisoning and tormenting, and for a while there seemed to be nothing that either of
us could do.

Instead of being able to own the disturbing and potentially violent reactions evoked in him when he felt badly treated by the
doctors, by the accountant, or by me, he silently nurtured his
sense of injury and his resentment, holding the threat of some
kind of "litigation" over me in a way that was intended to tyran-
nize and weaken me. While there seemed to be a gratifying,

compulsive, and deadly quality in this, I think the healthier aspect of the patient expressed itself in the fear that, like the doctors who were treating his mother, I, too, would give up hope in the face of the silent destructiveness. However, even this momentary protest against this possibility became overwhelmed once again by the gratification bound up in hopelessness and resignation.

In my interpretation, I referred to his initial silence and the desultory way he had begun to speak. I said I thought he had been acutely aware that we had started a couple of minutes late. He indicated that he could, like his mother, be upset and angry, but what seemed to emerge instead was a kind of hopeless resignation, where neither of us could do anything. I thought this situation was kept going by his silent resentment and thoughts about destructive retaliation, which gave him a feeling of gratification and power.

He responded by saying, "Well, I wasn't sure whether you were late or not, or how late. Because the watch was. . . . I had just changed the time, because the date on my watch does not move automatically, thirty-one days, and I wondered whether in changing it, er . . . I had moved it on a bit. I thought you might have been a minute late, but according to my watch it was three minutes late, but I wasn't sure. We can obviously split the difference. I was going to mention it, but I thought, well, what's the point. It's not exactly resignation, but what's the use, we've been here before. I think you've only ever kept me waiting two or three times, but . . . the last time I mentioned it, you said I was very demanding and hold you to the very second. Which is partly true. . . .

"The thing is, I wasn't actually in a rage about the accountant, funnily enough, I tried to get into a rage, but it just rang hollow. Before this I had felt the problem was entirely down to me, and now I felt I was off the hook. Now he is going to find it very difficult to hand me a bill, because it's his fault. There is a lot of money involved, all the work and time that has been spent, and I'm just not going to pay it. It's not my responsibility, so I'm off the hook."

This part of the session felt difficult and frustrating. Mr B claimed to be uncertain about the time we had started. His offer to "split the difference" was also manifest in the ambiguous and partial way he related to my interpretations. What was apparent in the way he spoke about the accountant was that when it was clearly the other person's failure, he didn't express his criticisms directly, but used his observations and his subjective experience in a more hidden way. He now felt he had something he could hold over his object, to control and intimidate in a superior, quietly menacing fashion. He had no responsibility: he didn't have to pay . . . he was "off the hook". His power depended in part on the other person's sense of guilt and responsibility. At times Mr B was now able to recognize the satisfaction he got from holding his objects in a tormenting grip that tyrannized and undermined them internally, and to some extent externally. This conscious and unconscious attack on his objects resulted in them often appearing weak, bed-ridden, and vulnerable.

I believe Mr B found the guilt inherent in this situation very difficult or impossible to bear, and he partially defended himself through the process of becoming identified with these attacked and weakened figures. It was the extent of his introjective identification with such objects that greatly contributed to the difficulty Mr B himself encountered in making proper use of his capacities.

I said I thought it gave him some relief and satisfaction when he could argue that I was the one in the wrong and wouldn't dare to present him with the bill. When he kept his observations and reactions ambiguous or hidden and could hold something over me, this gave him an even greater sense of power. However, I thought he never felt secure in this position, as he was always afraid I would reverse the situation and hold him responsible for everything that was wrong.

After a long silence, he said, "What occurs to me is that, if I was correct in my original guess when I was in the waiting room, that we started late, in fact later than any time I can think of, the timing of this was very strange, after yesterday's session. What came up in yesterday's session about my feeling of self-righteousness

and anger, well, I feel it is changing to something quite different, something more unpleasant and destructive."

At this point he demonstrated some knowledge of the contents
of the previous session and appeared to be in possession of the
capacity to observe and judge, which he could now acknowledge to his analyst. However, this more positive and insightful
contact with himself and with me changed. He first turned a
critical interpretive eye on me and then continued by commenting on what I had interpreted in the previous session (and
on other occasions), speaking in a superior explanatory tone.
Once again he conveyed that he was not concerned with understanding himself better or helping me understand him better,
but with asserting his knowledge and his superiority in a way
that felt provocative and undermining, rather than constructive. Nevertheless, I thought the recognition of the emergence
of anything unpleasant that was actually located within him was
disturbing, and in the session he became more irritable and
argumentative.

I felt subjected not so much to direct anger or criticism, but to
a silent, hostile, aloof destructiveness that undermined his own
understanding as well as mine, and that I thought had been
provoked by the evidence of life within him and his object. For
a while we both felt imprisoned, despairing of the presence of a
third, properly helpful object that might provide either him or
me with any way of dealing with the awfulness and hopelessness
of the situation.

After a while, when he said, "There is an obvious imbalance
between the analyst and the patient because of why they are
meeting, but there is a smaller imbalance that I think is worth
mentioning. I mean, if I had come two or three minutes late,
there would have been some significance in that, but if you are
two or three minutes late, that has no significance, apparently.
It's just a fact."

The delay at the start of the session did not give rise to the open
expression of anxiety, criticism, or anger, and Mr B went no further
in describing whatever thoughts or suspicions he had concerning

the reasons for it. Rather, he used his observations in a character-istic fashion to fuel his feelings of resentment at the "imbalance" between us. As I have tried to illustrate, I believe this gave rise to a malign attack on my functions and on his own mental capaci-ties: his ability to explore, to recognize, and to articulate his own thoughts and feelings. At several points when I was able to preserve or recover my functions, however, and was able to speak to him about the more malignant processes taking place within him and between us, he often seemed to recover his capacity for thought. At those moments the patient showed a greater capacity for insight and a greater inclination to acknowledge what he had recognized about himself and his object, in a way that felt more benign and more cooperative.

In this session, he continued,

> "I have never understood. . . . I remembered something that happened with Dr A that I think I have mentioned before. He just didn't turn up for a meeting one day, when I was at a criti-cal point in my work on the thesis, just ten days before he was leaving. There was some reason why he couldn't make it, but he didn't get hold of me: he could have got hold of me. Later that week I went to see Professor K, who had initially arranged for me to have Dr A as my tutor. The one thing that I regret is that I told Professor K that Dr A had not turned up, and I said that that had hurt me quite a bit. Telling Professor K about it in the way I did created a very strange balance. I'm not trying to compare a couple of minutes with somebody not turning up at all, but it reminds me of the way in which it coloured my whole experience of working with Dr A over the three years."

Both in the previous session and this one the patient came to ac-knowledge feelings of being let down and angry. However, it was very difficult for him to sustain this more reflective state within himself and the more positive contact with me. I suspect that the pain, humiliation, and envy provoked by what he called the "imbal-ance" contributed to his irritable defensiveness and the underlying destructive impulses. He could reverse this imbalance when he replaced feelings of helplessness or dependency with a gratifying and powerful sense of grievance. In this session he now seemed to recognize, with discomfort, that his hurt, confusion, and anger over his previous analyst's behaviour had mobilized his hatred and his desire for revenge. He now regretted that he hadn't been able to resist placing himself in a position where he not only registered an appropriate complaint, but internally exploited Dr A's lapse in or- der to twist the knife in a vengeful way that subsequently coloured his whole experience of the help and support he had received over the three years.

In the session I have been describing I thought this destruc- tive attack was not open but disguised in the ambiguity and doubt that Mr B assumed, even when he was in possession of quite ex- plicit thoughts and clear memories. His polite partial agreement or disagreement didn't feel like attempts to correct or clarify, but something much more hostile and undermining. He often seemed, in fact, to be speaking from a rather threatening position, as if in consultation with the powerful Professor K. I was made to feel in the wrong—the person who should feel uncomfortable, guilty, and weak.

It was only when we were able to address the extent to which Mr B became absorbed in these cruel and gratifying processes that the patient became more able to know, and to articulate quite clearly for the first time, how upset and disturbed he had been by the disruption at the end of his period of work with Dr A. He started speaking in a different way, describing how he had had to come to a different office for the last two or three weeks, and when his tutor failed to appear for the crucial meeting in the last week, he waited for the whole two hours, and it felt very strange and awful. He said: "When I gave the account of what had happened with Dr A to Professor K, it overshadowed all the good things that had happened over the course of the work on my dissertation." It was also clear that his resentment, hostility, and continuing destructive attacks on his tutor had also succeeded in attacking his own aware- ness of the pain, as well as the awful confusion and sense of loss to which his tutor's departure had exposed him. I believe the work that had gone on in the session allowed the patient more openly to acknowledge this to me.

Discussion

In this chapter I have mainly focused on the way in which, when the patient was threatened by experiences of pain and loss, a variety of early mechanisms were evoked, in particular his turning to a world in which a sense of unremitting grievance and injury led to cruel and gratifying destructiveness. His own mental functions were attacked, often resulting in a degree of confusion and fragmentation, where he could not understand, think, or work properly. His objects, too, were often attacked in a dispersed and invasive fashion, drawn into a cruel, tormenting, and gratifying imprisonment with him. This led, in turn, to his becoming identified not with parents who were vigorous, sexual, and creative, but with a father dying of cancer and a mother, as in his dream, whose reproach consisted in becoming progressively weakened. Similarly, he found himself in a relationship with his academic tutor or his analyst, not as strong and effective figures, but distracted and unreliable, speaking to him in incomprehensible and unhelpful ways.

I believe one can recognize in this patient's material evidence of an ongoing conflict between vital impulses leading him into more direct contact with, and knowledge about his own inner life, his links with his objects, and a destructive force operating within him. When he felt hurt or abandoned or made hatefully aware of an "imbalance", this greatly increased the pull of this force in ways I have tried to describe.

When, in the course of the session, it was possible to understand and articulate some of these processes, a shift sometimes took place, and Mr B seemed to recover aspects of his personality and mental functions that had either been attacked or projected, or both. The understanding of these aspects of his mental life, and the description in words that he was offered, seemed to make them more amenable to thought and enabled the patient to integrate them more fully, even though they aroused his anxiety and guilt. There was then a noticeable diminution in the enactment of these defensive and destructive mechanisms within his own mind, and within the transference relationship. He became more able to recognize and articulate his genuine anger, his resentment and grievance, but also the pleasure he derived from his destructiveness, both in the present and in the past. He became distressingly aware of the extent to which his good experiences could become poisoned by these processes. He referred once again to the time when he felt let down by his tutor, but now he spoke about it in a very different and more moving fashion, giving a real sense of his distress, panic, and confusion, which had become organized into his grievance.

Conclusion

There remains something very compelling about the concept of a primordial death instinct, the gratification of which involves the total annihilation of the self as a thinking, living being. Freud and Klein both felt that they could account for some of the clinical phenomena they encountered in terms of a fundamental struggle between forces that promoted life and a drive towards death. The deep biological resonances of these theories and the references to physical death may be important, even necessary.

However, the postulation of the instinctual drive towards death can be seen as an attempt to capture and to account for the mani-festation of a destructive psychological force that is part of our nature, and often very evident in many of our ill patients. I believe we need to continue to explore the nature of the experiences, ac-tivities, and aims that reflect this destructive psychic force and the conscious and unconscious gratification that is intrinsically bound up in it.

What is "deadly" is the way in which meaning, specificity differ-ences, are attacked and any developmental processes retarded or undermined. The vitality is taken out of the patient himself and his objects, and although in an important sense these drives are "anti-life", I am suggesting that their aim is not literally to kill or to annihilate, but to maintain a link with the object that often has a tormenting quality. I believe the gratification that is so bound up in these activities, which gives them such a compulsive quality, does not result from some fusion with the life instinct, with the consequent libidinization. The implication of this is that sexuality and sexual excitement are not necessarily bound to the life instinct, being recruited, or "hijacked" at times by the death instinct. On the contrary, the gratification obtained from attacking, spoiling, and undermining, whether directed to the self or the object, is an essential element of such a destructive drive.

It will be evident that the phenomena I am discussing are closely related to those that led Klein to recognize the importance of envy as a destructive force. The expression of this force results in a world of seriously weakened and devalued objects that the patient holds on to, controls, and triumphs over, in a way that is evidently gratify-ing. Thoughts about the death of the patient or his objects, or even acts of violence or suicide, can often be understood as expressions of this cruel, tormenting tie to the object, which the patient feels compelled to maintain.

There are times when the drive behind this is such that any attempt to intervene is undermined by the processes I have tried to describe. However, I hope I have briefly illustrated how the analyst's understanding and interpretation may bring these destruc-tive activities into the realm of thought and of language, thereby diminishing their silent destructiveness, and partially liberating his objects from their grip. This shift is partially brought about through the patient becoming more able to acknowledge and to tolerate his awareness of his own hatred and anger. This movement is often accompanied by the patient becoming able to make better contact with something more lively in himself and his object, capable of good experiences, including feelings of appreciation and gratitude towards someone else, as well as feelings of sadness and loss.

Note

This is an expanded version of a paper first published as "Some Views on the Manifestation of the Death Instinct in Clinical Work". *International Journal of Psychoanalysis, 81* (1) (2000): 53–65; a revised version of the paper was published in M. M. Feldman, *Doubt, Conviction and the Analytic Process*, ed. Betty Joseph. London: Routledge, 2009.

9

A Hindu reading of
Freud's *Beyond the Pleasure Principle*

Ashok Nagpal

Freud's celebrated if controversial work *Beyond the Pleasure Principle* (1920g) inaugurated a radical revision of his earlier theory of dualism between the pleasure principle and the reality principle. With the introduction of the death-instinct concept, Freud moved away from a theoretical position he had built up with painstaking care. That this was not a whimsical idea is evident in the consistency with which references to the death instinct appear in his post-1920 writings (Freud, 1923b, 1930a, 1940a [1938]). *Beyond the Pleasure Principle* also reveals a Freud who seems to muster every source at his command—clinical, biological, and philosophical—to persuade the reader of his new discovery.

In his work, Freud reassesses the pleasure principle and places it amidst a new matrix where unpleasure comes about not only through the reality principle but also in the very dynamics of the mental apparatus through its necessary conflicts and dissensions. In the early post-Freudian era, the fiercest battle was over the death instinct. Though Melanie Klein (1933, 1935) and her followers (Joseph, 1982—chapter 7, this volume; Segal, 1956, 1974; Spillius, 1988a, 1988b) championed it, others (Hartmann, 1939; Lear, 2005;

Marcovitz, 1973; Waelder, 1956) constituting the majority opinion in psychoanalysis, saw the death instinct as a speculative philosophical effort by an aging Freud that was insufficiently rooted in clinical experience and bypassed the need for a psychoanalytic postulation on human aggression. Could it be said that Freud "jumped over" an obstacle here by letting his intellect over-think without the necessary engagement within a relational frame such as is availed of in clinical work? In other words, if Freud had had an analyst take care of the anxieties erupting in his life, would he still have propounded the death instinct?

A question of this sort notwithstanding, from the perspective of Hindu thought there is something attractive about Freud's 1920 excursion. It is at once apparent that there are several possibilities in reading the relationship between Hindu philosophy and *Beyond the Pleasure Principle*. It could be a perfectly legitimate enterprise to locate the discussion of the essay in the light of civilizational and cultural processes other than those of the Judeo–Christian and Islamic one. One might begin with the analysis of Freud by one of India's eminent political psychologists, Ashis Nandy (1995), who positions Freud along with Marx as one of the "dissenting children of the enlightenment" and views psychoanalysis, with its critique of rationality and prudish morality, as an internal critique of the modern West. Indeed, despite his success, Freud was located somewhat at the edge of the centre of the world to which he belonged. The question could be asked whether Freud—a Jew, suffering from cancer, engaging with psychological suffering often of women, and witnessing the destruction of war through his somewhat de-centred location within the European world—may have acquired insights that echo those prevalent in the Eastern world for a long time.

It is evident that Freud was deeply influenced by the philosopher Schopenhauer, who had read extensively on aspects of Buddhism and Hindu thought. Parsons (1999) points out that Freud was also sympathetic to Yoga. He apparently recognized that yogic practices have the potential to alter the relations between the different regions of the mind. That Freud saw the possibility of other forms of understanding (e.g. via concepts such as *Nirvana*) is evident in the following communication between Freud and Goetz, a young Swiss poet impressed by aspects of Sanskrit literature.

> If however without the aid of a clear intellect you become im-
> mersed in . . . the *Bhagavad Gita*, where nothing seems to be
> constant and everything melts into everything else, then you
> are suddenly confronted by nothingness . . . And yet this very
> nothingness is simply a European misconception: The Indian
> *Nirvana* is not nothingness, it is that which transcends all con-
> tradictions. [Freud, cited in Parsons, 1999, p. 44]

Furthermore, in an apparent reference to the *Vedantic* practice of
neti,[1] Freud said, ". . . the most sensible thing is to keep on asking
questions. Hindu philosophers often went so far as to express their
answers in the form of questions. They knew why" (cited in Parsons,
1999, p. 45).

Freud's increasing interest in mysticism was also evident in his
correspondence with Romain Rolland (Parsons, 1999). Such statements indicate some new openness towards other world-views. Had
Freud pursued this line of thought further, this could have paved
the way for a more grounded trans-culturation of psychoanalysis.

Thus, in this spirit, I hypothesize three interrelated yet somewhat contradictory lines of reasoning in this chapter. First, I argue
that the treatment and understanding of the twin processes of
life and death in Hindu thought are distinctively different from
those seen in European thought. Second, I draw upon some aspects of *Beyond the Pleasure Principle* to comment upon the similarities between these bodies of thought. Finally, however, I argue
that although Freud may have produced in the death instinct a
concept that approximated some aspects of Hindu thought and
despite a more sophisticated response to the fear of death articulated in Hindu worldview, these do not match Freud's ability to
locate the philosophy of life in the very structure of the mental
apparatus—one that is less centred around pleasure and narcissism and asking for a greater acceptance of the forces of destruction and death. His plea posits that a greater acknowledgement
of death is a necessary regulatory step in the sublimation of human destructiveness. The processes of sublimation as left unelab-
orated in Freud's writings subsequent to this work and developed
more fully by later post-Freudians, particularly Green (1993a) and
Laplanche (1989), permit a more critical engagement with the
death instinct.

The Hindu worldview

To write a summarized version of an aspect that has preoccupied a civilization is itself a paradox, and is even more marked as I have been neither a devout practitioner nor professionally engaged with the metaphysics of Hinduism. Nevertheless, to live as a Hindu and to have spent one's childhood embedded in tales of Hindu gods and goddesses gives some understanding of the nuances of the worldview. Let me structure this contribution, therefore, by selecting some central renderings of death in Hindu writing. My attempt in making this selection is to:

▷ demarcate some critical differences between the dominant perspective towards death and destruction in the worldview in which Freud was embedded and those described in Hindu texts;

▷ illustrate how Freud the philosopher had begun to see the limitations of the civilization to which he largely belonged;

▷ develop a thesis that Freud's later writings reflect a more philosophical bent concerned with ethical issues.

Let me start with my first point. Hindu philosophy is a complex and changing body of thought. It is often described in terms of six schools, including, most prominently, *Yoga* and *Vedanta*. These schools of thought vary in several respects, particularly in relation to their positions on monism and dualism. However, despite these differences, the highest ideal posited for man in various strands of Hinduism is the idea of *moksha* [freedom from the chain of birth–death–rebirth] and its relationship to questions of desire, relationships, suffering, loss, and death. The earliest preoccupation with such eternal questions of humanity was probably seen in the *Vedas* (ca. 3000 BC). These tracts posited an automatic rebirth after death and a brief stay in the celestial home of the ancestors. One was trapped in unending cycles of life, death, and rebirth. The idea of escape from rebirth emerged during the *Upanishads* (ca. 500–700 BC) and was gradually linked to the nature of one's moral actions. If one was fortunate enough to have lived a life that was totally free of moral blemish, one did not have to be reborn. Rebirth, a second chance to live life right, was only required for the less-than-virtuous majority.

The fundamental thesis of *Vedanta* is that of a single reality that is observable in multiple manifestations, called *Brahman*. The nature of *Brahman* is best revealed by the process of negation—it is neither this nor that [*neti*]. *Brahman* appears as existent but formless, without beginning and end, indescribable. The underlying metaphysical position of *Vedanta* is that the entire world of phenomenal experience is a grand illusion, or *Maya*. Although cognitive and phenomenal reality has ontological status, its illusory character becomes evident to one who reaches an altered or higher state of consciousness. Such a person recognizes the identity of the Infinite Self with the Infinite or *Brahman*.

The core beliefs of Hinduism (Chakkarath, 2005; Kakar, 1981; Saraswathi, 2005) also include the notion of the cycle of birth, death, and rebirth through which the *atman* [soul] crosses from one life to another. The repeated efforts to live properly that are implicit in these cycles testify to the inherently blemished nature of human life. Liberation [*moksha*] from the cycle of birth and rebirth involves realization of the ultimate oneness of the phenomenal self [*atman*] with the cosmic self [*brahman*]. The concept of *karma*, the accumulation of good and bad deeds, provides another important coordinate within which the Hindu worldview functions. Although the ultimate goal of life is to attain *moksha*, the individual is expected to live as a social being through the paths of *dharma* [individual, social, and religious duties], *artha* [economic attainment], and *kama* [experience of desire and pleasure]. The purpose of life is to attain these goals within the overarching framework of *moksha*.

Contrary to the Western psychologies, which regard the lack of a well-evolved self as serious pathology, *Vedanta* regards the basic human problem to be the individual's over-identification with his phenomenal self and the consequent attachment, both material and psychological. Given the intrinsic finitude of objects in the material world, it is to be expected that the desire for these cause attachments, but the same attachments, in turn, make one susceptible to experiences of loss and hence suffering. However, most schools of Hindu thought do not privilege the model of detachment as the only goal of humanity, and yes, the conflict between the ideal of the householder and that of the renouncer has contributed to the specificities of Hindu religion and philosophy (Olivelle, 1993).

Let us take a step back and consider this in context. By 400 BCE the origins of the *Ashrama* theory had begun to emerge. This theory posited that life is to be lived in accordance with sequentially unfolding stages of *brahmacharya, grahastha, vanaprastha,* and *sanyasa.* These stages enable the fulfilment of the goals of *kama* and *artha* while seeking to advance the individual towards the attainment of *moksha.* Thus pleasure is not denied. Paranjpe (1984) points out that Hindu thought somewhat uniquely emphasizes *bhokta* [one who enjoys/suffers the fruits of one's actions], signifying both the experience of pleasure and the inevitable alteration to non-pleasure. Desire is explicitly accepted as an aspect of human nature but is placed within a stage, to be expressed and lived out in accordance with certain prescribed general aims.

For the various life stages [*ashramas*] of *brahmacharya* [student], *grihastha* [householder], *vanaprastha* [ascetic], and, finally, *sanyasi* [renouncer], along with a vast body of myths and tales not to mention the two great epics, the scriptures offer various prescriptions for guidance and actualization of the ideals. The student, for instance, is expected to live a disciplined life committed to the acquisition of knowledge. Sensual pleasure is to be subjugated in favour of devotion to sacred and professional texts. Drinking, eating meat, and having sex are discouraged. All this changes with the next stage. The householder is encouraged to have an intense and intimate investment in money, marriage, sex, childrearing, and family. As family obligations cease, the individual is expected to move towards an ascetic path and to groom the next generation to take over the economic and social dimension of family life. The following stage is that of renunciation, whereby the individual is encouraged to give up material concerns altogether and devote himself to meditating over existential issues. Thus an individual is expected to move several times between relatedness and separation within his life (Kakar, 1981).

The Hindu concept of death

The pre-eminent Indian psychoanalyst, Sudhir Kakar (1981), points out that Hindu civilization is characterized by a marked preoccupation with death. Of course, as in most other matters, there are many aspects of these conceptualizations that are

sometimes contradictory. The classical Brahminical theory re-
volves around reincarnation—where the individual form of each
life dies over and over again—while folk tales speak of the spirit
of the dead being transformed into one of the denizens of the
preta-loka [the world of ghosts] or in an ancestral spirit. In the
first view, there is no trace of a material body after death: the Sanskrit term for death, *dehanta*, means the end of the body. In the
second view, one still operates with some kind of material body
surviving. As in all other respects, there are many renderings of
Hindu thought, with many divergent currents developing differential aspects. Given the greater emphasis on the intellectual tradition of *Vedanta* in this chapter, it might be wise to remember
that Ramanujan (1993) points out that the notions of *karma* and
the attendant idea of rebirth are not found in the folk tales from
various regions of India.

The fact is that Hindu thought does not operate along the
distinction between life and death: rather, the significant duality is
between birth and death (Kakar & Kakar, 2007). Death does not
signify the end of existence, since with death one takes one's place
in the cycle of rebirth. The earliest preoccupation with eternal
questions of living and dying appears in the *Vedas*, which posit an
automatic rebirth after a brief stay in the home of the ancestors.
The idea of escape from rebirth, as stated above, emerged during
the *Upanishads* and was gradually linked to the extent of one's
moral actions.

The tale of *Prajapati,* cited by Kakar and Kakar (2007), begins in
a world that precedes the existence of death. *Brahma,* the creator,
had given life to a variety of beings. However, as time passed, they
aged and became unwell. As *Prajapati* (another name for *Brahma*)
sat down in meditation, the figure of Death emerged from within
him in the form of a daughter, *Nir-Riti. Brahma* explained the oner-
ous task to her. She resisted, however, arguing that it was unfair that
the responsibility of taking death, the ultimate source of sorrow,
be given to a woman. In the ensuing conflict between father and
daughter, Death performed severe ascetic practices. In response to
these, *Prajapati* yielded by creating diseases that would bring death
upon people. However, Death again protested that the sin of causing sorrow should fall upon her. At this, *Brahma* took away her sight
and hearing. Death thus became incapable of knowing the sorrow

she causes. She has no feelings, and in any case she doesn't need them: she is blameless and is summoned by people through their own *karma*—an idea that resonates with Freud's (1920g) thesis that we die due to internal reasons.

This tale points to the necessity of death as a process of renewing life. It is noteworthy that Death is created by the same forces that create Life. Hindu myths communicate the paradoxical fact that death will cause suffering, but death is preordained and death is for us to make some sense of our conduct as well as centring upon the goal of life in dialectical terms.

Indeed, death in the Hindu tradition is more popularly called *Yama*, who bears a close relationship to the other God of *Dharma*; the former means control and discipline, and the latter refers to the ethical implications rooted in a perfect sense of equality for all and assumes a metaphysical aspect. Appearances of control, frustration, and destruction do result in an awareness and self-possession of remaining on a righteous path despite the concerns and anxieties that one may suffer in the initial anguish and wailing. Death, as this underlying force, unknowable in its completeness, thus lies intimately close to the forces of living and life and navigates, albeit silently, the chart of events and experiences. Death in its feminine form, *Nir-Riti* (*Nir* meaning complete, and the root *ri* means walking; the word suggests complete walking away as an unimaginable disaster), as the daughter of *Prajapati*, the God of Creation, is that reluctant aspect of Death who is imagined as utterly disconsolate at the prospect of snatching away (one wonders whether she secretly wishes—as she is created/born, she, too, wishes to be able to live a full course) life from some and leaving others. Protesting vehemently at being assigned this role, she is first made to lose her sense organs of seeing and hearing and then even agency of touching and pulling, since people will die of diseases brought on them by the force of their bad karmas. They will be brought to her, or an impersonal form termed as IT, closer to the Freudian ID, and accept their destiny to die. So her father sends her to this fate—of no feelings and a passivity that has had to surrender its own desire to live! (In my opinion this completes the sense of total disaster: a part born that does not reap its potential to come alive and reach a consummation with loneliness in relationships.)

The analysis of death is also visible in the dialogue between *Krishna* and *Arjuna* that appears in the chapter of the most frequently accessed source of spiritual wisdom among Hindus, the *Bhagawad Gita*. The dialogue is located on the battlefield of *Kurukshetra,* where the two armies brace themselves for conflict. The battle of the *Mahabharata* is in fact a war between two sections of the same family. *Arjuna,* full of doubt regarding the justifiability of a war that would lead him to kill dearly loved ones, is reminded by *Krishna* about his role as a *kshatriya.* He then makes the famous argument that the *atman* [soul] is eternal and indestructible, and what dies is merely the body: that death is not the final reality. The *atman* sheds the form of a particular body, just as a body sheds a set of clothes to wear another. There is, therefore, no need for grief. *Krishna* also reminds *Arjuna* that actions must be performed dutifully, without thought of the consequences.

Freud's declaration that death does not exist in our unconscious is narrated in different ways in Hindu myths in terms of explicit inquiries about what death is—sometimes in a direct dialogue with it. *Yudhishthira,* the eldest brother of *Pandavas* and also the son of the God of Death—(popularly called *Yamaraj*)—remarks this as the greatest wonder, that human beings live in the delusion of their own immortality even though they can see its presence sooner or later terminating every living being. A reading of some selected myths, where human beings have a direct encounter with the God of death and show all the three—masculine, feminine, and impersonal—aspects is offered below in the three tales of *Nachiketa, Savitri,* and *Yudhishthira*—all from the great Hindu epic, *Mahabharata* (by Veda Vyasa, ca. 8th century BC).

The tale of Nachiketa

Nachiketa is the 8-year-old son of a sage. His father decides to organize a ceremony and offers cows to various sages as a ritual of developing good *karmas.* The boy notices his father's slyness in selecting old and useless cows to be gifted the God of Death and is affected by it. (Perhaps he has begun to feel the shudder at his own uselessness and the fate that awaits him.) This leads him to ask questions of his preoccupied father, including the one, "To whom would you donate me?" The father's response is an irritated, shocking one: to the God of Death! The boy decides to visit the land of Death: he waits outside the palace for a few days, without partaking of food, for the god, who is away at work. *Yama* returns from his journey, is told about this unlikely visitor, and grants him a reception. Impressed by the intellect and wisdom of the lad in not asking for worldly goods but inquiring and seeking the good of others (particularly of his own father who fails to be sincere in his observance of the ritual offerings of personal possessions!), *Yama* grants *Nachiketa* a long life and a boon: that forever after the fire of knowledge will be named after him. The boy is still not satisfied and asks *Yama* the secret: What happens in the afterlife? *Yama* tries to wriggle out of a reply, but in response to the boy's formidable tenacity the god relents and offers *Nachiketa* a mantra that reveals the essential truth of life.

The tale of Savitri

Savitri chooses *Satyavan* to be her husband but learns from a seer that he is doomed to die precisely one year from that day, of a curse of which he is unaware. Undeterred, she becomes his wife. The dreaded day arrives, and *Satyavan* finds his wife in torment. She is highly anxious but cannot tell him what is about to happen. He consoles *Savitri*, telling her that fear is only *Maya* [illusion]. She cannot settle down. However, when *Yama*, the God of Death—also referred to as the one who maintains perfect equality towards everyone (thus discipline) and is referred to as *Dharmaraja* (the king of *dharma*)—arrives to take *Satyavan's* life and soul, her reaction is quite unexpected. Instead of tears, she reacts with poise and dignity, as if practicing *neti* and saying that this is not yet the end. She speaks to *Yama* respectfully and solicits his friendship both by walking with him (reminiscent of walking with the dead part in patients) and through an acknowledgment of the need to obey the law of Death and its relationship with the renewal of life. The reader senses this moment of epiphany: *Yama* is enchanted by this luminous being, *Savitri*, and her steadfastness as a wife who is completely rooted in the *dharma* of life and accepts that her husband has to die following his *karma* but generates her own love and trust towards a perspective of saintliness resident in Death. Feelings are generated in the God, out of his anxiety that, while he would like to grant her as many boons as he can to mitigate the attendant loneliness in her life, he would not be in a position to offer her husband's life back. Hearing that she has asked for a hundred sons (it needs to be pointed out that the tale is placed in a context where widows were not allowed to remarry), he is more than relieved to grant this. Lest this gives rise to an impression that the God of Death was hoodwinked (a popular comprehension drawing from the childhood memories of the tale), I hasten to add the parts of the original verse where *Savitri* has heard, and noted, the boon being granted thus:

> Always rooted in *dharma*, the *santa*, the Saints are never troubled in mind, nor are they ever distressed. Being with them is never in vain. Neither do those who are good, fear them ever . . . . It is from the saints that the present, the past, and the future derive their support. Being with the saintly, people do not suffer . . . In the nearness of the saints the three get united: blessings, self-esteem and self-interest. [Chaturvedi, 2008, p. 69]

Yama experiences a transformation here and says:

> "The more you speak, and say in words most elegant things that have a deep meaning and are agreeable to the mind and the heart, the greater grow my feelings of *bhakti* [reverential devotion] for you. Ask from me therefore, some exceptional boon." [Chaturvedi, 2008, p. 69]

Here *Savitri* has to point out to *Yama* that she cannot realize the previous boon of having hundred sons without *Satyavan* being restored to life.

Sri Aurobindo, one of India's greatest sages, combining in his vision a blend of mysticism and occult science, devoted an epic effort to an interpretation of this brief tale of 700 lines, and wrote 24,000 lines of exquisite poetry, titled "*Savitri*"—the coaxial theme being the Ascent of Man and the Descent of the Divine—*Bhakti* flowing from the human to the divine. A Freudian would be content to sense in the popular depictions of Death in Hindu myths a nascent inclination towards feelings human contact and not be blamed for its mediation of loss and suffering! But the more crucial aspect that we need to represent here is the unbinding aspect of the death drive: existing units of relatedness are to be unbound, and striving towards binding is checkmated. Further this process cannot be adequately formulated, contingent as it is on the very binding processes. An exception occurs where an interlocutor has partially overcome his/her own predominant fears of loss and trauma in contact with an affective constellation emanating from imagining one's death—so *Savitri* can walk with death and is in no hurry to get God to give what has already been granted. She says: "I seek from you this last boon, that *Satyavan* be restored to life, for without him I am like the dead" (p. 70).

The tale of Yudhishthira

Arguably the ideal figure, *Yudhishthira*—meaning "steady in war", from *yuddha* [war] and *sthira* [steady]—the son of Lord *Yama*, God of Death himself, has been sketched in multiple complex shades of human characters. Compared, in his righteous qualities and steadfastness to pursue a course of Truth and *Dharma*, to Lord *Rama* himself, *Yudhishthira*, along with his four brothers and the common wife, *Draupadi*, decide to go to *Vanaprastha*. Their dog follows them. On the way all of them die one by one, except *Yudhishthira* and his dog; when the two reach the peak of the mountain, Lord *Indra* comes to receive *Yudhishthira* himself so as to take him to the heavens [*swarga*]. *Yudhishthira* refuses to leave the dog behind, asserting that the dog has stayed with him in unmatched loyalty. *Indra* assents to this righteous assertion and allows *Yudhishthira* to take the dog with him. Once inside the heavens, another shock awaits him: he comes upon the sight of all of his cousins, the *Kauravas*, and other enemies who had fought them in the famous war of *Kurukshetra*, where they were defeated. He is enraged to see them bedecked with such honour and embellishments and can't fathom the underlying rationale. Even as he is fuming and casting doubts on this heaven, a voice tells him that there is no place for animosity and hate here. Everyone deserves some celebration and festivity due to whatever goodness they have displayed in their lives. He asks for his own family and his wife. He is now led to a dark and dingy place that stinks: here he can't see any human faces but soon manages to hear barely audible voices, somewhat familiar, asking him to stay on, since his arrival has brought them some relief! Soon he recognizes in them his own family members. He is maddened further by this perverse order of justice: he is then offered the choice between staying here or going back to where the *Kauravas* had been lodged and decorated. As he chooses to settle amidst the stink and the rot in order to be with his family, Lord *Indra* appears again, declaring this to be a delusion, set up to ascertain his integrity. All of them now finally settle in peace and equanimity worthy of the lives they have led in pursuit of *dharma*—thanks to *Yudhishthira's* nearly impeccable righteousness.

Three images of encounter with death in these myths suggest other meanings too. Death appears as a complement to wherever life needs correction: to *Nachiketa* it appears as a mothering God who embraces the boy and offers gifts and love and even displays a desire to adopt him. In the admiration so openly expressed, there is a good substitution of the father who did not reciprocate the curiosity and almost killed him by sending him to Death. Here the God gifts him with a transitional symbol to his central question of the relation of life and death: that of sound echo and voice embodied in the God's almost human presence.

In the myth of *Savitri*, *Yama* appears as too masculine, but in a position to notice the feminine and experiencing a desire to be communicated with by her. In the process, *Yama* can come upon a new interpretation of his own anxieties about his impeccable reputation of perfect justice becoming besmirched. Hearing those moving words in which *Savitri's* own sense of deadness upon having lost her husband in the prime of her youth begins to come alive touches him deeply, and the boon is granted. Death truly renews life even as its own deadness is recognized in undesignated places where the two walk together in no hurry to leave and await the dawn of saintliness.

The third myth refers to an over-conscious deliberateness as manifested in the character of *Yudhishthira,* who is too omnipotent:

as everyone is walking towards the mountain and they start collaps-
ing one by one, *Yudhishthira* displays this omnipotence by recounting to the still living members of his entourage why and due to
what transgression that particular member had forfeited his/her
right to join him on the pinnacle. He breaks down through this
delusion and the accompanying loss of face and dignity, since he
is too conceited to follow the moral precepts, regardless of what
these had done to his brothers and his wife, who had died earlier
than he. Only when he settles down in the decay and darkness can
he feel the sprouting of love that he has so missed while living on
earth. It also makes him accept the impersonality of the world most
critically—a renewal most acutely full of struggle since it requires
the comprehension of the earliest consciousness emerging from
what is now distinguishable as the inanimate.

In some ways these stories parallel the processes of provision,
challenge, and transformation that occur in psychodynamic therapy
and psychoanalytic clinical practice, especially in the deadness and
perversions in contemporary syndromes and character pathologies.
What one avidly wishes to come upon in Hindu thought and narratives is the presence of a dialogic documented account showing the
translation of awareness into interpersonal conduct in the wake of
despairing dilemmas of life.

Back to Freud

Writing of the death instinct in *Beyond the Pleasure Principle*, Freud
says that "an instinct is an urge inherent in organic life to restore
an earlier state of things" (p. 308). Somewhat later he argues that,
ultimately,

> What has left its mark on the development of organisms must
> be the history of the earth we live in and of its relation to the
> sun. Every modification which is thus imposed upon the course
> of the organism's life is accepted by the conservative organic
> instincts and stored up for further repetition. [Freud, 1920g,
> p. 36]

He adds that there is a deceptive appearance that forces are propel-
ling the individual towards

Change and progress, whilst in fact they are merely seeking to
reach an ancient goal by paths alike old and new . . . It must be
an old state of things, an initial state from which the living entity has at one time or other departed and to which it is striving
to return by the circuitous paths along which its development
leads. [Freud, 1920g, p. 36]

Let me examine whether these resonate somewhat in Hindu
thought. Freud's first concern is with a return to the point of
origin, a relationship with that which is inanimate. This implies
that there is another principle beyond—or before—the pleasure
principle that produces the repetition compulsion. This principle
is more primordial: the organic being restaged back into the inanimate. Freud's reference to the inanimate has an echo in Hindu
thought and practice but one of a different kind. Here it starts
from our popular instruction to reach equanimity through various
meditative practices. We are enjoined to overcome our passions
and in the process sense the self-need and the dependence on the
other(s). The ethical injunction that pervades Hindu consciousness
is to sense the intrinsic suffering associated with attachment and
to follow the pursuit of detachment. The most advanced state of
consciousness belongs to the seer who attempts to reach *Samadhi*,
or complete identification even with the inanimate. Such a seer has
unbounded compassion for all the sorrows and *dukhas* of the world.
Evil and corrupt aspects of the mind also find a home in the seer's
ashram [monastery]. This is based on his cosmic view that all human
deeds are rooted in something that is unconscious into eternity!

Of course, what Freud calls the inanimate is the material in Hinduism. Freud argues that "almost all the energy with which the apparatus is filled arises from its innate instinctual impulses" (1920g,
p. 10). Compare this with the Hindu belief that energy comes from
the cosmos through the *Brahman* and is leased to a body to bring it
alive through the entry of *atman*. Further, as in Hindu thought, life
and death are intrinsically interwoven in the latter (1930a, 1940a
[1938]). As Freud points out:

In the course of things it happens again and again that individual instincts or parts of instincts turn out to be incompatible
in their aims or demands with the remaining ones, which are
able to combine into the inclusive unity of the ego. The former

> are then split off from this unity by the process of repression,
> held back at lower levels of psychical development and cut off,
> to begin with, from the possibility of satisfaction. If they succeed
> subsequently, as can so easily happen with repressed sexual in-
> stincts, in struggling through, by roundabout paths, to a direct
> or to substitutive satisfaction, that event, which would in other
> cases have been an opportunity for pleasure, is felt by the ego as
> unpleasure. . . . The details of the process by which repression
> turns a possibility of pleasure into a source of unpleasure are
> not yet clearly understood or cannot be clearly represented; but
> there is no doubt that all neurotic unpleasure is of that kind—
> pleasure that can not be felt as such. [Freud, 1920g, p. 11]

Since the sexual is erotic, something in the nature of evolving and
binding one with the other, it does have a place in Hindu thought.
The striving for a state of *ananda*—a more pervasive experience of
bliss and heightened awareness of others' relatedness to I/me—as
well as a certain freedom to remain non-focused here about specific vicissitudes of pleasure as well as directions, is comparable to a
more radical transformation such as Freudian thought offers. The
very destiny of the instincts then can become a part of the ego and
attain a different aesthetic experience. Freud's last three statements
above portray a resistance to speculation about the exact sources
of unpleasure and its dynamics and acknowledge the limits of dynamic research. Hindu thought, on the other hand, is metaphysical
and posits the *Karmic* theory with much greater facility.

One of the events that triggered this preoccupation in Freud
is the image of the battle-wearied, disoriented soldier of his time
whose traumatic nightmares neither completely relieve him by being re-staged in the mental theatre nor get absorbed and assimi-
lated in some somatic resource. If the injury had happened, Freud
reminds us, then the soldier may not have been caught in this
dread. He reaches the notion of death instinct as silent work being carried out at the cellular level so that all this immeasurable,
unspeakable dread can be discharged and the state of quiescence
re-established. It is, of course, interesting to note that war is the
setting in which Freud writes, just as war forms the background for
the dialogue between *Krishna* and *Arjuna*.

Freud reassesses the pleasure principle and places it amidst a
new matrix where unpleasure comes about repeatedly not only

through the reality principle but also in the very dynamics of the mental apparatus through the necessary conflicts and dissensions that take place there. In the Hindu system is there an application concerning the mental apparatus? The judgement for *Arjuna* (as the representative of acute dissensions and conflicts) is set against the *Karmic* principle, whereas in the latter's case, there is the conscience that is severely paralysed; he is unable to deploy the principle in questions and instead turns to *Krishna*.

Reading the representation of a conflictual conversation between *Arjuna*, the warrior king, faced with the dilemma of having to kill his own kin in the *Bhagawad Gita*, it may be possible to dwell upon the different psychic characteristics of *Arjuna* and *Krishna*.

The references to the traumatic neuroses as well as to the child's game of *fort–da*, including the description that he had discovered a way of making himself disappear in front of a mirror, are aspects that require special emphasis/mention: the war veterans' dreams and their functions, the child's special way of creating a symbolic expression of his mother having been away, or throwing things and declaring that they were to disappear to the front (where his father has been): all of these aspects either require a distinctive, unreplicable perspective, since they are highly unlikely to be engaged with by a Hindu system, or they should be interpreted in the mythical language of religious thought!

> As the child passes over from the passivity of the experience to the activity of the game, he hands on the disagreeable experience to one of his playmates and in this way revenges himself on a substitute. . . . a reminder may be added that the artistic play and artistic imitation carried out by adults, which, unlike children's, are aimed at an audience, do not spare the spectators (for instance, in tragedy) the most painful experiences and can yet be felt by them as highly enjoyable. [p. 17]

This is convincing proof that, even under the dominance of the pleasure principle, there are ways of making what is in itself unpleasurable into a subject to be recollected and worked over in the mind. The consideration of these cases and situations, which have a yield of pleasure as their final outcome, should be undertaken by some system of aesthetics with an economic approach to its subject-matter. They are of no use for *our* purposes, since they presuppose the existence and dominance of the pleasure principle; they give no evidence of the operation of tendencies *beyond* the pleasure principle—that is, of tendencies that are more primitive than it and are independent of it. It does not require a deep engagement with Hindu philosophy to experience a shudder of (mis)recognition as one notes some ideational similarities between Hindu thought and psychoanalysis.

> ▷ The death drive is a correction on Freud's earlier overemphasis on narcissism. Thus Freud seems to be moving away from the centrality he has always given to pleasure and wishes. At the same time, while recognizing the non-pleasurable nature of certain traumas, he emphasizes reality. This reality, however, is not that of adaptation but, paradoxically, of suffering. Suffering, and even renunciation, are built into his conceptualization of being human. This has clear linkages to Hindu mysticism, which holds a more romantic view of the transformation that the individual undergoes in courting and evolving in this perspective. (Kakar, 1981)

> ▷ Freud argues that death is the true aim of life. However, Freud corrects this hypothesis in *New Introductory Lectures on Psychoanalysis* (1933a) by pointing out that death exists alongside life. It is mingled with the process of living. This, too, resembles the ideas contained in Hindu philosophy, as shown above in the very terms used to name the various gods of life—death as silently working to complement life but opposed to perpetuating the chain of birth and rebirths. (Kakar & Kakar, 2007; Rao, Paranjpe, & Dalal, 2008)

In the end, a philosophy is only good to the extent that it can set up a dialectic between the ordinary moments of living and the extraordinary engravings of consciousness. Freud posits that the chronic skirmish between the life instincts and death instincts informs every possible lived moment and has the potential to generate/accomplish a unique transformation of human relationship, human communication, and self-awareness into points of consciousness marked by pure energy, thus mutating itself into "meeting" even the inanimate as a part of the otherness in the world.

Concluding remarks

I was brought up in a Hindu–Islamic–Buddhist neighbourhood. My atheism has been changed somewhat by this encounter; one fine day, I may find myself adapting the Winnicottian prayer: "Oh God! May I be alive when I die" (in C. Winnicott, 1989, p. 4)—thus:

> May I be able to cry silently when I die; may this silent cry not shake my body with any vehemence so as to make me lose its awareness as my last conscious possession; this is the material which has kept my loyalty like nobody else and enabled an ex-cruciating slow dawn that things are inseparable from the spirit and soul, that mechanics must be the deepest foundation that I can't do without and also do nothing to. No, that is not true fully: I lay myself on it as an eternal prince of my fantasyland and receive imprints and create shapes and forms while coming alive in sense and feelings of time, space, and my humanness; I change my affinities to the earliest and preserve the deepest as a paradox now as unknowable but intimately contiguous, nah inseparable and deadly stuck while protecting my earliest sense of aliveness, my aloneness. May this cry be an acknowledgment that so many will be left aggrieved with the small–big me that they will continue to live but the lack of the real me with them will dominate their senses; the silent cry will also be for all those, including things, in this world whose otherness I could not touch and will never be able to touch in the way I have intimately known my own touch in diverse variations; and finally, cry for myself for the fact that I can not any more live and love with that infinite presumptuousness that masks my dependence on others and uses writing arts and the loftiest things and crafts to not let it become actual even for me. But then what is "actual" if life itself turns out to be a mere wave in Time's river and death remains unknown?"

Note

1. *Neti* refers to a search that is interminable and weds itself to no particularity as wishes often require of us to settle upon. The crucial step is to be drawn to "instead" unceasingly and remain conscious of the energy of searching while one minimally remembers what one started with. Comparable to a state of a perpetual preconception simultaneously

experienced as belonging to or put outside, the search/ answer for which is sought but never to be succeeded with/upon. This is not it; this is not it; this is not it . . . Endless repetition willed towards a state of tireless energy in the matrices of subjects, objects and processes! Experiences of durable recognition are to be discounted.

10

The trauma of lost love in psychoanalysis

Elisabeth Young-Bruehl

Most historians agree that in the history of psychoanalysis Freud's *Beyond the Pleasure Principle* (1920g) marks a juncture, even perhaps *the* juncture. Until 1920, no one could be a Freudian without subscribing to his libido theory—in its evolving formulation—and to the centrality of the sexual instinctual drive in the aetiology of the neuroses. Non-subscribers left the movement. Adler's and Jung's withdrawals became like traumas that Freud kept trying to master in writing about them. But in *Beyond the Pleasure Principle,* Freud himself brought into question the defining position of the libido theory. He disagreed with himself, and the disagreements his interior debate provoked among his followers have, to this day, not ceased reverberating. But, because the Master's revision was so problematic and became no less so as he elaborated his new theory in some later works while rejecting it in others, his followers have felt free to disagree without needing to become schismatics. *Beyond the Pleasure Principle* was more a statement of intense theoretical need than a *Dictat.*

To me, the text seems like the great missed opportunity of psychoanalysis, a moment when an elementary form of love—long known and named—might have been described in dynamic psychoanalytic terms: it might have been shown to have a developmental course, growing to be foundational for mature human relations and political life. To make this argument briefly, I am going to pay particular attention to how this form of love slipped away, became nameless, as Freud proposed his startling hypothesis that there is a "death instinct" in all humans and, indeed, in all nature: a hypothesis of *Naturphilosophie*, not a psychoanalytic hypothesis.

* * *

Let me begin with a few remarks explicating the text's overdetermined title: *Jenseits des Lustprinzips*. All the psychoanalysts who read Freud's *Beyond the Pleasure Principle* in 1920 were familiar with his 1911 paper "Formulations on the Two Principles of Mental Functioning". They knew Freud's claim that the *Lustprinzip* operates on a newborn's sexual drive or libido with few constraints, as long as the newborn is cared for. That is, the well-cared-for newborn's sexual drive produces tensions and excitations that the newborn can discharge unconstrainedly, with libidinal *wishes*—hallucinations—attached to memories of pleasures past. By contrast, there are drives, like the prototypical drive hunger, that cannot be satisfied with a wish for more than a brief while: they are dependent for their satisfaction on real food, a real breast, a real caretaker's responsiveness to baby communications. These drives are more governed by a second *Prinzip*, called the *Realitätsprinzip*. The sexual drive always retains some of its initial capacity to be satisfied, so to speak, "beyond (or before) the *reality* principle"—or to be satisfied by phantasy. Libido's initial manifestations are like a tribe living without any constitution, and its later manifestations may be like anarchists who hark back to the state of nature and reject constitutions as constraints.

The self-preservative drives need reality from the start (as Ferenczi pointed out, even *in utero* they need the reality of the mother's whole body's functioning), and thus they come to adapt more to reality at every stage of the child's life: they become tamed by reality, educated to work with it, to postpone satisfaction while real—or, perhaps, better—satisfactions can be found. These drives were called by Freud the ego instincts, because they preserve the baby's developing "I"—as well as its life—and because the developing ego allies with the reality principle to satisfy the ego instincts—

and the sexual drive, too—in a progressively more "civilized" way, using thought, judgement, imagination, and, ultimately, scientific reasoning. The self-preservative drives and the ego can thus come into conflict with the phantasy-prone sexual drive, and then the ego becomes the director of repression of the sexual drive and its phantasy objects. In *Beyond the Pleasure Principle* Freud invokes this opposition and remarks (1920g, p. 10) that the *Realitätsprinzip* is "under the influence of the ego's instincts of self-preservation". But that is all that Freud says about the ego instincts in the opening pages of *Beyond the Pleasure Principle*—thus missing his opportunity to keep them in his view and in psychoanalysis.

His 1911 theoretical picture of two basic drives—libidinal and ego instinctual—and two basic governing principles was quite clear and unproblematic to Freud, although he had ended his summary statement with a host of questions that needed exploring. His theoretical house seemed in order and consistent with what he had been thinking for years, frequently announcing his agreement with the poet Schiller, with the great Darwin, and with common psychological sense and language since the Greeks. Human beings are ultimately moved by sex and hunger—that is, by a sexual instinct that eventually leads them as they mature to reproduce (to preserve the species) *and* by an instinct that moves them to preserve themselves: initially, to satisfy their hunger, but also to live in safety, security, with healthy functioning of all organs, in a state of well-cared-for-ness or psychic holding. Crucially, Freud acknowledged that self-preservation requires the affection or love or sociality of real—not phantasy—preserving caretakers: that is, it is a relational drive. Human beings are, as Aristotle had said long before, *by nature* sociable and desiring to live together in polities. Affection cannot be got by a baby from a hallucination, or from a wire mother with a bottle, as Harlow's little experimental monkeys knew; it cannot even be satisfied—as Ferenczi's pupil Rene Spitz (Spitz, 1945) showed experimentally—by a well-intentioned hospital nurse with a bottle who shows no warmth or affection for her baby charge and thus causes the baby to suffer from and even die of "hospitalism".

In the early editions of *Three Essays on the Theory of Sexuality* (1905d), Freud had declared that the libidinal energy in children should be called "the sensual current", and the self-preservative drive energies should be called, collectively, "the affectionate current". Similarly, he distinguished sensuality—*Sinnlichkeit*—from tenderness or affection—*Zärtlichkeit*. Both currents of desire have as their first object the maternal breast, but when a baby is nursing, the affectionate current leads the way, and the sensual current leans upon it (or is "anaclitic" on it). The breast is the "anaclitic" object, *Anlehnungsobjekt*, literally the object leaned upon, depended upon, by the affectionate desire, because the baby cannot survive without the breast—or, as Freud would later stress, because the baby is helpless without it. Winnicott put the matter more wittily by saying that "there is no such thing as a baby"—there is only a baby-and-mother. For the sexual instinct the breast is an erotic object, pleasurable but not essential to life.

As a child develops, Freud argued, the sexual instinctual drive (the sensual current), at first so strong in the mouth, concentrates in the site of the anus, and then in the genitals. But he did not note a corresponding stage development or site-specificity for the self-preservative drives, although he sometimes associated a self-preservative drive with each of the major bodily organs. Generally, he left these drives very little explored once he had described their satisfaction as getting physiological needs met and getting affection.[1] Crucially, Freud did not explore an object relational line of development for the affectionate current, even though he had said clearly that it is object-related before the sensual current is.

When Freud wrote about sex and hunger, he always interpreted sex very broadly, using the Greek word *eros*, as the qualitative dimension for what he would describe quantitatively as tension reduction. But he never assigned hunger a general name comparable to *eros*—although such a word was available in ancient Greek, where *eros* was always contrasted to but entwined with *philia*—affection or love of the sort that exists first between parents and children, but later between children and mentors, between friends who care for each other, citizens who appear before each other in councils and are bound by respect or *philia politike*, and so forth. *Philia* refers to all bonds without which humans do not survive or do not survive *as humans*.[2] In all the European languages with which Freud was familiar it is very obvious that a distinction between libidinal desire and needs that require loving care is registered as fundamental. Further, that lexical line separates desire—chiefly sexual desire—

which you must actively reach out to satisfy (even if only to touch your own body) or go after, from desire that is satisfied by taking in or binding to yourself and which originally came *to you* in your helpless, dependent infant state. It is from the taking in or binding desire that the higher capacities of people in their relations with each other derive. The two forms of desire are analogized with words like "appetite", which you can have for sex as well as for food, but the satisfactions are understood to be quite different. *Eros* and *philia*—desire directed actively outward and desire directed inward (as incorporative, receptive)—are, in non-technical German, *Begierde* (*sinnliche*) and *Wunsch*, in Italian *concupiscenza* and *desiderio*, in Spanish *lujuria* and *deseo*. These distinctions are like the one in English between lust and desire, where lust indicates acquisitive sexual desire (and also inordinate activity, avidity, greed) and desire is closer to need.

But, even though Freud's first instinctual drive theory had the virtues of clarity and simplicity, the weight of poetic and scientific authority, and the wisdom of common speech to recommend it, he renovated it. The period of Freud's thought between 1911 and 1920 can be characterized in many ways, but for the argument I am making here it is most important to note that this is the period in which the self-preservative instinctual drives were unexplored, then marginalized, and finally redefined into unimportance. From 1911 to 1920, Freud's attention was on the emergent ego as intently as it had been, until then, on the sexual drive, and, even more, it was on the relationship of the ego and the sexual drive (not the self-preservative ones). His burning question was, how does the ego form (and also misform) and grow *in relation to the sexual drive*? This striking de-emphasis on the self-preservative drives came just after Freud had geared up to defend his libido theory against Adler, who had been very concerned with the ego instincts (which he thought included an aggressive drive) and just as he was beginning to realize that he had to get ready to argue with Jung, who thought (monistically) that there was but one type of energy moving human beings. The Jungian single energy was not specifically sexual—indeed, it was more self-preservative, more affectional (even though Jung had the impertinence to call it "libidinal"). It may well be that Freud (consciously or unconsciously) steered away from the ego instinctual drive territory where he thought his opponents had set up their theoretical camps in order to attack his libido theory. They seemed more concerned theoretically with security (or, in Adler's case, insecurity) and with social power than with sex.

As he realized that he and Jung had substantial and potentially irreconcilable differences, Freud was also very concerned to clarify his own thinking about obsessionality and particularly about psychosis—that is, about ego distortion and pathology, Jung's speciality. So it was his work on Schreber (Freud, 1911b) that led Freud to the hugely consequential work on narcissism (1914c). This paper is too complex to go into in detail here, but for my purposes its final declaration, that there are but two kinds of love, is the nub. Freud described the sexual drive, under the direction of the ego, as going to objects and hanging on them—that is, as directed towards the "anaclitic object" (which, of course, had once been the ego instinctual drive's object). And he described the sexual drive (not the ego instinctual) as directed towards the ego itself, both in the ego's initial emergent state ("primary narcissism") and in later states subsequent to the sexual drive having gone out towards an anaclitic object and then retreated, either unable to hang there or suffering a loss of the object. The ego has either anaclitic objects or a narcissistic object (itself). In a normal developmental course, the child grows from narcissistic love to love of another. If the normal child must retreat into narcissistic love after a loss, it can do so without "narcissistic neurosis" (which basically means that it manages to master its loss of an object and is able to go forth again to love others, not getting stuck in pathological mourning but being strengthened by reinvesting its salvaged libidinal investment in its ego[3]).

After 1914, when Freud had added to his theoretical edifice these ideas about normal primary narcissism and psychotic retreat into narcissism, he offered a crucial redefinition of the self-preservative "affectionate current". In his last revision of the *Three Essays*, the affectionate current lost its distinctiveness from the sensual current and changed into inhibited *sexual* desire, It became sexual desire that cannot proceed to full object love but remains fixed in self-investment or retreats to narcissistic love of the self. The theory of narcissism really erased the independence and the importance of the self-preservative drive as it demoted affectional love to a kind of narcissism. The new developmental theory (from primary

narcissism to object love) then required a slight renovation or de-
velopmentalizing of the *Lustprinzip*: autoerotic tension reduction
normally gives way developmentally to altererotic tension reduction
(and this vastly increased the pathological significance of masturba-
tion and of the perversions, which fall short of altererotic tension
reduction). The helpless newborn baby's need for, search for, and
reception of sustenance and affection in relation to its care-givers
(particularly the mother) was replaced with primary narcissism conceived of as an explanation for the newborn's search for pleasure in
autoeroticism, which requires no dependency, no other, no mother.
There is such a thing as a baby, alone.

So when, in 1920, Freud came to looking *Beyond the Pleasure Principle*, it was hardly to be expected that he would find a new version
of the old ideas that had been demolished during the years when
he was extending and broadening in every way that he could his
"libido theory", his postulation of the omni-causality and centrality
of the sexual instinct, in general and in the development of the
ego. Freud was not going to return to or reconsider or rebuild the
old idea that there are two instincts, sex and hunger, particularly
as such a return might have weakened his ability to distinguish his
theory from Adler's or Jung's. And, besides, the self-preservative
instincts were not at all what Freud thought he needed to deal with
the pieces of evidence he catalogued in *Beyond the Pleasure Principle*,
claiming that they did not fit with even the revised *Lustprinzip* postulation. Apparently, it did not occur to him that the pieces of evidence he was cataloguing were without a theoretical place because
he had been so busy demolishing their place—the self-preservative
instinct theory.

* * *

Let me turn now to the pieces of evidence. They are of different
sorts, but all have in common that they involve repetition—what
Freud called "the compulsion to repeat"—of painful activities,
some of which do finally end in pleasurable relief, but some bring
discharge but no relief, and some bring only perpetual pain. He
noted that children play games in which they repeat actions, over
and over. This seems to have the function of allowing them (usually) to cope with or master loss, particularly separation from the
mother (in the instance of the "*fort–da*" game he describes in de-

tail). Then Freud noted that people who suffer traumatic injuries, as well as soldiers who suffer from war neurosis (where no physical injury is involved), repeatedly dream their traumas—but seldom to any relief. In psychoanalytic treatments, he adds, recurring to a feature he had noted in his papers on technique, neither interpreting the content of patients' free associations nor analysing their resistances to interpretations brings about a cure. Cure must arise from allowing patients to repeat in the analytic situation their childhood experiences of defeat, loss, rivalry with parents or siblings, or failure to fulfil their wishes because of physical immaturity or prohibitions. Repetition of painful childhood experiences takes place in treatment and with the analyst (where it is called the "transference neurosis"), but it also takes place in the lives of some normal people, who "give the impression of being pursued by a malignant fate or possessed by some 'daemonic' power" (1920g, p. 21). They have a character trait or formation that produces repetitive patterning or "perpetual recurrence of the same thing" (p. 22).

Every analyst knows that compulsive repetition is evident in every treatment, crucially, and is everywhere in people's lives (and, many would say, as Freud himself later did, in the collective lives of groups). The quarrel over *Beyond the Pleasure Principle* that began in 1920 and continues is not over the commonness of the repetition compulsion or its paramount significance, but over the explanation. For Freud, the phenomenon points to the limits of the *Lustprinzip*, which cannot regulate and reduce the tension these games and dreams and enactments are themselves trying to contain or master. The *Lustprinzip* cannot, as Freud puts it, "bind" the energy—so far unnamed—that *must* be invidiously active in these activities, which have run unchecked, he suggests, because the precipitating traumas have broken through the mind's "protective barrier" against shocking stimulation and overstimulation. The traumas have, so to speak, returned the mind to formlessness and void, like pre-life. The mind has to be somewhat regulated, somewhat constant, before it can carry through the process of finding peace and quiet; internal chaos cannot bring about the end of chaos produced by trauma or returned to in trauma. So these traumas must release an instinctual drive lying deep in the mind, there *before* the *Lustprinzip*.

At this point in the argument, the Freud of the first instinct theory might have been able to say: what is released by a trauma is the self-preservative drive, screaming, so to speak "Let me live! Help me! Take me in your arms!" But that is not the step Freud took in 1920. Rather, he took one that caused the trauma to the psychoanalytic community that it has been repeating compulsively ever since.

His thoughts about traumatic breakthrough had been propelled by the question: if the compulsion to repeat can override the *Lustprinzip* ("to which, after all, we have hitherto ascribed dominance over the course of the processes of excitation in mental life" [p. 23]), does that not mean that this compulsion is "more primitive, more elementary, more instinctual than the pleasure principle which it over-rides"? Freud then asks: "But how is the predicate of being 'instinctual' related to the compulsion to repeat? (p. 36)" His next, fateful, cluster of questions was: Does the compulsion to repeat express an instinctual drive towards an earlier state of things, towards a state of dissolution, breakdown—ultimately, towards death? Does it express an inertia inherent in organic life? And might this instinctual drive towards dissolution even have brought the ego into being in the first place—that is, might the ego have grown up to try to control this dissolving energy (not to try to preserve itself by getting love and care)?

A fragile ego trying to control this dissolving energy would naturally have to have its own energy, and that would, of course, have to be an energy of binding and building up. Such an energy would have to be, Freud argued, none other than the sexual instinctual drive, the species preservative drive that eventually brings sperm to ovum, creating new life. *Eros*. So *Eros*, which had once been the source of disruption in the psychic economy, the source of ego pathology, because it resisted the reality principle and maintained its phantasy-proneness following the *Lustprinzip*, becomes now the redemptive force of binding, unification, building up (on its eventual way to reproduction[4]).

The biological speculations and reviews of contemporary biologists' speculations that Freud offered as he took up his questions and began to construct his theory of "the death instinct" (later to be called *Thanatos* in contrast to *Eros*) are not, I think, of great interest now. What seems to me most important in the theory construction is the act of demolition required to make way for it. Specifically, the self-preservative instincts, long under threat of theoretical superfluity, had to be completely broken up and recycled. Remarkably, they do not appear with *Eros* as forces of binding and building up, but as forces that serve the death instinct! Freud himself seemed shocked at this strange development:

> The hypothesis of self-preservative instincts, such as we attribute to all living beings, stands in marked opposition to the idea that instinctual life as a whole serves to bring about death. Seen in this light, the theoretical importance of the instincts of self-preservation, of self-assertion and of mastery greatly diminishes. They are component instincts whose function it is to assure that the organism shall follow its own path to death, and to ward off any possible ways of returning to inorganic existence other than those which are immanent in the organism itself. We have no longer to reckon with the organisms puzzling determination (so hard to fit into any context) to maintain its own existence in the face of every obstacle. What we are left with is the fact that the organism wishes to die only in its own fashion. Thus these guardians of life, too, were originally the myrmidons of death . . . [p. 39]

As they struggle against dangers and threats to life, the self-preservative instincts may *seem* to serve life—as the sexual instincts actually do, Freud believed, by leading to unification, reproduction. But, in fact, self-preservation serves only to stave off any externally dealt death blow while the death instinct follows its inevitable immanent or interior course, which is so inexorable that it does not even require a *Todesprinzip*, a regulatory principle (although, in effect, it follows a principle of inertia). As we compulsively repeat, we struggle mightily to take *our own* path to death.

Not surprisingly, this idea soon seemed to Freud himself to be far-fetched, and he eventually redeemed the much-diminished self-preservative drives somewhat by saying that, really, they must serve the sexual instinctual drive—they must be *its* guardians.[5] But he did not then, as he might have, realize that the compulsion to repeat can very well be seen—as I suggested before—to be manifesting these very "instincts of self-preservation, of self-assertion and of mastery" as they go about trying to heal the effects in children and adults of traumas (which may be traumas primarily effecting the sensual current or the affectionate current or, more usually, both). He did not say that if reality is traumatic to a sufficient degree, reality will overcome the *Lustprinzip*, reality itself will be beyond the pleasure principle. And the self-preservative drive, rather than serving the reality principle, will have to fight it; survival will depend upon the self-preservative drive not being knocked completely out of commission. If, in a manner consistent with Freud's first instinct theory, in which his notion of the "protective barrier" was framed, we describe a trauma as an event (or series of events) that, producing psychic chaos, cuts a person off from caretakers, security, safety, allegiances, comrades, civility—all the aims of the affectionate current—as well as from any sexual desire satisfaction, then a compulsion to repeat is a compulsion on the part of the drives for preservation to heal, to overcome, to make a different outcome, to reconnect. The compulsion to repeat is attempted self-care-taking or solicitation of care-taking from others. The traumatized person wants her own *path to life*, which has been obscured, demolished.

In fact, this line of argument that I have imagined had been taken by Freud himself back in the 1911 Schreber case, where Freud had described the psychotic's symptoms as manifestations of an effort to return to a benign reality and to other people, a self-preservative effort or an effort at self-healing. And the line of argument was also taken *after 1920*. It shapes the 1926 text *Inhibitions, Symptoms and Anxiety*, where Freud constructed a brilliant definition of anxiety as—in effect—a signal that an elemental expectation of love had been or was about to be disappointed. He even constructed a developmental line for anxiety. This definition and this developmental line obviated the need for a death-instinct theory.[6] But Freud compulsively repeated the theory anyway.

* * *

In the history of psychoanalysis beyond *Beyond the Pleasure Principle*, two roads eventually parted in the woods. At first, there was some agreement. All Freudians were impressed with the emphasis that Freud put after 1920 on aggression, because everyone who had survived the First World War realized that aggression and aggression against the self (masochism) had been underemphasized and undertheorized in psychoanalysis. But there agreement ended. And most subsequent psychoanalysts have either followed Klein and Lacan in elaborating the death-instinct theory in various ways or followed Hartmann and Fenichel and others among the ego psy-

chologists in repudiating the biological theory while accepting the
idea that sex and aggression are fundamental drives. (Anna Freud
stood diplomatically aside, speaking of sex and aggression as fundamental drives but neither embracing nor rejecting the biological
death-instinct theory, which she said needed to be confirmed or
disconfirmed by empirical research.[7])

In only one camp did refusing the death-instinct theory flow
from recognition that the theory had cost psychoanalysis its path to
exploring the self-preservative drives or the ego instincts and thus
to developing a philosophy of love and a moral–political theory:
this was the Budapest School, starting in the 1930s, after Ferenczi's death.[8] Ferenczi himself had opened the way for his trainees
with his asides in *Thalassa* about a self-preservative longing for
the nourishing protective enclosure of the womb. But he had also
emphasized a *sexual* drive for return to the womb and accepted a
version of the death-instinct theory. Most significant for his trainees
were his efforts to theorize about protective, affectional love in the
therapeutic situation, although these efforts were disturbing when
they veered off into reflections on eroticism in the therapeutic situation and to dangerous experiments with "mutual analysis".

The most empirically oriented Hungarian explorer of the self-
preservative relational drives was Imre Hermann, a researcher well-
versed in ethology and primatology, who wrote a famous 1936 paper
on the self-preservative drive pair "to cling" and "to go in search".[9]
Michael Balint recognized that the original affectionate current
had a developmental history that needed exploring (and he eventually thought that the developmental history might be clearest
in group relations—hence the Balint Groups). As children grow
more complex, they do so on the basis of an original relational
love, which he called "primary passive object love" or sometimes
just "primary love" (Balint, 1937). Depending on the reality—the
traumas—they encounter and how they react, children become
characterologically "ocnophile" (loving to cling to objects) or tend
towards "philobatism" (orientation towards open spaces that are
free of dreaded, anxiety-producing obstacles). Balint's first wife,
Alice Balint, spoke of "archaic, egoistic object love" in a 1931 book
called *The Early Years of Life*, which, when it was finally translated
into English in 1954, contained an appreciative Preface by Anna
Freud.

To my knowledge, the difficulties of finding an adequate single noun for the affectionate current (as a range and development of drives, not just in its prototype, hunger) have been considered only by a psychoanalyst who did not think in the lexicon that Freud inherited from German philosophy and physics. Takeo Doi (1973) notes that in his mother tongue, Japanese, there is an everyday noun, *amae*, which means "the expectation to be sweetly and indulgently loved". *Amae*, Doi argued (and Michael Balint accepted the argument in his 1968 book *The Basic Fault*), is Freud's old ego instinctual "affectionate current", and it is a template for all later affectionate love, in children, in adults, and in societies. But neither Michael Balint nor Takeo Doi recognized, it seems to me, that the distinction Freud drew in his early work between "the sensual current" and "the affectionate current"—like the one he drew between the sexual instincts and the ego instincts—actually represents the common sense of the European *eros/philia* tradition as well as of the Japanese.

The relative silence in psychoanalysis over the lost ego instincts has not been recognized in recent years because those who have felt the need for an "affectionate current" have thought that such was supplied by John Bowlby's attachment theory, which was developed by Mary Ainsworth but also by the contemporary Freudians at the Anna Freud Centre, like Peter Fonagy and Mary Target. Bowlby had posited an attachment drive that must be satisfied for normal development, while pathology flows from its frustration or its traumatization by environmental factors. Others have felt that Winnicott's distinction between the object mother (recipient of erotic love) and the environmental mother (supplier of vital needs and protector from trauma) recognizes the love that had no name other than hunger. These are crucial contributions, which have inspired most of the fruitful work in child analysis in recent decades, but the Bowlbyan line really has no theory of the unconscious, and the Winnicottian line has no drive theory.

So, it seems to me, what was lost in 1920 has not really been refound, and psychoanalysis remains relatively unconnected to the ethical and political insights first articulated in the West by the Greek explorers of *philia*. The ways in which we are supplied with the necessities of life—the ways in which we are lovingly fed and cared for tenderly—set the developmental stage for mature life when people are no longer under the sway of necessity, no longer helpless and dependent, and can tend to others, including their parents, in a well-regulated polity that guarantees their freedom to act or to direct their own actions according to worthy principles like courage and magnanimity. Affectionately reared children, Aristotle says in the *Nichomachean Ethics* (IX.ii.8), will later impart to their parents "nourishment" [*trophe*] and find this care more beautiful than they find caring for themselves. Receiving affectional love is the root of altruism.

And in our world it would be a great benefaction, it seems to me, were altruism to be understood this way: as the great life-sustaining attainment of our inborn expectation of love.

Notes

1. Sándor Ferenczi noticed this absence, and wrote a paper in 1913, after the *Prinzip* concept had entered the Freudian lexicon, called "Stages in the Development of the Sense of Reality" (1913a). He set out a preliminary sketch for a line of ego instinctual development that had great influence in the Budapest School, particularly upon Michael Balint.

2. *Philia* was the word used by Aristotle to reflect an earlier Homeric system of words focused around the verb *trepho*, cherish or nurture, which was translated as *colere* in Latin, the verb underlying the noun *cultura*. The *philia* bonds are the cultural bonds, compassing child-rearing methods, education, mentoring from older to younger citizens, and creating cultural objects, monuments, and cities (cf. Young-Bruehl, 2003).

3. In the technique papers contemporary to his work on narcissism, Freud recommended to analysts who felt erotically drawn to their female patients that they withdraw, mastering their "countertransference" (a new term) and enhancing their ego-strength thereby. This was another matter on which he and Jung disagreed, particularly as they both treated an incurable extreme obsessional patient, Elfriede Hirschfield (cf. Falzeder, 1994).

4. In his writings on sexual development after 1920, Freud emphasized the normality and importance of reproductive sexuality and heterosexuality more than he ever had before, because homosexuality and the perversions made no contribution to opposing the death instinct. The consequences of this emphasis were disastrous for psychoanalytic understanding of homosexuality and the perversions.

5. In the unfinished *An Outline of Psycho-Analysis* (1940a [1938]), Freud

wrote: "The contrast between the instincts of self-preservation and the preservation of the species, as well as the contrast between ego-love and object-love, fall within Eros" (p. 148).

6. Anna Freud seems to have understood this significance of signal-anxiety and its developmental line, as she built it into the framework of her *The Ego and the Mechanisms of Defense* (1936), in which she did not need to mention of the death-instinct theory.

7. Then, in 1971, upon her first return to Vienna after the war, speaking about aggression to the IPA Congress, Anna Freud asked her colleagues to "agree to acknowledge the gap between clinical fact and biological specu-lation instead of enforcing direct causal links between the two fields" (A. Freud, 1981, p. 174).

8. There was American interest in the ego instincts after World War II, but that interest focused on the ego instincts as instincts of mastery or "effectence" (Robert White's word, 1963), not on their modality of love. This was a kind of Pragmatist Darwinism.

9. Hermann has a contemporary advocate in the Belgian analyst To-mas, but Geyskens does not see the ego instinctual line of development outlined in Hermann's work (Geyskens & Van Haute, 2007).

Epilogue

Mary Kay O'Neil

> Go, said the bird, for the leaves were full of children,
> Hidden excitedly, containing laughter.
> Go, go, go, said the bird: human kind
> Cannot bear very much reality.
> Time past and time future
> What might have been and what has been
> Point to one end, which is always present.
>
> T. S. Eliot, Burnt Norton (1935)
from The Four Quartets (by permission of Faber & Faber)

T. S. Eliot realized we all live with pleasure, reality, and the passage of time while holding the awareness of one inevitable end. For life, this end is death. Freud in 1920 struggled with this ambiguous and contradictory awareness. Yet the question remains: What occurs between the beginning of life and its ending by death, and towards which does "humankind" lean?

Beyond the Pleasure Principle (1920g) is long, difficult to read, and rather obtuse theoretically. It is "arguably the least plausible, the most inscrutable and speculative of all of Freud's major theoretical contributions" (Greenberg, 1990). It demonstrates Freud's

uncertainty, his struggle with inconsistencies, his dilemmas, his un-
answered questions, and his daring to speculate and be wrong.
Historically, it is an odd essay, unlike Freud's more assertive, less
ambiguous theorizing from clinical material, and, in spite of the enduring controversy engendered, it says much about dilemmas with
which psychoanalysts still struggle. Freud's new concept, "the death
instinct", central to his thesis has been questioned, repudiated,
dismissed as untenable biologically, and theoretically unintegrated.
However, *Beyond* . . . offers much more than this new concept. It is
a rich, challenging essay! It is revisionist and prescient of what is
to come. Many of the psychoanalytic seeds planted in *Beyond the
Pleasure Principle* have matured since 1920.

As is well known, at the end of this essay Freud challenged his
followers and today's psychoanalysts to question, to put forth their
views, to dare to be right and/or wrong.

> We must be patient and await fresh methods and occasions of
> research. We must be ready, too, to abandon a path that we have
> followed for a time, if it seems to be leading to no good end.
> Only believers, who demand that science shall be a substitute
> for the catechism they have given up, will blame an investiga-
> tor for developing or even transforming his views. We may take
> comfort, too, for the slow advances of our scientific knowledge
> [Freud, 1920g, p. 64]

The authors of the ten chapters presented here, with advanced scientific knowledge and having different psychoanalytic perspectives,
address Freud's ambiguities. They agree and disagree. They highlight current theoretical developments, demonstrate how to teach,
they discuss the clinical and cultural implications; and they present
their contemporary views of *Beyond the Pleasure Principle*. As well as
psychoanalysts, the readership of the book will include teachers,
pupils, and scholars of psychoanalysis, as well as interested laypeo-
ple. The variations in authors' thoughts will speak to some more
than to others, but their combined contributions bring *Beyond the
Pleasure Principle* alive, thereby perhaps reducing its inscrutability.
This is a timely volume, given the current sociocultural and clinical
attention to post-traumatic syndromes, including traumatic dreams,
the psychoanalytic attention to narcissism and severe psychopathology, the repetition of genocide in today's world, the persistence of
destructive aggression, the desperate attempts at peace, and the

courageous moves, socially and clinically, to channel aggression constructively. This epilogue serves to comment on the rich ideas communicated in the volume's chapters.

Craig Tomlinson begins with his chapter on teaching Freud's late work as it evolved from his 1920 mind-set as revealed in *Beyond the Pleasure Principle*. Tomlinson challenges teachers to know the particularities of their audience and to communicate accordingly. He astutely guides not only teachers and pupils of psychoanalysis but also the readers of this volume. By placing this "watershed work" as an "equal among firsts" of psychoanalytic classics, he signifies its "monumental" and evolving implications while recognizing that it must be read both in past time—the social, clinical, and scientific context within which it was written—and in present time—the sociocultural context within which today's reader lives. This historical perspective underlines the role that *Beyond . . .* plays in the divergent social and intellectual history of psychoanalysis. Freud intended *Beyond . . .* to generate debate, not to resolve it. He had not anticipated its significant influence on tensions within psychoanalytic organizations, nor could he have predicted the richness and diversity of psychoanalytic contributions that would be stimulated.

Tomlinson also draws attention to little-recognized details that facilitate understanding of and ongoing debate over this Freudian work. For example, "Freud conspicuously left the death drive as a 'drive without a name'"; it was others who coined the phrase "death instinct"/*Thanatos* to capture Freud's central concept. Translation generates its own meaning, a fact often forgotten as the English version of Freud's works became widely read. To begin with the first word in the title, *Jenseits* [beyond] could also be translated as "the other side" or "the far side", containing an allusion to traditional German philosophy and theology—that is, "other-worldly", a reference to a religious afterlife. The consideration of such small details gives much food for thought and debate.[1] As Tomlinson concludes, Freud left his audience with significant scientific issues with which to grapple. Yet, "one need not accept the details of Freud's speculations here as scientifically credible in the twenty-first century", but it is possible "to share in a sense of wonder at the scope of Freud's thinking about the human condition . . .".

Tomlinson's opening chapter sets the stage for readers to consider the varied views of the other authors, in the light of what, in his Introduction, *Salman Akhtar* refers to as altered concepts—life instinct, self-preservative instinct, death instinct, aggression, sadism, and masochism—as well as an enriched dream theory and "psychic incorporation of death in life".

Fàtima Caropreso and *Theisen Simanke*, coming from Brazil and their classical Freudian frame of reference, take an historical view of Freud's 1920 essay. Comparing his first and second dual instinct theories, they note, "Freud recognizes in *Beyond the Pleasure Principle* that this new instinctual dualism does not offer the same degree of certainty as his earlier efforts in instinctual theory. Some hypotheses he developed in later writings seem to make the death and life instinct duality more problematic and to reinforce the impression that there is in fact no difference between these two types of instinct." Commenting on Freud's thoughts about "instinctual dualism" after *Beyond . . .,* they insist that a reappraisal of life and death instincts within Freudian metapsychology logically requires a different balance between the two. Their reappraisal of Freud's second instinctual dualism accepts his most debated and controversial concept, the "death instinct", not only as valid but, indeed, as primary; they argue that, "No matter how hard Freud tried to accord the life instinct the same status as the death instinct, it seems difficult to avoid the conclusion that death lurks behind all life." Certainly, their view alters the "life instinct" concept. One can only applaud their final words that full appreciation and reappraisal of Freud's theorizing on the "death instinct" needs to be based on a dialogue between contemporary biology and psychoanalysis. This challenges psychoanalysts to bring Freud's 1920 concept into the twenty-first century in the light of current research in neuroscience.

"Repetition compulsion"—a second important concept that Freud introduced in *Beyond . . .*—was stimulated by what he observed in the behaviour of children, war veterans, and others who suffered painful, traumatic past experiences. Responding to the post-war world around him, Freud's observations led to the theory that this repetitive behaviour was a self-destructive "daemonic force" (p. 35), opposed to the pleasure principle with the purpose of reducing the organism to a quiescent, inorganic state: the "death instinct". *Ira Brenner,* being of the opinion that Freud in his development of the meaning of repetition compulsion was too theoretical and autobiographical, is in accord with subsequent analysts (Bibring, 1943; Casement, 1991; Loewald, 1971), as noted by Akhtar (2009a, p. 245), who consider this behaviour to be in the "service of mastering a trauma". Brenner, using case material and experience with patients in dissociative states, neither labels nor theorizes but brings one case example alive to show how symptoms and extreme desperate dissociative defences (fugue states and switching or dual personalities) allow his patient to deal with unbearable emotions arising from the terrible reality of past traumatic experiences and triggered by a current threatening event. Not only does Brenner cut through the controversy over the "death instinct" to illustrate the clinical meaningfulness of "repetition compulsion", but he also elucidates technical handling of deep psychopathology and the mobilization of extreme defences in the face of trauma. As well, he sheds light on the collapse of time—past, present, and future—due to severe trauma: that is, the traumatic experience can be so intense that a person cannot appreciate the passage of time between past and present and fears similar harm in the future. Brenner understands the "quiescence, quiet, or calm" that is sought through "repetition" not as the "daemonic force" of the death instinct but as a way of coming to terms with disturbing traumatic experiences—indeed, being able to live. Brenner goes beyond Freud clinically and, with his discussion of traumatic dreams, he provides an opening for the next chapter, which elucidates and integrates Freud's two dream theories.

Joshua Levy continues where Freud left off by bringing together, in a lucidly unique way, Freud's two dream theories. The first well-known theory in *The Interpretation of Dreams* considers dreams as disguised wish-fulfilment, whereas the second *independent* theory occurring in traumatic neuroses represents compulsive repetition of the traumatic event as it occurred. The purpose here is to release tension and belatedly master the trauma. Freud's two theories, significantly different in structure and function, have rarely been brought together and remain un-integrated. Levy uses the conclusions of those few analysts (Loewenstein, Adams-Sylvan and Sylvan, Lansky, Brenneis) who proposed that traumatic dreams can have the dual function both of mastering the threatened reality and as a wish-fulfilment, "as building blocks towards *his* attempt to find the base for the coexistence of Freud's two dream theories". Levy notes: "There is a vast difference in the clinical evidence that

Freud provided for his two dream theories: while in 1900 his well-reasoned clinical evidence allows for scrutiny of the development and conceptual clarity of Freud's original dream theory, the lack of clinical evidence for his 1920 theory, in contrast, precludes assessment of the grounds for this second theory."

Apparently, the self-psychological approach to dreams is akin to Freud's second dream theory, and some clinical evidence is provided (e.g. Kohut, Ornstein). However, there are limitations to understanding and interpreting dreams with one or the other theoretical framework. Levy asks: "Is it possible to find space in the analyst's mind for the coexistence of Freud's two dream theories?" If so, then the integration of Freud's dream theories requires that the analyst listen to the patients' free associations to their dreams, be in tune with potential multiple day residues that might have triggered the dreams, and try to process the clinical material, relying on the operations of the dream-work. By first astutely re-analysing Freud's three dreams (the "Irma" dream, "R is my uncle", and the "botanical monograph") utilizing both theories, and then by providing detailed clinical evidence of his own, Levy not only fills the clinical evidence gap but provides the reader with an opportunity to make an individual assessment of the value of integrating the two theories clinically and conceptually. In keeping with the contemporary emphasis on transference and countertransference, interpersonal aspects of the dream as embedded in the analytic relationship are highlighted.

"Freud presented his theory of the manifest content of traumatic dreams without clinical evidence and without reference to the pivotal concepts of his earlier dream theory—the latent content, the dream-work, and unconscious wish-fulfilment. Consequently there were no grounds for assessing the validity of his second dream theory and no conceptual basis for integrating his original dream theory." Levy concludes that traumatic dreams, like any other dream, can be understood as being constructed through the dream work. To achieve a clinically meaningful dream theory, a systematic comparison is needed between current diverse theories and Freud's theories.

Henri Parens, perhaps unintentionally, recognizes, like Freud and T. S. Eliot, that humankind cannot bear much reality. In contrast to analysts who wish to depend on—even reify—Freudian concepts,

Parens notes that Freud was speculative rather than dogmatic when he postulated the "death instinct". Throughout his career, while accepting much of what Freud has written, Parens took Freud's invitation to "consider or dismiss (the "death instinct") according to his individual predilection". He doubts the validity of Freud's death-instinct-based theory of aggression and is in agreement with psychoanalysts who hold that it is not possible to prove that humans are driven by a death instinct. In fact, he believes that the "death-instinct" concept is unnecessary for a sound and valid understanding of human aggression.

Based on extensive research with children, Parens' chapter is not only enlightening but offers fresh findings about the nature of aggression. He proposes, after much cogitation, deliberation, testing, and dreaming, four categories of aggressive behaviours:

1.   unpleasure-related destructiveness;
2.   non-affective destructiveness;
3.   nondestructive aggression;
4.   pleasure-related destructiveness.

Parens then conceptualizes three trends in aggression: hostile destructiveness (1 & 4); non-affective destructiveness (2); and nondestructive aggression (3). His observations of children's repetitive behaviour lead back to what Freud hypothesized and then rejected—that the compulsion to repeat represents an effort to make passive into active—an effort to master rather than return to an inorganic state. It is excessive unpleasure—intense frustration and narcissistic injury—that generates hostile destructiveness, but aggression, in contrast, can lead to creativity when it seeks restitution. The unpleasure can be both internal and external. In essence, aggression related to the "death instinct" does not align with Parens' observations of children who use their repetitive assertive behaviour for growth, mastery, and living. Parens holds that Freud's first drive theory—the dichotomy of the sexual instincts and the ego (self-preservative) instincts—holds up much better with regard to the multi-trends theory of aggression than does his second instinctual drive theory—the dichotomy of the sexual drive (based on the "life instincts") and the aggressive drive (based on the death instinct). In that sense, by aligning aggression with the life instinct, he disagrees with Caropreso and Simanke, who feel that life is subsumed in death. Nodding to the Kleinians' clinical use of the concept of the death instinct to understand aggression, Parens supports his multi-trend theory of aggression with carefully gathered evidence not only from his own research with children but from other analysts and students of adjacent fields addressing psychoanalytic questions.

Otto Kernberg, with his imitable point form clarity, deconstructs Freud's hypothesis of the death drive. The phenomena that led Freud to this concept include the repetition compulsion, sadism and masochism, suicide in severe depression and in non-depressive characterological structures, and destructive and self-destructive developments in group processes and their social implications. He discusses Freud's theory and explores each of these phenomena in the light of clinical experience with severely self-destructive personality disorders and of contemporary object relations theory. As Freud encouraged, Kernberg develops an understanding of the death drive within a contemporary biopsychosocial context: individually and socially, affects (positive and negative) are "primary motivational systems in the sense that their activation, under certain circumstances, by mechanisms of the limbic brain, initiates strong motivation to movement towards other objects or away from them. . . . All affects are embedded in mental representations: that is, a cognitive organization. . . . The very fantasies that reflect unconscious conflicts between love and hatred are always representations embedded in respective positive or negative affects." He proposes more in that the unconscious function of self-destructiveness is not simply to destroy the self, but to destroy significant others as well and, further, that triumphant pleasure can be experienced in the aggression against the self and others. In this way "the death drive is not inconsistent with the pleasure principle, as evidenced by the triumphant pleasure some patients get in defeating all efforts to help them". Here, perhaps unwittingly, Kernberg is integrating both of Freud's dual instinct theories. To summarize, the concept of the death drive is clinically relevant, but this condition needs to be traced to the general dominance of aggressive affects as the primary etiological factor. Only under severely pathological circumstances does this dominance lead to a focused drive to self-destruct. It remains to be seen whether growing psychoanalytic understanding of aggressive and self-aggressive behaviour of large groups and its relation to regressive processes in the social realm will lead to a contribution to their prevention and management. Kernberg concludes succinctly: "Freud's dramatic concept of the death drive may not reflect an inborn disposition as such, but is eminently relevant in clinical practice."

Betty Joseph's eminence is unquestionable, and any discussion of *Beyond* . . . and its primary concept, the "death instinct", would be less meaningful if her seminal paper "Addiction to Near-Death" were not included. Joseph, from her Kleinian model of the mind, brings clinically alive what Kernberg stated theoretically. In keeping with Levy, she underlines the importance of the analyst's countertransference—that is, how the patient's powerful masochism through projective identification evokes despair in the analyst. The straightforwardness of her language brings clinical clarity to the concepts Freud introduced in "*Beyond* . . .". For example, her use of "chuntering"—to mutter, mummer, grumble, find fault, complain—not only adds meaning to "repetition compulsion", but the sense of "going over and over" supports her notion of addiction. For Joseph "near-death" is a malignant type of self-destructiveness, seen in a small group of patients, which addictively dominates their lives, their internal relationships, their thinking and the way they communicate and relate in the analysis. The analytic interaction (verging on a sadomasochistic relationship) goes beyond "negative therapeutic reaction". In fact, both patient and analyst feel tortured to the point of near-destruction. Her lucid description of how she works with such patients and their dreams includes her recognition that these patients are not driven towards a Nirvana type of peace or relief from problems but have a felt need to have the satisfaction of seeing oneself being destroyed. The sheer, undeniable, unequalled sexual delight of the grim masochism fuels the addiction to self-object annihilation. Indeed, any pull towards life and sanity is located in the analyst, which, if "split off", can account for the patient's apparent extreme passivity and indifference to progress. Technically, Joseph offers astute guidance when she underlines that the analyst must first deal with the masochistic use and exploitation of the analyst and analytic situation before a clear connection can be made with the patient's underlying anxieties about real life and the fears of rejection. The question "towards which end does humankind lean?"—life or death—is resolved, in such severe cases as Joseph describes, in that the person leans towards death, and the move towards life and more real object-related enjoyments, which means that giving up the all-consuming addictive gratifications is extremely difficult.

Michel Feldman, also a Kleinian, harkens back to Freud's concept of "the uncanny" and notes that a patient's compulsion to repeat overrules pleasure and evokes the "daemonic character" of the mind, which involves annihilation of the self as a thinking, living being. He recognizes that both Freud and Klein tried to account for certain clinical phenomena in terms of a "fundamental struggle between forces that promoted life, and a drive towards death". Calling on Segal, Rosenfeld, and Joseph, all of whom have struggled with the concept of the death drive, where it fits with the life instinct and its clinical implications, Feldman provides succinct summaries of their clinical contributions. Segal calls attention to the conflict between life and death instincts in seeking satisfaction for needs. The life-promoting side leads to object-seeking, love, and object concern. The other side seeks to annihilate the perceiving self and other. When the "compromise" to solve the conflict fails, the death instinct triumphs in destruction of the self. Rosenfeld feels that the death instinct manifests itself as a destructive process directed against the objects and the self, and Feldman suggests that with certain patients "their primary aim is not totally to destroy life, but to take the life out". The link with Joseph is made through the idea that "life is allowed to continue just so long as nothing is really alive and functioning". Like Brenner and Levy, Feldman uses very detailed case material to exemplify these processes. His patient was caught in "a vicious interplay between actual frustration and disappointment, and the gratification and sadistic pleasure he obtained from using experienced suffering and despair to undermine and torment his objects, and himself." Feldman offers hope for the efficacy of the analyst's intervention. The death instinct found in minor/tiny interactions is lessened by bringing the patient's destructive attacking, spoiling, undermining of the self and other into conscious thought and language, thereby diminishing its subtle silent self-destructiveness and liberating tormented objects. The patient becomes more able to tolerate his own hatred and anger and to make improved contact with something more lively, appreciative, and empathetic in himself and his objects.

In "A Hindu Reading of Freud's *Beyond the Pleasure Principle*", *Ashok Nagpal* provides a broad survey of the Hindu world view(s). He does so in a manner that makes this complex subject remarkably accessible to the reader whose background, in the main, will be the Judaeo–Christian world. He also effectively connects and contrasts the several strands of Freud's concept of a death instinct with various Hindu ideas on death—the God of Death, saintliness in death, death as equanimity, Nirvana, and so on. Although Nagpal states firmly that "the treatment and understanding of the twin processes of life and death in Hindu thought are distinctly different from those seen in European thought", he seems to make an exception for Freud, as exemplified in "*Beyond . . .*". The explanation for Nagpal seems to be that Freud was located "at the edge" rather than at the centre of his European world and thus was able to be more open to mysticism and to Eastern religions and philosophy. The overview of Hindu thought about death is lucidly illustrated by three classical tales that are not likely to be familiar to most Western readers: *Nachiketa*, the boy who confronts the God of Death; *Savitri*, the faithful wife who extracts from *Yama*, the God of Death, a hundred sons (epitomizing rebirth), thereby saving her husband from death; and *Yudhishthira*, the righteous warrior, who finds peace and equanimity amidst the dead. In all three tales death is seen to renew life in the endless cycle of birth–life–death–birth. The parallel to Freud's speculation of the urge to revert to the inorganic, to what-was-there before, a cosmic homeostasis, is not far-fetched. There is, however, a difference of emphasis in the Freudian and Hindu ways of thinking about death. For Freud, death subsumes life (recall Caropreso and Simanke: "No matter how hard Freud tried to accord the life instinct the same status as the death instinct, it seems hard to avoid the conclusion that death lurks behind all life."). For the Hindu, life is not marginalized. How well one lives through life's phases takes prominence over death in that in a well-lived life, there will be no need for rebirth.

Elizabeth Young-Bruehl brings the reader back full circle to "*the juncture*" when Freud's internal debate with his psychoanalytically defining "libido theory" led to not only his "new theory" expressed in "*Beyond . . .*" but also evoked disagreement reverberating through time within the profession. Young-Bruehl's thesis is that Freud missed the great *opportunity* of psychoanalysis—a moment when an infantile form of love might have been shown to have a developmental course towards mature human relations and political life. She asserts that the missed opportunity was his failure to keep the influence of the ego's instincts of self-preservation within psychoanalytic theory. As is well accepted, the ego instincts need reality—a way of satisfying self-preservation needs, including sexual needs. She states succinctly that "self-preservation requires the affection or love or sociality of real (not phantasy) preserving caretakers—that is, it is a relational drive". Development through relationship involves growth from narcissistic love to love of another, and within this (relational) love growth is the development of the self. Trauma, repetition compulsion, and aggression enter into Young-Bruehl's thinking, but again in the service of life, when she comments that Freud might have said: "what is released by a trauma is the self-preservation drive, screaming, so to speak 'Let me live! Help me! Take me in you arms!'" For her, aggression can be used creatively, repetition leads to mastery, and, in fact, through the transference in the analytic relationship patients relive and understand childhood and life traumas to develop a more secure inner self. Paying her respects to those analysts—Ferenczi, Bowlby, Balint, Winnicott, the little-known Imre Hermann, the Japanese analyst, Takeo Doi, Fonagy, and others—who recognized the importance of relational needs, she asserts, nevertheless, that none recognized "the distinction Freud drew in his early work between 'the sensual current' and the 'affectionate current'". Further, Bowlby's attachment theory has no theory of the unconscious, and Winnicottian proposals have no drive theory. It seems there is a need to go "beyond" attachment theory and return to early Freud where he left off. Indeed, for Young-Bruehl, psychoanalytic theory needs to return and incorporate the European *eros/philia* tradition and the Japanese *amae* (to be sweetly and indulgently loved). Perhaps, if Freud had not missed this opportunity, the life instinct would not have been marginalized, and there might have been, within psychoanalytic theory, less controversy over attempts to go beyond Freud to develop a lively creative and integrated theory.

Questions remain. Is there a thread of consensus among these ten psychoanalytic authors about Freud's thinking in *Beyond the Pleasure Principle*? Can psychoanalysis grow from time past—what has or might have been—and from time present—what is—into a future that includes acceptance of the natural inevitability of death but preserves and promotes life in the interim? It would not be implausible to suggest that the answer comes from our patients and our clinical experience and that, like Freud, we will continue to have professional and individual internal struggles to agree and disagree theoretically. The consensus among the authors of this volume appears to be that the concept of the "death instinct" has therapeutic—perhaps also theoretical—relevance in those few patients who need to repeat aggressive, sadomasochistic, self/other destructive tendencies but whose drive to self-preserve leads them to seek psychoanalysis. Ironically, Freud's concept of the death instinct—life seeking death—meets opposition in the very purpose of psychoanalytic treatment: to assist analysands to self-preserve—to live life more fully, creatively, and relationally.

A less evident consensual thread is that Freud's dual instinct and two dream theories need integration, a task he left to his followers. As has been seen, major attempts have been made by these authors to bring together the theories, to understand, clinically and theoretically, the nature of aggression and the purpose of the repetition compulsion, and to restore the importance of humankind's self-preservative drive and relational need. These are difficult tasks for several reasons. No other profession harkens back, to the extent that psychoanalysis does, to the theories of its founder in developing theory for future generations. Nor do other professions reify their founder's ideas to the same extent. Some authors of this volume dare to disagree especially with Freud's central concept of the death instinct. Although with certain patients they find this concept clinically useful, few analysts seem to believe that humankind has a continual drive towards death. This does not mean that psychoanalysis denies the inevitability of death and the need to come to terms with the fact that eventually we all die but in the meantime strive to live life fully and satisfactorily. Certainly, analysts aim to assist analysands in this endeavour. By proposing the "death instinct", Freud, perhaps unwittingly, tapped into an unconscious conflict inherent in our profession. Psychoanalysts when beginning an analysis promise to be there "for as long as the person needs them". Yet it is well known that analysts deny their own vulnerability to sudden death or unexpected incapacitation or illness, nor does well-planned retirement come easily, and analysts do not readily make professional wills or prepare in other ways for the eventuality that they can no longer practice (O'Neil, 2007; Schwartz & Silver, 1990). To return to T. S. Eliot, Freud's *Beyond the Pleasure Principle* has forced us as analysts to think further theoretically and clinically within the context of what has come before, what is now, and what psychoanalysis will offer future generations.

Note

1. Did Freud question an "*other side*"? As Akhtar commented in O'Neil and Akhtar (2009), Freud was both a believer and non-believer (p. 3). Was he struggling with his ambivalent belief system *as well as* the other disturbing events in his life—the First World War, the death of his daughter, and his cancer when writing *Beyond the Pleasure Principle*?

REFERENCES

Abend, S. M. (2007). Therapeutic action in modern conflict theory. *Psychoanalytic Quarterly, 76S*: 1417–1442.

Adams-Silvan, A., & Silvan, M. (1990). A dream is the fulfillment of a wish: Traumatic dream, repetition compulsion, and pleasure principle. *International Journal of Psychoanalysis, 71*: 513–522.

Adler, A. (1908). Der Aggressionsbetrieb im Leben und in der Neurose. *Fortschritte der Medizin, 19*: 53.

Adler, A. (1910). Beitrag zur Lehre vom Widerstand. *Zentralblatt für Psychoanalyse, 1*: 214–219.

Akhtar, S. (1995). Aggression. In: B. Moore & B. Fine (Eds.), *Psychoanalysis: The Major Concepts* (pp. 364–380). New Haven, CT: Yale University Press.

Akhtar, S. (2009a). *Comprehensive Dictionary of Psychoanalysis*. London: Karnac.

Akhtar, S. (2009b). *Good Feelings: Psychoanalytic Perspectives on Positive Attitudes and Emotions*. London: Karnac.

Akhtar, S. (2010). Freud's *Todesangst* and Ghalib's *ishrat-e-qatra*: Two contrasting perspectives on death. In: *The Wound of Mortality: Fear, Denial, and Acceptance of Death* (pp. 1–20). Lanham, MD: Jason Aronson.

Akhtar, S. (2011). *Matters of Life and Death: Psychoanalytic Reflections*. London: Karnac.

Akhtar, S., & Brenner, I. (1979). Differential diagnosis of fugue-like states. *Journal of Clinical Psychiatry, 40*: 381–385.

Anzieu, D. (1981). *Le groupe et l'inconscient. L'imaginaire groupal.* Paris: Dunod.

Balint, A. (1931). *The Early Years of Life: A Psychoanalytic Study.* New York: Basic Books, 1954.

Balint, M. (1937). Early developmental states of the ego: Primary object love. In: *Primary Love and Psychoanalytic Technique.* London: Hogarth Press, 1955; reprinted London: Karnac, 1994.

Balint, M. (1955). *Primary Love and Psychoanalytic Technique.* London: Hogarth Press.

Balint, M. (1968). *The Basic Fault: Therapeutic Aspects of Regression.* London: Tavistock Publications.

Bandura, A., & Walters, R. H. (1959). *Adolescent Aggression.* New York: Ronald.

Bandura, A., & Walters, R. H. (1963). Aggression. In: *National Society for the Study of Education, 62nd Yearbook, Part I: Child Psychology.* Chicago: The National Society of the Study of Education.

Barrett, D. (1995). The dream character as prototype for the multiple personality alter. *Dissociation, 8*: 61–68.

Bibring, E. (1941). The development and problems of the theory of the instincts. *International Journal of Psychoanalysis, 22*: 102–131.

Bibring, E. (1943). The conception of the repetition compulsion. *Psyche Quarterly, 12*: 486–519.

Bion, W. R. (1957). Differentiation of the psychotic from the non-psychotic personalities. *International Journal of Psychoanalysis, 38*: 266–275.

Bion, W. R. (1961). *Experiences in Groups.* London: Routledge.

Bion, W. R. (1965). *Transformations.* London: Karnac, 1984.

Bowlby, J. A. (1958). The nature of the child's tie to his mother. *International Journal of Psychoanalysis, 39*: 350–373.

Brenneis, C. B. (1994). Can early childhood trauma be reconstructed from dreams? On the relationship of dreams to trauma. *Psychoanalytic Psychology, 11*: 429–447.

Brenneis, C. B. (1997). *Recovered Memories of Trauma: Transferring the Present to the Past.* Madison, CT: International Universities Press.

Brenneis, C. B. (2002). Apparitions in the fog: Commentary on paper by Adrienne Harris and Barbara Gold. *Psychoanalytic Dialogues, 12*: 987–999.

Brenner, C. (1971). The psychoanalytic concept of aggression. *International Journal of Psychoanalysis, 52*: 137–144.

Brenner, C. (1982). *The Mind in Conflict.* New York. International Universities Press.

Brenner, C. (2003). Is the structural model still useful? *International Journal of Psychoanalysis, 84*: 1093–1096.

Brenner, C. (2009a). In his own words: Charles Brenner (1913–2008). Personal memoir, 2007. *Psychoanalytic Quarterly, 78*: 637–673.

Brenner, C. (2009b). Interview with Robert Michaels, 2006. *Psychoanalytic Quarterly, 78*: 675–700.

Brenner, I. (1994). The dissociative character: A reconsideration of "multiple personality". *Journal of the American Psychoanalytic Association, 42*: 819–846.

Brenner, I. (1995). Letter to the editor. *Journal of the American Psychoanalytic Association, 43*: 300–303.

Brenner, I. (1997). Letter to the editor. *Journal of the American Psychoanalytic Association, 45*: 1285–1287.

Brenner, I. (2001). *Dissociation of Trauma: Theory, Phenomenology and Technique.* Madison, CT: International Universities Press.

Brenner, I. (2004). *Psychic Trauma: Dynamics, Symptoms and Treatment.* Lanham, MD: Rowman & Littlefield.

Brenner, I. (2009a). *Injured Men—Trauma, Healing and the Masculine Self.* Lanham, MD: Rowman & Littlefield.

Brenner, I. (2009b). On "splitting of the ego": A history of the concept. In: *On Freud's Splitting of the Ego in the Process of Defense* (pp. 9–26), ed. T. Bokanowski & S. Lewkowitz. London: Karnac.

Britton, R. (2003). *Sex, Death, and the Superego.* London: Karnac.

Brun, R. (1953). Über Freuds Hypothese vom Todestrieb [On Freud's hypothesis of the death instinct]. *Psyche, 7*: 81–111.

Caropreso, F., & Simanke, R. T. (2006). Compulsão à repetição: Um retorno às origens da metapsicologia Freudiana [Repetition compulsion: A return to the origins of Freudian metapsychology]. *Ágora— Estudos em teoria psicanalítica* [Agora—Studies in psychoanalytic theory], *9* (2): 207–224.

Casement, P. (1991). *Learning from the Patient.* New York: Guilford Press.

Chakkarath, P. (2005). What can Western psychology learn from indigenous psychology? In: W. Friedlmeier, P. Chakkarath, & B. Schwarz (Eds.), *Culture and Human Development: The Importance of Cross Cultural Research to the Social Sciences* (pp. 31–52). New York: Psychology Press.

Chaturvedi, B. (2008). *The Women of the Mahabharata: The Question of Truth.* New Delhi: Orient Longman.

Compact Oxford English Dictionary (1979). London: Oxford University Press.

Dawkins, R. (1976). *The Selfish Gene.* Oxford: Oxford University Press.

De Wit, J., & Hartup, W. W. (Eds.) (1974). *Determinants and Origins of Aggressive Behavior.* The Hague: Mouton.

Doflein, F. (1919). *Das Problem des Todes und der Unsterblichkeit bei den Pflanzen und Tieren.* Jena.

Doi, T. (1973). *The Anatomy of Dependence.* New York: Kodansha.

Dollard, J., Doob, L. W., Miller, N. E., Mowner, D. H., & Sears, R. R. (1939). *Frustration and Aggression.* New Haven, CT: Yale University Press.

Erikson, E. (1954). The dream specimen of psychoanalysis. *Journal of the American Psychoanalytic Association, 2*: 5–56.

Fairbairn, W. R. D. (1944). Endopsychic structure considered in terms of object-relationships. *International Journal of Psychoanalysis, 25*: 70–93.

Fairbairn, W. R. D. (1952). *Psychoanalytic Studies of the Personality.* London: Routledge.

Falzeder, E. (1994). My grand-patient, my chief tormenter: A hitherto unnoticed case of Freud's and the consequences. *Psychoanalytic Quarterly, 63*: 297–331.

Falzeder, E. (Ed.) (2002). *The Complete Correspondence of Sigmund Freud and Karl Abraham, 1907–1925.* London: Karnac.

Falzeder, E., & Brabant, E. (1996). *The Correspondence of Sigmund Freud and Sándor Ferenczi, Vol. 2, 1914–1919,* trans. P. T. Hoffer. Cambridge, MA: The Belknap Press of Harvard University Press.

Fechner, G. T. (1873). *Einige Ideen zur Schöpfungs- and Entwicklungsgeschichte der Organismen.* Leipzig.

Feldman, M. (2000). Some views on the manifestation of the death instinct in clinical work. *International Journal of Psychoanalysis, 81*: 53–65.

Fenichel, O. (1945). *The Psychoanalytic Theory of Neurosis.* New York: Norton.

Ferenczi, S. (1913a). Entwicklungsstufen des Wirklichkeitssinnes. *Internationale Zeitschrift für Psychoanalyse, 1*: 124. English version: Stages in the development of the sense of reality. In: *First Contributions to Psycho-Analysis.* London: Karnac, 1994.

Ferenczi, S. (1913b). To whom does one relate one's dreams? In: *Further Contributions to the Theory and Practice of Psycho-Analysis.* London: Karnac, 1994.

Ferenczi, S. (1924). *Thalassa. Versuch einer Genitaltheorie.* Leipzig and Vienna: Internationaler Psychoanalytischer Verlag. English: *Thalassa: A Theory of Genitality,* tr. H. A. Bunker. Albany, NY: Psychoanalytic Quarterly, 1938.

Ferenczi, S. (1933). Confusion of tongues between adults and the child. In: *Final Contributions to the Problems and Methods of Psycho-Analysis*. London: Karnac, 1994.

Feshbach, S. (1970). Aggression. In: P. H. Mussen (Ed.), *Carmichael's Manual of Child Psychology, Vol. 2* (pp. 159–259). New York: Wiley.

Figueiredo, L. C. (1999). *Palavras cruzadas entre Freud e Ferenczi* [Words exchanged between Freud and Ferenczi]. São Paulo: Escuta.

Fleiss, R. (1953). *The Revival of Interest in the Dream*. New York: International Universities Press.

Fliess, W. (1906). *Der Ablauf des Lebens*. Vienna.

Freud, A. (1936). *The Ego and the Mechanisms of Defense*. London: Hogarth Press.

Freud, A. (1958). Child observation and prediction of development. *Psychoanalytic Study of Child, 13*: 92–124.

Freud, A. (1963). The concept of developmental lines. *Psychoanalytic Study of the Child, 18*: 245–265.

Freud, A. (1972). Comments on aggression. *International Journal of Psychoanalysis, 53*: 163–171.

Freud, A. (1981). *The Writings of Anna Freud, Vol. 8*. New York: International Universities Press.

Freud, S. (1893a) (with Breuer, J.). On the psychical mechanism of hysterical phenomena: Preliminary communication. *S.E., 2*: 3.

Freud, S. (1895d) (with Breuer, J.). *Studies on Hysteria. S.E., 2*.

Freud, S. (1900a). *The Interpretation of Dreams. S.E., 4–5*.

Freud, S. (1905c). Jokes and their relation to the unconscious. *S.E., 8*.

Freud, S. (1905d). *Three Essays on the Theory of Sexuality. S.E., 7*: 125–245.

Freud, S. (1905e). Fragment of an analysis of a case of hysteria. *S.E. 7*: 15–122.

Freud, S. (1909b). Analysis of a phobia in a five-year-old boy. *S.E., 10*: 5–149.

Freud, S. (1910i). The psycho-analytic view of psychogenic disturbance of vision. *S.E., 11*: 211.

Freud, S. (1911b). Formulations on the two principles of mental functioning. *S.E., 12*: 213–226.

Freud, S. (1914c). On narcissism: An introduction. *S.E., 14*: 69–102.

Freud, S. (1914g). Remembering, repeating and working-through (Further Recommendations on the Technique of Psycho-Analysis, II). *S.E., 12*: 147.

Freud, S. (1915c). Instincts and their vicissitudes. *S.E., 14*: 111–140.

Freud, S. (1915d). Repression. *S.E., 14*: 141–158.

Freud, S. (1915e). The Unconscious. *S.E., 14*: 161.

Freud, S. (1916–17). *Introductory Lectures on Psycho-Analysis. S.E. 15–16*: 243–462.

Freud, S. (1917d). A metapsychological supplement to the theory of dreams. *S.E., 14*: 217–235.

Freud, S. (1917e). Mourning and melancholia. *S.E., 14*: 237–58.

Freud, S. (1918b [1914]). From the history of an infantile neurosis. *S.E., 17*.

Freud, S. (1919a). Lines of advance in psycho-analytic therapy. *S.E., 17*: 167–168.

Freud, S. (1919d). Introduction to *Psycho-Analysis and the War Neuroses. S.E., 17*: 207.

Freud, S. (1919e). A child is being beaten: A contribution to the study of the origin of sexual perversions. *S.E., 17*: 219–258.

Freud, S. (1919h). The "uncanny". *S.E., 17*.

Freud, S. (1920g). *Beyond the Pleasure Principle. S.E. 18*.

Freud, S. (1921c). *Group Psychology and the Analysis of the Ego. S.E., 18*: 65–143.

Freud, S. (1923a). Two encyclopaedia articles. *S.E., 18*: 235–259.

Freud, S. (1923b). *The Ego and the Id. S.E., 19*: 3–68.

Freud, S. (1923c). Remarks on the theory and practice of dream-interpretation. *S.E., 19*: 109–121.

Freud, S. (1924c). The economic problem of masochism. *S.E., 19*: 155–170.

Freud, S. (1925a [1924]). A note upon the "mystic writing-pad". *S.E., 19*: 227.

Freud, S. (1925j). Some psychical consequences of the anatomical distinction between the sexes. *S.E., 19*: 243–260.

Freud, S. (1926d). *Inhibitions, Symptoms and Anxiety. S.E., 20*.

Freud, S. (1927c). *The Future of an Illusion. S.E., 21*: 3.

Freud, S. (1930a). *Civilization and Its Discontents. S.E., 21*: 59–145.

Freud, S. (1933a). *New Introductory Lectures on Psycho-Analysis. S.E., 22*: 5–182.

Freud, S. (1937c). Analysis terminable and interminable. *S.E., 23*.

Freud, S. (1937d). Constructions in analysis. *S.E., 23*: 257–269.

Freud, S. (1940a [1938]). *An Outline of Psycho-Analysis. S.E., 23*: 141–207.

Freud, S. (1940d [1892]) (with Breuer, J.). On the theory of hysterical attacks . *S.E., 1*: 151.

Freud, S. (1941a [1892]). Letter to Josef Breuer. *S.E., 1*: 147.

Freud, S. (1942a [1905 or 1906]). Psychopathic characters on the stage. *S.E., 7*: 305.

Freud, S. (1950 [1895]). Project for a scientific psychology. *S.E., 1.*

Freud, S. (1955c [1920]). Memorandum on the electrical treatment of war neurotics. *17*: 211.

Geyskens, T., & Van Haute, P. (2007). *From Death Instinct Theory to Attachment Theory.* New York: Other Press.

Ginsberg, B. E. (1982). Genetic factors in aggressive behavior. *Psychoanalytic Inquiry, 2*: 53–75.

Goette, A. (1883). *Über den Ursprung des Todes.* Hamburg.

Goodall, J. (1979). Life and death at Gombe. *National Geographic, 155*: 592–620.

Green, A. (1983). *Narcissisme de vie, narcissisme de mort.* Paris: Minuit.

Green, A. (1993a). *The Work of the Negative.* London: Free Association Books, 1999.

Green, A. (1993b). *On Private Madness.* Madison, CT: International Universities Press.

Greenacre, P. (1960). Considerations regarding the parent–infant relationship. *International Journal of Psychoanalysis, 41*: 571–584.

Greenacre, P. (1971). Notes on the influence and contribution of ego psychology to the practice of psychoanalysis. In: J. B. McDevitt & C. F. Settlage (Eds.), *Separation–Individuation: Essays in Honor of Margaret S. Mahler* (pp. 171–200). New York: International Universities Press.

Greenberg, D. E. (1990). Instinct and primary narcissism in Freud's later theory: An interpretation and reformulation of beyond the pleasure principle. *International Journal of Psychoanalysis, 71*: 271–183.

Grosskurth, P. (1991). *The Secret Ring: Freud's Inner Circle and the Politics of Psychoanalysis.* Boston, MA: Addison-Wesley.

Grotstein, J. (2009). Dreaming as a "curtain of illusion": Revisiting the "royal road" with Bion as our guide. *International Journal of Psychoanalysis, 90*: 733–752.

Gunther, M. (1980). Aggression, self psychology, and the concept of health. In: A. Goldberg (Ed.), *Advances in Self Psychology.* New York: International Universities Press.

Hamburg, D. A., & Trudeau, M. B. (Eds.) (1981). *Biobehavioral Aspects of Aggression.* New York: Alan R. Liss.

Hartmann, H. (1939). *Ego Psychology and the Problem of Adaptation,* transl. D. Rapaport. New York: International Universities Press, 1958.

Hartmann, H. (1950). Psychoanalysis and developmental psychology. *Psychoanalytic Study of the Child, 5*: 7–17.

Hartmann, H., Kris, E., & Loewenstein, R. M. (1949). Notes on the theory of aggression. *Psychoanalytic Study of the Child, 3/4*: 9–36.

Hartmann, M. (1906). *Tod und Fortpflanzung*. Munich.

Hermann, I. (1936). Sich Anklammern—Auf Suche gehen. *Internationale Zeitschrift für Psychoanalyse und Imago, 26*: 252–274.

Holt, R. R. (1962). A critical examination of Freud's concept of bound vs. free cathexis. *Journal of the American Psychoanalytic Association, 16*: 475–525.

Jacobi, R. (1983). *The Repression of Psychoanalysis: Otto Fenichel and the Freudians*. Chicago, IL: University of Chicago Press.

Jacobs, J. (2009). Obituary: Charles Brenner, M.D. *International Journal of Psychoanalysis, 90*: 953–955.

Janet, P. (1907). *The Major Symptoms of Hysteria*. New York: MacMillan.

Jones, E. (1927). The early development of female sexuality. *International Journal of Psychoanalysis, 8*: 459–472.

Jones, E. (1957). *The Life and Work of Sigmund Freud, Vol. 3*. New York: Basic Books.

Joseph, B. (1982). Addiction to near-death. *International Journal of Psychoanalysis, 63*: 449–456. Also in: M. Feldman & E. Bott Spillius (Eds.), *Psychic Equilibrium and Psychic Change* (pp. 127–138). London: Routledge, 1989.

Jung, C. G. (1909). Die Bedeutung des Vaters für das Schicksal des Einzelnen. *Jahrbuch für psychoanalytische und psychopathologische Forschungen, 1*.

Kakar, S. (1981). *The Inner World: A Psychoanalytic Study of Childhood and Society in India* (2nd edition). New Delhi: Oxford University Press.

Kakar, S., & Kakar, K. (2007). *The Indians: Portrait of a People*. New Delhi: Penguin/Viking.

Kernberg, O. (1975). *Borderline Conditions and Pathological Narcissism*. New York: Jason Aronson.

Kernberg, O. (1982). Self, ego, affects and drives. *Journal of the American Psychoanalytic Association, 30*: 893–917.

Kernberg, O. (1991). The psychopathology of hatred. *Journal of the American Psychoanalytic Association, 39*: 209–238.

Kernberg, O. (1992). *Aggression in Personality Disorders and Perversion*. New Haven, CT: Yale University Press.

Kernberg, O. (2001). Recent developments in the technical approaches of English-language psychoanalytic schools. *Psychoanalytic Quarterly, 70* (3): 519–547.

Kernberg, O. (2003a). Sanctioned social violence: A psychoanalytic view, Part I. *International Journal of Psychoanalysis, 84*: 683–698.

Kernberg, O. (2003b). Sanctioned social violence: A psychoanalytic view, Part II. *International Journal of Psychoanalysis, 84*: 953–968.

Kernberg, O. (2004a). The concept of drive in the light of contemporary psychoanalytic theorizing. In: *Contemporary Controversies in Psychoanalytic Theory, Techniques, and Their Applications* (pp. 48–59). New Haven, CT: Yale University Press.

Kernberg, O. (2004b). Hatred as a core afect of aggression. In: *Aggressivity, Narcissism, and Self-Destructiveness in the Psychoanalytic Process* (pp. 27–44). New Haven, CT: Yale University Press.

Kernberg, O. (2004c). Psychoanalytic object relations theory. In: *Contemporary Controversies in Psychoanalytic Theory, Techniques, and Their Applications* (pp. 26–47). New Haven, CT: Yale University Press.

Kernberg, O. (2004d). A technical approach to eating disorders in patients with borderline personality organization. In: *Aggressivity, Narcissism, and Self-Destructiveness in the Psychoanalytic Process* (pp. 205–219). New Haven, CT: Yale University Press.

Kernberg, O. (2007). The almost untreatable narcissistic patient. *Journal of the American Psychoanalytic Association, 55* (2): 503–539.

Kernberg, O. (2009). The concept of the death drive: A clinical perspective. *International Journal of Psychoanalysis, 90*: 1009–1023.

Kestenberg, J., & Brenner, I. (1996). *The Last Witness: The Child Survivor of the Holocaust*. Washington, DC: American Psychiatric Press.

Klein, M. (1933). The early development of conscience in the child. In: *Love, Guilt and Reparation and Other Works 1921–1945* (pp. 262–289). London: Hogarth Press, 1985.

Klein, M. (1935). A contribution to the psychogenesis of manic depressive states. In: *Love, Guilt and Reparation and Other Works 1921–1945* (pp. 262–289). London: Hogarth Press, 1985.

Klein, M. (1940). Mourning and its relation to manic-depressive states. In: *Contributions to Psychoanalysis, 1921–1945* (pp. 311–338). London: Hogarth Press.

Klein, M. (1952). The mutual influences in the development of ego and the id. In: *Envy and Gratitude and Other Works 1946–1963* (pp. 57–60). London: Hogarth Press, 1987.

Klein, M. (1957). *Envy and Gratitude*. New York: Basic Books.

Kluft, R. P. (1987). Unsuspected multiple personality disorder: An uncommon source of protracted resistances, interruption and failure in psychoanalysis. *Journal of Clinical Psychiatry, 9*: 100–115.

Kohut, H. (1971). *The Analysis of the Self*. New York: International Universities Press.

Kohut, H. (1977). *The Restoration of the Self.* New York: International Universities Press.

Kris, E. (1950). Notes on the development and on some current problems of psychoanalytic child psychology. *Psychoanalytic Study of the Child, 5*: 24–46.

Lacan, J. (1966). Position de l'inconscient [Position of the unconscious]. In: *Écrits* [Writings] (pp. 829–850). Paris: Seuil.

Land, L. (1991). Thanatos: The drive without a name: The development of the concept of the death drive in Freud's writings. *Scandinavian Psychoanalytic Review, 14*: 60–80.

Lansky, M. R. (1995) (with Bley, C. R.). *Posttraumatic Nightmares: Psychodynamic Explorations.* Hillsdale, NJ: Analytic Press.

Lansky, M. R. (1997). Posttraumatic nightmares: A psychoanalytic reconsideration. *Psychoanalysis and Contemporary Thought, 20*: 501–521.

Lansky, M. R. (2004). Trigger and screen: Shame dynamics and the problem of instigation in Freud's dreams. *Journal of the American Academy of Psychoanalysis, 32*: 441–468.

Lantos, B. (1958). The two genetic derivations of aggression with reference to sublimation and neutralization. *International Journal of Psychoanalysis, 39*: 116–120.

Laplanche, J. (1970). *Vie et mort en psychanalyse* [Life and death in psychoanalysis]. Paris: Flammarion. (*Vida e morte em psicanálise* [Life and death in psychoanalysis]. Porto Alegre: Artes Médicas, 1985.)

Laplanche, J. (1989). *New Foundations for Psychoanalysis.* Oxford: Blackwell.

Laplanche, J., & Pontalis, J. B. (1973). *The Language of Psychoanalysis.* London: Karnac, 1988.

Laub, D., & Auerhahn, N. (1993). Knowing and not knowing massive psychic trauma: Forms of traumatic memory. *International Journal of Psychoanalysis, 74*: 287–302.

Laub, D., & Lee, S. (2003). Thanatos and massive psychic trauma. *Journal of the American Psychoanalytic Association, 51*: 433–463.

Lear, J. (2005). *Freud.* New York: Routledge.

Leveton, A. (1952). *Psychoanalytic Studies of the Personality.* London: Routledge.

Leveton, A. (1961). The night residue. *International Journal of Psychoanalysis, 42*: 506–516.

Levy, J. (1996). On learning and teaching dream interpretation. *Journal of Clinical Psychoanalysis, 5*: 561–579.

Levy, J. (2009). Studying *The Interpretation of Dreams* in the company of analytic candidates. *Journal of the American Psychoanalytic Association, 57* (4): 847–870.

Lewin, B. D. (1955), Dream psychology and the analytic situation. *Psychoanalytic Quarterly, 24*: 169–199.

Lichtenberg, J. D. (1989). *Psychoanalysis and Motivation.* Hillsdale, NJ: Analytic Press.

Lifton, R. J. (1976). *The Life of the Self: Toward a New Psychology.* New York: Simon & Schuster.

Lipschütz, A. (1914). *Warum wir sterben.* Stuttgart.

Loewald, H. W. (1971). Some consideration of repetition and repetition compulsion. *International Journal of Psychoanalysis, 52*: 59–66.

Loewenstein, R. M. (1949). A post-traumatic dream. *Psychoanalytic Quarterly, 18*: 449–454.

Lorenz, K. (1963a). *L'aggression: Une histoire naturelle du mal* [Aggression: A natural history of evil]. Paris: Flammarion, 1969.

Lorenz, K. (1963b). *On Aggression.* New York: Harcourt, Brace & World, 1966.

Low, B. (1920a). *Psycho-Analysis.* London.

Low, B. (1920b). A revived sensation-memory. *International Journal of Psychoanalysis, 1*: 271–272.

Makari, G. (2008). *Revolution in Mind: The Creation of Psychoanalysis.* New York: HarperCollins.

Marcinowski, J. (1918). Die erotischen Quellen der Minderwertigkeitsgefühle. *Zeitschrift für Sexualwissenschaften, 4*: 313.

Marcovitz, E. (1973). Aggression in human adaptation. *Psychoanalytic Quarterly, 42*: 226–233.

Mark, D. (2009). Waking dreams. *Psychoanalytic Dialogues, 19*: 405–414.

Marmer, S. S. (1980). Psychoanalysis of "multiple personality". *International Journal of Psychoanalysis, 61*: 439–459.

Marmer, S. S. (1991). Multiple personality: A psychoanalytic perspective. *Psychiatric Clinics of North America, 14*: 677–693.

McCord, W., McCord, J., & Zola, I. K. (1959). *Origins of Crime.* New York: Columbia University Press.

Meltzer, D. (1973). *Sexual States of Mind.* Strath Tay: Clunie Press.

Modell, A. (1975). The ego and the id. *International Journal of Psychoanalysis, 56*: 57–68.

Monzani, L. R. (1989). *Freud: O movimento de um pensamento* [Freud: The movement of a thought]. Campinas, Brazil: Ed. da Unicamp.

Moyer, K. E. (1968). Kinds of aggression and their physiological basis. *Communications in Behavioral Biology, 2*: 65–87.

Nandy, A. (1995). *The Savage Freud and Other Essays on Possible and Retrievable Selves*. Delhi: Oxford University Press.

Nunberg, H. (1932). *Principles of Psychoanalysis: Their Application to the Neuroses*. New York: International Universities Press.

Nunberg, H., & Federn, E. (Eds.) (1962–75). *Minutes of the Vienna Psychoanalytic Society* (4 vols.). New York: International Universities Press.

Olivelle, P. (1993). *The Asrama System: The History and Hermeneutics of a Religious Tradition*. Oxford: Oxford University Press.

O'Neil, M. K. (2007). Confidentiality, privacy and the facilitating role of psychoanalytic organizations. *International Journal of Psychoanalysis*, *88*: 1–20.

O'Neil, M. K., & Akhtar, S. (Eds.) (2009). *On Freud's "The Future of an Illusion": Contemporary Freud Turning Points & Critical Issues*. London: Karnac.

Ornstein, P. H. (1987). On self-state dreams in the psychoanalytic process. In: A. Rothstein (Ed.), *The Interpretation of Dreams in Clinical Work* (pp. 87–104). New York: International Universities Press.

Panksepp, J. (1998). *Affective Neuroscience*. New York: Oxford University Press.

Paranjpe, A. C. (1984). *Theoretical Psychology: The Meeting of East and West*. New York: Plenum Press.

Parens, H. (1973). Aggression: A reconsideration. *Journal of the American Psychoanalytic Association, 21*: 34–60.

Parens, H. (1979). *The Development of Aggression in Early Childhood* (1st edition). Lanham, MD: Jason Aronson/Rowman & Littlefield [revised edition, 2008].

Parens, H. (1984). Toward a reformulation of the theory of aggression and its implications for primary prevention. In: J. Gedo & G. H. Pollock (Eds.), *Psychoanalysis: The Vital Issues, Vol. 1* (pp. 87–114). New York: International Universities Press.

Parens, H. (1989). Toward a reformulation of the psychoanalytic theory of aggression. In: S. I. Greenspan & G. H. Pollock (Eds.), *The Course of Life, Vol. II: Early Childhood* (pp. 83–127). Madison, CT: International Universities Press.

Parens, H. (1994). *Comments on Kernberg's "Hatred as a Core Affect of Aggression"*. Paper presented at the Twenty-Fifth Annual Margaret S. Mahler Symposium on Child Development, Philadelphia, PA, 30 April.

Parens, H. (2008). *The Development of Aggression in Early Childhood* (revised edition). Lanham, MD: Jason Aronson/Rowman & Littlefield.

Parens, H., Pollock, L., & Prall, R. C. (1974). *Toward an Epigenesis of Aggres-*

sion in Early Childhood [Film #2]. Philadelphia, PA: Audio-Visual Medical Section, Eastern Pennsylvania Psychiatric Institute.

Parens, H., & Saul, L. J. (1971). *Dependence in Man.* New York: International Universities Press.

Parens, H., & Weech, A. A., Jr. (1966). Accelerated learning responses in young patients with school problems. *Journal of the American Academy of Child Psychiatry, 5*: 75–92.

Paris, J. (2009). *Childhood Adversities and Borderline Personality Disorder.* Unpublished manuscript.

Parsons, W. B. (1999). Freud's encounter with Hinduism: A historical–textual overview. In: T. G. Vaidyanathan & J. J. Kripal (Eds.), *Vishnu on Freud's Desk: A Reader in Psychoanalysis and Hinduism.* New Delhi: Oxford University Press.

Patterson, G. R., Littman, R. A., & Bricker, W. (1967). Assertive behavior in children: A step toward a theory of aggression. *Monographs of the Society for Research in Child Development, 32* (5): 1–43.

Pfeifer, S. (1919). Äusserungen infantil-erotischer Triebe im Spiele. *Imago, 5*: 243.

Ramanujan, A. K. (1993). *Folktales from India.* India: Penguin/Viking.

Rangell, L. (1972). Aggression, Oedipus, and historical perspective. *International Journal of Psychoanalysis, 53*: 3–11.

Rank, B. (1949). Aggression. *Psychoanalytic Study of the Child, 3/4*: 43–48.

Rao, K. R., Paranjpe, A. C., & Dalal, A. K. (2008). *Handbook of Indian Psychology.* New Delhi: Foundation Books.

Rapaport, D. (1949). *Emotions and Memory.* The Menninger Clinic Monograph Series No. 2. Baltimore, MD: Williams & Wilkins.

Reik, T. (1911). Fusion of sex and death: "The ring that is sexual guilt and formed by coming into being and punishing, by Eros and Thanatos". In: H. Nunberg & E. Federn (Eds.), *Minutes of the Vienna Psychoanalytic Society* (4 vols.). New York: International Universities Press, 1962–75.

Reis, D. J. (1973). *The Chemical Coding of Aggression in the Brain.* Manuscript circulated for the Colloquium on Aggression of the American Psychoanalytic Association, Chairman Leo Stone, New York, December.

Reis, D. J. (1974). Central neurotransmitters in aggression. *Research publications: Association for Research in Nervous and Mental Disease, 52*: 119–148.

Reiser, M. F. (1994). *Memory in Mind and Brain.* New Haven, CT: Yale University Press.

Roazen, P. (1975). *Freud and His Followers.* New York: Knopf.

Rochlin, G. (1973). *Man's Aggression: The Defense of the Self.* Boston, MA: Gambit.

Rosenfeld, H. (1971). A clinical approach to the psychoanalytic theory of the life and death instincts: An investigation into the aggressive aspects of narcissism. *International Journal of Psychoanalysis, 52*: 169–178. Also in: E. Bott Spillius (Ed.), *Melanie Klein Today, Vol. 1* (pp. 239–255). London: Routledge, 1988.

Saraswathi, T. S. (2005). Hindu worldview in the development of selfways: The "atman" as the real self. *New Directions for Child and Adolescent Development, 109*: 43–50.

Schopenhauer, A. (1851). Über die anscheinende Absichtlichkeit im Schicksale des Einzelnen. *Parerga and Paralipomena, 1.* In: *Sämtliche Werke,* ed. Hübscher. Leipzig, 1938.

Schur, M. (1972). *Freud: Living and Dying.* New York: International Universities Press.

Schwartz, H. J., & Silver, A. L. (1990). *Illness in the Analyst: Implications for the Treatment Relationship.* Madison, CT: International Universities Press.

Segal, H. (1956). Depression in the schizophrenic. *International Journal of Psychoanalysis, 28*: 139–145.

Segal, H. (1974). *Introduction to the Work of Melanie Klein.* New York: Basic Books.

Segal, H. (1977). Psychoanalysis and freedom of thought. In: *The Work of Hanna Segal* (pp. 217–227). New York: Jason Aronson, 1981.

Segal, H. (1991). The royal road. In: *Dream, Phantasy and Art* (pp. 3–15). London: Tavistock/Routledge.

Segal, H. (1993). On the clinical usefulness of the concept of the death instinct. *International Journal of Psychoanalysis, 74*: 55–61.

Segal, H. (1997). On the clinical usefulness of the concept of the death instinct. In: *Psychoanalysis, Literature and War* (pp. 17–26). London: Routledge.

Seife, C. (2000). *Zero: The Biography of a Dangerous Idea.* New York: Penguin.

Shane, M., & Shane, E. (1982). The strands of aggression: A confluence of data. *Psychoanalytic Inquiry, 2*: 263–281.

Silber, A. (1970). Functional phenomenon: Historical concept, contemporary defense. *Journal of the American Psychoanalytic Association, 18*: 519–538.

Silber, A. (1979). Childhood seduction, parental pathology and hysterical symptomatology: The genesis of an altered state of consciousness. *International Journal of Psychoanalysis, 60*: 109–116.

Silberer, H. (1909). Report on a method of eliciting and observing certain symbolic hallucination-phenomena. In: D. Rapaport (Ed.), *Organization and Pathology of Thought* (pp. 195–207). New York: Columbia University Press, 1957.

Silbersweig, D., Clarkin, J. F., Goldstein, M., Kernberg, O., Tuescher, O., Levy, K., et al. (2007). Failure of frontolimbic inhibitory function in the context of negative emotion in borderline personality disorder. *American Joutrnal of Psychiatry, 164* (12): 1832–1841.

Simmel, E. (1918). *Kriegsneurosen und psychisches Trauma.* Munich.

Slap, J. W., & Trunnell, E. E. (1987). Reflections on the self state dream. *Psychoanalytic Quarterly, 56*: 251–262.

Solnit, A. J. (1970). A study of object loss in infancy. *Psychoanalytic Study of the Child, 25*: 257–272.

Solnit, A. J. (1972). Aggression: A view of theory building in psychoanalysis. *Journal of the American Psychoanalytic Association, 20*: 435–450.

Sperling, O. (1963). Exaggeration as a defense. *Psychoanalytic Quarterly, 32*: 533–548.

Spielrein, S. (1912). Die Destruktion als Ursache des Werdens. *Jahrbuch für psychoanalytische und psychopathologische Forschungen, Vol. 4.* Leipzig & Vienna. English: Destruction as a cause of coming into being. *Journal of Analytical Psychology, 39* (1994): 155–186.

Spillius, E. B. (Ed.) (1988a). *Melanie Klein Today, Vol. I: Mainly Theory.* London: Routledge.

Spillius, E. B. (Ed.) (1988b). *Melanie Klein Today, Vol. II: Mainly Practice.* London: Routledge.

Spitz, R. (1945). Hospitalism. *Psychoanalytic Study of the Child, 1.*

Spitz, R. (1969). Aggression and adaptation. *Journal of Nervous and Mental Diseases, 149*: 81–90.

Stärcke, A. (1914). Introduction to Dutch translation of S. Freud, "'Civilized' Sexual Morality and Modern Nervous Illness" [*S.E., 18*: 55]. Leyden.

Stechler, G., & Halton, A. (1983). *Assertion and Aggression: Emergence during Infancy.* Paper presented at Winter Meetings of the American Psychoanalytic Association, New York.

Steiner, J. (1982). Perverse relationships between parts of the self: A clinical illustration. *International Journal of Psychoanalysis, 63*: 241–252.

Steiner, J. (1993). *Psychic Retreats: Pathological Organizations in Psychotic, Neurotic, and Borderline Patients.* London: Routledge.

Stekel, W. (1911). *Sex and Dreams: The Language of Dreams,* trans. J. S. Van-Teslaar. Boston, MA: Gorham Press, 1922.

Storr, A. (1968). *Human Aggression.* New York: Atheneum.

Storr, A. (1972). *Human Destructiveness*. New York: Basic Books.

Strachey, J. (1955). Editor's note. In: S. Freud, *Beyond the Pleasure Principle* [1920g]. *S.E. 18*: 3–6.

Strachey, J. (1957). Editor's note. In: S. Freud, "Instincts and Their Vicissitudes" [1915c]. *S.E. 14*: 111–116.

Sulloway, F. (1979). *Freud, Biologist of the Mind: Beyond the Psychoanalytic Legend*. Cambridge, MA: Harvard University Press, 1992.

Tinbergen, N. (1969). On war and peace in animals and man. *Reflections, 4* (1): 24–49.

Tomkins, S. S. (1962). *Affect, Imagery, Consciousness, Vol. I: The Positive Affects*. New York: Springer, 1992.

Tomkins, S. S. (1991). *Affect, Imagery, Consciousness, Vol. III: The Negative Affects, Anger and Fear*. New York: Springer.

Tomlinson, C. (1992). G. C. Lichtenberg: Dreams, jokes, and the Unconscious in eighteenth-century Germany. *Journal of the American Psychoanalytic Association, 40*: 761–799.

Turquet, P. (1975). Threats to identity in the large group. In: L. Kreeger (Ed.), *The Large Group: Dynamics and Therapy* (pp. 87–144). London: Constable.

Volkan, V. (2004). *Blind Trust: Large Groups and Their Leaders in Times of Crisis and Terror*. Charlottesville, VA: Pitchstone.

Waelder, R. (1930). The principle of multiple function: Observations on over-determination. *Psychoanalytic Quarterly, 5*: 45–62.

Waelder, R. (1956). Critical discussion of the concept of an instinct of destruction. *Bulletin of Philadelphia Association of Psychoanalysis, 6*: 97–109.

Weismann, A. (1882). *Über die Dauer des Lebens*. Jena.

Weismann, A. (1884). *Über Leben und Tod*. Jena.

Weismann, A. (1892). *Das Keimplasma*. Jena. English edition: *The Germ-Plasm*. London, 1893.

White, R. (1963). *Ego and Reality in Psychoanalytic Theory*. Psychological Issues, 7. New York: International Universities Press.

Winnicott, C. (1989). D.W.W.: A reflection. In: *Psychoanalytic Explorations* (pp. 1–19). London: Karnac.

Winnicott, D. W. (1947). Hate in the counter-transference. *International Journal of Psychoanalysis, 30*: 69–74.

Winnicott, D. W. (1950). Aggression in relation to emotional development. In: *Through Paediatrics to Psychoanalysis: Collected Papers* (pp. 204–218). London: Karnac, 1990.

Winnicott, D. W. (1960). Ego distortion in terms of true and false self.

In: *The Maturational Processes and the Facilitating Environment* (pp. 140–152). London: Karnac, 1990.

Winnicott, D. W. (1971). *Playing and Reality.* London: Routledge.

Wolf, E. (1988). *Treating the Self: Elements of Clinical Self Psychology.* New York: Guilford Press.

Yorke, C. (1986). A pulsão de morte. Posição pessoal [The death drive: Personal position]. In: A. Green et al., *A pulsão de morte* [The death drive] (pp. 85–90). São Paulo: Escuta, 1988.

Young-Bruehl, E. (2003) (with J. Russo). *Amae* in Ancient Greece. In: *Where Do We Fall When We Fall In Love?* New York: Other Press.

Ziegler, K. (1913). Menschen- und Weltenwerden. *Neue Jahrbücher für das klassische Altertum, 31:* 529.

INDEX

Made in the USA
Middletown, DE
17 December 2022

19185203R00186